Culturally Relevant
*E*thical Decision-Making
in Counseling

Culturally Relevant
Ethical Decision-Making
in Counseling

Rick Houser ◆ Felicia L. Wilczenski ◆ MaryAnna Ham

University of Massachusetts Boston

SAGE Publications
Thousand Oaks ▪ London ▪ New Delhi

For information:

Sage Publications, Inc.
2455 Teller Road
Thousand Oaks, California 91320
E-mail: order@sagepub.com

Sage Publications Ltd.
1 Oliver's Yard
55 City Road
London EC1Y 1SP
United Kingdom

Sage Publications India Pvt. Ltd.
B-42, Panchsheel Enclave
Post Box 4109
New Delhi 110 017 India

Printed in the United States of America

Library of Congress Cataloging-in-Publication Data

Houser, Rick.
Culturally relevant ethical decision-making in counseling / Rick Houser,
Felicia L. Wilczenski, MaryAnna Ham.
        p. cm.
Includes bibliographical references and index.
ISBN 1-4129-0586-9 (cloth)—ISBN 1-4129-0587-7 (pbk.)
    1. Counseling—Moral and ethical aspects. 2. Counseling—Decision making.
3. Cross-cultural counseling—Moral and ethical aspects. I. Wilczenski, Felicia L.
II. Domokos-Cheng Ham, MaryAnna. III. Title.

BF637.C6H676 2006
174′.91583—dc22   2005030922

This book is printed on acid-free paper.

06 07 08 09 10 9 8 7 6 5 4 3 2 1

Acquisitions Editor:	Kassie Graves
Editorial Assistant:	Veronica Novak
Production Editor:	Laureen A. Shea
Copy Editor:	Cate Huisman
Typesetter:	C&M Digitals (P) Ltd.
Proofreader:	Theresa Kay
Indexer:	Nara Wood

Contents

Acknowledgments

First, we want to take the opportunity to thank several individuals who were instrumental in the completion of this book. Ms. Manisha Vijayaraghavan provided extensive quality assistance with reference research, accuracy of references, and compilation of the indexes. She tirelessly completed these tasks with enthusiasm and in a timely fashion. We also want to thank Susan Coomey, who also provided invaluable assistance with reference research and compilation of indexes. Additionally, the copyediting of Cate Huisman was exceptional. Her concise editing and diligent efforts were greatly appreciated. Finally, we want to thank Serena Houser for developing the figure used in illustrating the hermeneutic model.

Sage Publications gratefully acknowledges the contributions of the following individuals:

Juan Kenigstein
Breyer State University

James J. Messina
Counselor Educator, Argosy University/Tampa

Jeffrey A. Miller
Duquesne University

Margie Rodriguez Le Sage
School of Social Work, Michigan State University

Sally D. Stabb
Texas Woman's University

William E. Stilwell, III
University of Kentucky

Patricia Wolleat
Professor Emerita, University of Wisconsin–Madison

Chapter 1

Introduction

Ethics and morality are commonly used terms, both in our everyday lives and in our professional lives. Although these are common terms, actual definitions of these terms may not be as readily discernable. What are the formal definitions of these two terms?

Ethics have been defined as "a generic term for several ways of examining the moral life" (Beauchamp & Childress, 1989, p. 9). *Merriam Webster's Collegiate Dictionary* (11th edition) defined ethics as "the discipline dealing with what is good and bad and with moral duty and obligation. A set of moral principles." Corey, Corey, and Callahan (2003) stated "ethics pertain to the beliefs we hold about what constitutes right conduct. Ethics are moral principles adopted by an individual or group to provide rules for right conduct" (p. 11). Professional associations generally set the ethical standards for a profession.

Rest (1983) defined morality as "standards or guidelines that govern human cooperation—in particular, how rights, duties, and benefits are to be allocated" (p. 558). Corey et al. (2003) wrote that morality is "concerned with perspectives of right and proper conduct and involves an evaluation of actions on the basis of some broader cultural context or religious standard" (p. 11).

A difference between these two concepts concerns to some degree the objective versus subjective interpretation of right behavior, in the case here professionally acceptable or desirable behavior. Ethics, theoretically, are generated from a more general standard set of guidelines outlined and set forth by professional organizations, whereas morality is more narrow and based on cultural and possibly religious beliefs. The problem becomes differentiating the two, because professional organizations have used certain broad ethical theories to develop codes that have been based to a large extent on cultural and religious beliefs or morality. Because morality has influenced the development of ethics, we want to propose that ethics includes morality—cultural and religious beliefs, as well as broader perspectives that are sanctioned by professional organizations—professional ethical codes. We live in a diverse and a multicultural society, and developing professional ethical codes from one or two philosophical perspectives (professional codes have been developed from Western philosophies and religious beliefs) is limiting and potentially discriminatory. We propose that ethics should be objective and based on agreed upon professional standards of practice, but include additional moral philosophies that are representative of wider cultural and geographical perspectives than just a few Western views.

Ethics and ethical decision-making are a critical part of the training and practice of professional counselors (Corey et al., 2003; Cottone & Claus, 2000; Neukrug, Miliken, & Walden, 2001; Scott, 2000). Training in ethics typically focuses on professional codes of ethics, ethical decision-making, and general theories of ethics (Corey et al., 2003; Freeman, 2000; Welfel, 2002).

One characteristic of a profession is the formulation of a professional code of ethics (Walden, Herlihy, & Ashton, 2003). Lunt (1999) stated, "codes may provide bottom-line rules or proscriptions for behavior or aspirational guidelines" (p. 251). She further stated that there are two different purposes of ethical codes: One purpose is the regulation of inappropriate behavior whereby minimal expectations and rules are stated; a second purpose is the promotion of quality services by counselors and psychologists. All ethical decision-making models include a review of professional codes of ethics (Cottone & Claus, 2000).

A substantial portion of educational training for counselors is based upon professional codes of ethics and ethical decision-making (Corey et al., 2003; Freeman, 2000; Knapp & Sturm, 2002). Freeman proposed that "Ethical standards are self-imposed regulations that provide rough guidelines for professional behavior and attempt to specify the nature of the ethical responsibilities of members, at least minimally" (p. 19). Hadjistavropoulos, Malloy, Sharpe, and Fuchs-Lacelle (2003) suggested the importance of educational training that involves a socialization process designed to instill professional values and ethics. These professional values and ethics are formulated in professional codes of ethics. Professional codes of ethics are founded on broader ethical theories, specifically western theories of ethics (Malloy, Hadjistavropoulos, Douaud, & Smythe, 2002). Professional codes of ethics for various disciplines within counseling are prevalent (American Counseling Association [ACA], 2005; American Association of Marriage and Family Therapists [AAMFT], 2001; American Mental Health Counseling Association [AMHCA], 2000; American Psychological Association [APA], 2003a; Commission on Rehabilitation Counseling Certification [CRCC], 1997).

A profession is defined in part by its development and proclamation of professional ethical codes (Lindsay, 1996; Lunt, 1999; Malloy et al., 2002). Malloy et al. noted that the content of these different professional codes varies to some degree across professions. It is interesting that there are such variations because many of the professions interact and consequently ethical decision-making may differ as a result of these differences. An important question is: How do professionals resolve conflicts based upon their own professional codes of ethics? Professionals interact in teams and frequently must agree on clinical decisions; at times this may result in conflicts between their professional codes, for example, between the codes of social workers, counselors, and psychologists.

Several authors noted the limitations of professional codes of ethics in ethical decision-making (Cottone & Claus, 2000; Danzinger & Welfel, 2001; Welfel, 2002). Keith-Spiegel & Koocher (1985) suggested that professional codes of ethics were blunt instruments and may increase conceptual confusion. For instance, Tjeltveit (2000) concluded that professional codes of ethics when narrowly interpreted do not address many issues regarding managed care. Danzinger and Welfel found that only one-third of licensed counselors surveyed consulted with professional codes of ethics regarding managed care issues. Also, only four percent of the licensed counselors indicated that referring to professional codes was useful in dealing with managed care issues. Corey et al. (2003) indicated that simply learning professional ethical codes will not prepare counselors for ethical practice.

In addition to studying professional codes of ethics, another focus of educational training for counselors is in ethical decision-making (Bowers & Pipes, 2000; Corey et al., 2003; Cottone, 2001; Cottone & Claus, 2000; Garcia, Cartwright, Winston, & Borzuchowska, 2003; Mattison, 2000; Rest, 1994). Cottone and Claus provided a comprehensive review of several ethical decision-making models. The models vary with regard to complexity and focus. In general, most decision-making models include the following steps: identification of the ethical dilemma, review of professional codes of ethics, consultation with peers and supervisors, determination of risks and benefits of choices of action, and evaluation of decision after implementation. Cottone and Claus noted that there has been minimal research into the effectiveness of ethical decision-making models. Another criticism by Cottone and Claus was that the models do not include steps that focus on the use and review of ethical theories, that is, they are not grounded in philosophical ethical theories.

Welfel (2002) offered a sound ethical decision-making theory that incorporated several recommended approaches to ethical decision-making (Cottone & Claus, 2000). Welfel proposed ten steps to ethical decision-making (see Figure 1.1). The first step is for the professional to become sensitive to ethical issues. Welfel

Figure 1.1   Traditional Ethical Decision-Making Model

Step 1:	Develop ethical sensitivity.
Step 2:	Define dilemma and options.
Step 3:	Refer to professional standards.
Step 4:	Examine relevant laws and regulations.
Step 5:	Search out ethics scholarship.
Step 6:	Apply ethical principles to the situation.
Step 7:	Consult with supervisor and respected colleagues.
Sept 8:	Deliberate and decide.
Step 9:	Inform supervisor; implement and document actions.
Step 10:	Reflect on the experience.

Source: Welfel, E. (2002). *Ethics in counseling and psychotherapy: Standards, research and emerging issues.* Pacific Grove, CA: Brooks/Cole.

suggested that counselors/psychologists need to identify the potential ethical issues beginning in the first session, particularly since issues of legally mandated clients, or other relevant concerns, such as dual relationships and confidentiality, are prevalent in the profession. Counselors should begin their work with an awareness of what ethical issues may come up. Welfel noted that one way for counselors to be aware is through education and training, so that when they are making this initial assessment they will be able to identify important ethical dilemmas that may arise.

A second step is the definition of the ethical dilemma and the options for action (Welfel, 2002). This step involves concretely defining the ethical dilemma and identifying potential options for action. For example, a counselor may define the problem as possibly violating confidentiality with a client who has been violent in the past. Options might include first informing the client of the limitations of confidentiality. A second option may be to violate confidentiality and report a dangerous situation when it occurs.

A third step in the Welfel (2002) model is to refer to professional codes of ethics. As was mentioned earlier, there are numerous professional codes. The counselor may find more than one code that applies and the codes may conflict with each other. However, the task is to identify all codes that apply and use the information in later decision-making.

A fourth step according to Welfel (2002) is the review of relevant state and federal regulations and case law that may apply. For example, many states require counselors to report suspected child abuse. This action potentially violates client confidentiality if one is working with a child or parent and the abuse is detected.

A fifth step according to Welfel (2002) is a review of relevant professional ethics literature. This may involve reviewing research articles in professional journals that apply to the situation. A sixth step is the application of ethical principles based on *virtue ethics* (see further explanation of virtue ethics in Chapter 2) such as beneficence, nonmaleficence, etc.

A seventh step is consultation with colleagues and supervisors (Welfel, 2002). As Welfel noted, it is important to consult with trusted supervisors and seasoned colleagues to obtain feedback about the ethical dilemma confronting a counselor.

The eighth step is to decide what to do and, as Welfel (2002) noted, this is done alone. The counselor must decide based upon the information gathered and bear the responsibility for the course of action.

The ninth step is to inform appropriate people, such as supervisors, of the decision and action to be taken (Welfel, 2002). As Welfel noted, supervisors must be informed because they are legally responsible for the outcome that results from the counselor's decision. The final step is reflection on and evaluation of the decision and the actions taken. Each step of the process should be evaluated and repeated if necessary (Welfel, 2002).

The Welfel model is comprehensive and addresses most of the steps of other models. Kitchener (1984) suggested that ethical decision-making models provide a guide for the process of decision-making and not for explicit outcomes or ethical decisions. Corey et al. (2003) stated that "your own ethical awareness and problem-solving skills will determine how you translate these general guidelines into day-to-day practice" (p. 6). However, Cottone and Claus (2000), in reviewing the practice of ethical decision-making and related research, found that little investigation has been completed. They conclude, therefore, that ethical decision-making models should be used with caution when training students.

Another recent decision-making approach proposed to improve ethical reasoning is based upon hermeneutics (Betan, 1997; Fowers & Richardson, 1996). The concept of hermeneutics is the study of interpretation based upon context (Follesdal, 2001). Follesdal suggested that hermeneutics is defined by first establishing interpretational hypotheses and then determining whether the hypotheses conflict with the text that is being interpreted.

Betan (1997) pointed out that an important omission from many of the current ethical decision-making models, e.g., Welfel's model, is that the steps do not address the context in which the ethical issue is being interpreted. Betan further stated that

> applying this hermeneutic understanding to ethics in psychotherapy, the task is not, and cannot be, simply to apply principles a priori, but instead to work toward an understanding of how the principles fit within the context, the alternatives, and the interpersonal demands of a particular ethical situation. (p. 356)

Garcia et al. (2003) proposed an ethical decision-making model that incorporates a contextual orientation, but they do not identify clearly the relevant issues.

What might be some of the contextual issues that should be addressed? Our beliefs are similar to those of Cottone and Claus (2000) that "an understanding of underlying philosophy and theoretical tenets" (p. 281) provides a basis of contextual connection to ethical decision-making. We live in a society that is not bounded by geographic limitations and cultural backgrounds. Through easy worldwide mobility, the media, and the Internet, geographic and temporal boundaries are removed. Consequently, those individuals receiving counseling services bring various backgrounds—cultural, racial, etc.—that create many more complex ethical dilemmas. Fowers and Richardson (1996) discussed components of a hermeneutic view and stated that "every culture's traditions have some vision of the good life at their core that provide touchstones of meaning and directions for living" (p. 617). For example, the number of Asians entering and living in the United States has dramatically increased, and their ethical orientations are much different than traditional Western views; therefore, counselors must be better prepared to apply ethical decision-making that is based upon context and upon philosophical and theoretical approaches that are pertinent to the situation.

We are proposing training counselors in ethical decision-making using a hermeneutic approach. This contextualized approach is unique in the field of ethics. Specifically, we offer a model that includes a foundation in Western, Eastern, Middle Eastern, and Southern Hemisphere philosophical ethical theories. Our model of ethical decision-making incorporates considering the context of the situation, including a client's worldview that matches a particular ethical orientation, e.g., a relevant Western, Eastern, Middle Eastern, or Southern Hemisphere view. Included in this model are a review of appropriate professional codes and an interpretation of how the various philosophical and theoretical views fit within the codes. The intent is to give practitioners a firmer foundation and understanding of the ethical issues that confront them, so decisions can be made that are based upon solid knowledge and context.

SUMMARY

Professional counselors benefit from systematic training in ethics and ethical decision-making. An important issue is forming a foundation upon which to make ethical decisions. We propose that such a foundation begins with an in-depth understanding of general culturally relevant ethical theories that represent most world philosophical views. Such an approach facilitates an understanding of the contextual issues surrounding ethical dilemmas in counseling. Cottone and Claus (2000) stated, "It is surprising to find the number of practice-based models developed apparently without attention to underlying philosophical and theoretical tenets" (p. 281). As Danzinger and Welfel (2001) discovered, counselors actually may not be using professional codes of ethics and, therefore, preparation in ethical theories may provide a broader source of information for ethical decision-making. The model provided here attempts to provide the practitioner with just such a broad-based approach to ethical decision-making, and ultimately a model to improve the ethical decision-making process.

SECTION I

Western Theories of Ethics

In the first section, we introduce Western views of ethics, covering the following theories: *virtue ethics, natural law, utilitarian ethics, feminist ethics, Native American ethics,* and *respect for persons.* Chapter 2 concerns virtue ethics. Virtue ethics provides one of the oldest Western perspectives (Shanahan & Wang, 2003). The ancient Greeks developed this particular orientation, e.g., Plato, Aristotle, and Socrates. The primary focus of this theory is on an understanding of the person's character and related virtues.

Chapter 3 is a discussion of *natural law* (Harris, 2002; Shanahan & Wang, 2003). Natural law is grounded for the most part on Christian principles. Thomas Aquinas is one of the original contributors to this orientation. The primary basis of this theory is human nature and natural inclinations. These inclinations are defined in terms of biological and human values.

In Chapter 4, we discuss *utilitarian ethics*, which is founded upon the idea of the "most good for the most number of people." John Stuart Mill is one of the major contributors to this theory (Harris, 2002). Many Western laws are founded in part upon utilitarian perspectives.

The next chapter, Chapter 5, is a presentation on *respect for persons ethics* (Harris, 2002). Much of the theory of respect of persons is based upon the writings of the German philosopher Immanuel Kant. The primary foundation of respect for persons is a universal principle that agreement on ethical behavior is dependent upon actions being acceptable to you if you consent to others behaving that way toward you.

In Chapter 6, we discuss *feminine ethics.* According to feminine theorists, women hold a subordinate position in patriarchal society (Gilligan, 1982; Noddings, 1992; O'Brien-Hallstein, 1999; Page & Tyrer, 1995). In addition to oppression, another underlying principle of feminine ethics is that of caring. Caring accordingly includes responsiveness, sensitivity to others, acceptance, and a feeling of relatedness to others (Gilligan; O'Brien-Hallstein).

The seventh chapter is a focus on *Native American ethics*. There are many groups within Native Americans, but there are basic concepts that can be emphasized (Marshall, 2002). For example, a key belief is to show respect or show honor for all life. Other important views include showing respect for elders and community leaders.

Chapter 2

Virtue Ethics and Counselor Decision-Making

Virtue ethics is an important perspective for professional conduct because of its emphasis on the central role of motives in moral questions. To act from virtue is to act from some particular motivation; correct moral decisions require correct motives. For the virtue ethicist, helping a person in need should be motivated by charity or benevolence. Virtue ethics focuses on the process by which moral attitudes and character develop. Since character development continues over the life span, there is an emerging or evolving quality to it. As such, according to Meara, Schmidt, and Day (1996), virtue ethics can be viewed as a moral psychology, as well as a theory about making moral choices (as deontological or teleological theories). Virtues are neither situation specific nor universal maxims, but rather they are character and community specific. They are habits or intuitions that are nurtured in the context of a community, starting in childhood and continuing throughout life. Virtues are acquired qualities mediated by communities and religions. Modern virtue ethics still retains the key Aristotelian questions (Miller, 1991):

- What type of person do I want to be?
- What virtues are characteristic of the person I want to be?
- What actions will cultivate those virtues?

Western ethical thinking began with the Greek philosophers, Socrates, Plato, and, in particular, Aristotle, in the fifth century BCE. Socrates focused attention on the nature of a good life and how human beings ought to live; Plato questioned the standards for goodness; and Aristotle sought to define the good life and the means of attaining happiness.

Virtue, knowledge, and happiness are the central tenets in Greek ethics. The distinguishing feature of their ethical thinking was the emphasis on the nature and attainment of moral virtue. Virtues are ingrained habits of behavior and one's virtues make up one's character. In fact, the word *ethics* is derived from the Greek word *ethos,* which means character (Blackburn, 1996). A person's character is the key element of morality. Virtue is knowledge and acquiring virtue is vital for a life that is truly human. Shanahan and Wang (2003) explained that when a person chooses evil, it is with the mistaken belief that the choice is good. That is, if an individual does what is wrong, it is because the individual thought it was right. Evil actions are the result of ignorance. This idea is sometimes hard to reconcile with the lived experience of people who deliberately choose evil, for example, consider the events of September 11, 2001.

A corollary to Socrates' "virtue is knowledge" doctrine is that human beings should be regulated by rationality to bring emotions and desires under control. Genuine happiness is a harmony of the parts of the soul: reason, spirit, and appetites. Since Victorian times the word *virtue* has taken on a meaning suggesting sexual restraint; however, for the Greek philosophers, virtue meant excellence.

Although there are other virtue traditions (e.g., Christian, Hindu, Confucian, Buddhist, and Sioux, among others), Aristotle is the primary source, and his viewpoint receives the most attention in recent works on virtue ethics (Fowers & Tjeltveit, 2003; MacIntyre, 1999). The first systematic description of virtue ethics was summarized by Aristotle in his *Nicomachean Ethics.* Happiness or *eudaimonia* is the central concern in Aristotle's ethical theory. Eudaimonia is the activity of living well. It is not a temporary feeling or momentary sense of well-being, but rather the attainment of a lifetime, acquired by exercising appropriate virtues. Aristotle offers a prescription for a good life by engaging in activities that make one a virtuous person (striving for excellence) and pursuing a goal of happiness.

Aristotle believed that no action is virtuous unless the actor intends it to be virtuous, so that this intention can place the actor's perfection ahead of the other's good. Meilander (1984) suggested that virtue ethics is inherently egoistic because the individual's self-interest in gaining happiness coincides with fulfilling moral obligations. Spohn (1992) also pointed out how an individual's motivation can be an undependable source of virtue because humans are subject to self-deception and pride.

Modern virtue ethics still retains the three major concepts of virtue, knowledge, and happiness derived from the ancient Greek philosophy (Miller, 1991). According to virtue ethics, the origin of ethical action is a holistic blend of purpose, disposition, affect, cognition, and social participation (Fowers & Tjeltveit, 2003). Many different virtues have been identified and emphasized in the writings of contemporary ethicists, for example, self-understanding, honesty, compassion, and love. Virtue ethics is one approach in normative ethics. In contrast to the approach that emphasizes duties or rules (deontology) or to that which emphasizes the consequences of actions (teleological), virtue ethics emphasizes the virtues or moral character of the person. It shifts the emphasis from an appraisal of the act to an appraisal of the person who acts. Virtue ethics focuses on helping people develop good character traits, such as kindness and generosity. In turn, these character traits allow a person to make morally correct decisions in life. People need to break bad habits of character, such as greed or anger, because such vices stand in the way of becoming a good person. Of course, there are problems in deciding what constitutes a "good" character. Virtue ethicists have treated this issue as self-evident, but that position is problematic in that it suggests moral relativism: A virtue for one person or for one set of circumstances may be a vice for another. Bersoff (1996) points out that if acting ethically depends on character, then ethical reasoning and actions may be too individualized and idiosyncratic.

MAJOR CONCEPTS

Meara et al. (1996) differentiate virtue ethics from principle (or rule) ethics. The latter are espoused by various professions in their codes of ethical conduct and are typically used to facilitate solving ethical dilemmas. Principles allow for professional distance and objectivity. Conversely, professional virtues are values and purposes shared by practitioners and are acquired through socialization in the professional culture. Those virtues become the "character" of the profession as well as the "character" of its individual practitioners (Jordan & Meara, 1990). An essential difference between the two is that principles are obligations whereas virtues are ideals.

Principle ethics addresses the competing rights of clients and practitioners, answering the question, "What should I do?" in problematic situations, and is predominant in ethical decision-making among counselors in the United States. The five prima facie ethical principles (Beauchamp & Childress, 2001; Kitchener, 1984), which provide moral choices that can be applied when faced with moral dilemmas in counseling practice, include

1. Nonmaleficence, the duty to do no harm;

2. Beneficence, the duty to do good both individually and for all;

3. Fidelity, the duty to be truthful; to honor others, their rights, and their responsibilities;

4. Justice, the duty to treat all fairly; and

5. Autonomy, the duty to maximize the individual's right to make decisions.

Nonmaleficence is the basis of the Hippocratic oath taken by ancient Greek physicians. This principle requires that, *in addition to not intentionally harming others, professionals refrain from any action that may cause harm.* Because counselors are privy to information that could potentially harm a client either intentionally or unintentionally, they must be vigilant about confidentiality.

In contrast to nonmaleficence, which suggests a passive stance, *beneficence* refers to *taking positive action to promote the welfare of others.* It involves an obligation to help members of society who are in need of assistance. Counselors must make decisions that will result in the client's growth and well-being. An important responsibility for the counselor is to attain and maintain an appropriate level of professional competency.

Trust is the cornerstone of an effective counseling relationship. *Fidelity* requires counselors to *respect trust by keeping commitments and being honest with their clients.* Maintaining confidentiality, informed consent, and avoiding dual relationships (i.e., associating with clients in more than one relationship whether professional, social, or business) are obligations subsumed under this principle.

Justice refers to *fairness and equality.* Counselors must ensure that they do not practice in a way that discriminates against a particular individual or group. They have the further responsibility to advocate for change when they recognize inequities.

The principle of *autonomy* is the *right to self-determination and freedom* from the control of others. Counselors have an obligation to present information to clients in a manner that they can understand and not to interfere unnecessarily in the client's decision. Practices related to this competency include confidentiality, rights to privacy, and informed consent.

Ethical decision-making using a principle approach is carried out in the context of solving dilemmas. The approach claims to be objective and universal because it relies on rationality rather than subjective and socially constructed virtues. Pincoffs (1971) called this type of ethical reasoning *quandary ethics.* The decision-making process involves reviewing the various principles, examining the actions of the participants in the situation, and determining what the appropriate actions should be in the situation based on the relevant principles. Many professionals mistakenly believe that they have met their moral requirements when they diligently follow the principles. However, Jordan and Meara (1990) as well as others (Kilpatrick, 1986; Pincoffs, 1971) cautioned that this narrow focus on problem-solving risks viewing ethical dilemmas as puzzles to be analyzed according to a set of rules rather than human problems that might involve considerable pain for the parties involved.

Multicultural scholars challenge the Western, scientific, individualistic, male-dominated worldview assumed by these principle ethics. What happens when we confront people from different ethical traditions in a counseling context? Winston (2003) pointed out that cultivating abilities in two types of reflection are indispensable given the increasing need for communication across cultures. He refers to *double reflection* as the ability to discern what something might mean to a person from a different culture, especially when it is at variance with one's own cultural view, while simultaneously thinking about the contestability of one's own worldview.

The multicultural movement has renewed interest in virtue ethics (MacIntyre, 1984), resulting in a vast number of theories. Generally, the theories agree that a virtue is a disposition to act and that virtue ethics stands in opposition to utilitarian concerns about the consequences of action (Oakley, 1996; Spohn, 1992). Virtue ethics suggests that counseling is a professional discipline with moral as well as scientific dimensions, and the moral dimensions are intimately tied to the moral character of the practitioner. In contrast to principle ethics, the problem for virtue ethics is focused on personal qualities and on deciding the answer to the question, "What type of counselor should I be?" This virtue perspective enriches ethical reasoning and can better encompass the positions of people from culturally diverse backgrounds. Virtue ethics impels professionals to think ethically at all times (What is in the best interest of the client?) rather than just when confronted with a dilemma (What should I do in this situation?).

Those two preceding questions are related and there are parallels between virtues and ethical principles. It is not that ethical principles are unimportant; they are, however, seen as insufficient by virtue ethicists. From the virtue perspective, character is more important than conformity to principles. Beauchamp and Childress (2001) provide a rough outline of the correspondence between principles and virtues: nonmaleficence with nonmalevolence, beneficence with benevolence, fidelity with faithfulness, justice with fairness, and autonomy with respectfulness. For example, it is impossible to meet the obligation of fidelity without the virtue of faithfulness. The prima facie principles are moral obligations, that is, they direct courses of action. Virtues, however, are ideals rather than guides to specific actions. Campbell (2003) notes that, taken together, virtue ethics and principle ethics are complementary approaches: Principles are clear, simple, objective, and to some extent universal; virtues attend to emotional and personal factors.

Principle ethics focuses on the moral questions faced by individual practitioners, and as such has been criticized as being more concerned about professionals than about the public (Vasquez, 1996). In our litigious society, principle ethics may be used by professionals as a legal minimum—a contract to protect against lawsuits, for example, obtaining a signature of "informed consent" for release of confidential information. The signature may protect the professional legally, but how that confidential information is communicated to others may profoundly affect the client's life. A respectful, compassionate report conveying intimate information from a counselor will give a different view of the client than one based on the motive of self-protection alone. Also, principle ethics do not generally examine broader ethical issues involving systems or institutions.

If principles do not provide clear answers for resolving ethical dilemmas, how does one decide which principle should prevail in cases where more than one ethical principle may apply? In those cases, virtues are needed for the competent application of principles (Jordan & Meara, 1990). Virtues are not simply correlates of principles; they go beyond principles, encompassing those human qualities needed when there are disputes over principles. For instance, two different principles—the client's right to know versus the client's welfare—may be relevant in a dilemma about the issue of the "therapeutic lie." A counselor may decide at a particular point in the counseling relationship that it may not be in the client's best interest to reveal how the client is enabling a problematic situation (say, substance abuse) within the family. Proponents of the prima facie principles might argue that truthfulness is the client's right. But what would be considered truthful in this situation? How much would the counselor have to reveal in order to be "truthful"? On the other hand, the counselor may fear that the truth would result in premature termination of counseling. Here the issue of truthfulness not only involves clients' rights but also the counselor's virtues such as prudence, discretion, and integrity. The counselor's motives must be examined. In order to be considered a virtuous act, the concern about early termination of counseling must stem from a concern about the client's welfare and not from a concern about loss of income.

May (1984) and Meara et al. (1996) provided examples of professional *virtues,* including *fidelity* (truthfulness, keeping one's promises), *prudence* (exercising good judgment), *discretion* (knowing what is at stake), *courage* (firmness in the face of adversity), *integrity* (acting for the right reasons), *respectfulness* (determining how others wish to be respected), *public-spiritedness* (ensuring professional help to those in need), *benevolence* (wanting to do good), and *humility* (reciprocity of giving and receiving). These virtues are not obligatory but rather are ideals that professionals should strive to attain (APA, 2003a). Virtues become meaningful only in context. For instance, when working in multicultural communities, the justice principle needs to be understood at a societal as well as an individual level to truly understand a minority client's position. A prudent counselor in a multicultural setting is aware that the client's perspective on a situation may be very different from that of the counselor.

Virtues are character strengths that encompass both personal and professional domains—virtue ethics focuses on the expression of character in an individual's life as a whole (Fowers & Tjeltveit, 2003). Punzo and Meara (1993) differentiated *self-regarding* virtues, such as integrity and humility, which benefit the counselor, from *other-regarding* virtues, such as respectfulness and benevolence. The self-regarding virtues actually enable other-regarding virtues that are oriented toward producing moral good for the client or community rather than for the counselor who possesses them.

May (1984) highlighted integrity and humility as especially important virtues for professionals. Integrity is seen as synonymous with character—at the core of one's identity as a person and a professional. Integrity refers to how one behaves when no one is watching. Ethical codes address threats to integrity as issues that impair competence, such as misrepresenting credentials, inappropriate dual relationships, or imposing one's personal beliefs in one's work. As May pointed out, in this age of specialization and lengthy educational training, professionals are in powerful positions because of their knowledge. Professionals need to be virtuous because few people are in a position to discredit them.

Most of the virtues address how professionals should work with the client. However, the virtue of humility recognizes the reciprocity of a professional relationship (May, 1984). Counselors must acknowledge that their professional lives depend upon what they receive as well as give to a relationship. The need is two-way: The counselor needs the client as much as the client needs the counselor. In multicultural contexts, counselors may not be as knowledgeable as they would like to believe. Humility recognizes the need of the counselor to learn a different perspective from the client.

The saying, "virtues are caught as much as they are taught," reflects the idea that virtues are transmitted informally within communities. Questions then arise about how one defines community. There is considerable heterogeneity between and within cultural groups, so it is unlikely that a single moral code will adequately represent the view of the entire culture. Another question centers on the factors that are involved in decision-making from a virtue ethics perspective. One might ask whether a virtue ethics perspective practiced in multicultural settings would loosen or tighten professional boundary issues in certain situations, for example, bartering for payment for counseling services.

ADDITIONAL READINGS: VIRTUE ETHICS

Cates, D. E. (1996). *Choosing to feel: Virtue, friendship, and compassion for friends.* Notre Dame, IN: University of Notre Dame Press.

Freeman, S. J. (2000). *Ethics: An introduction to philosophy and practice.* Belmont, CA: Wadsworth/Thomson Learning.

Hursthouse, R. (2003). Virtue ethics. In E. N. Zalta (Ed.). *The Stanford encyclopedia of philosophy.* Retrieved February 23, 2006, from http://plato.stanford.edu/archives/fall2003/entries/ethics-virtue/

Hutchinson, D. S. (1995). Ethics. In J. Barnes (Ed.), *The Cambridge companion to Aristotle* (pp. 195–232). Cambridge, England: Cambridge University Press.

MacIntyre, A. C. (1984). *After virtue: A study in moral theory* (2nd ed.). Notre Dame, IN: University of Notre Dame Press.

Pence, G. (1993). Virtue theory. In P. Singer (Ed.), *A companion to ethics* (pp. 249–258). Malden, MA: Blackwell.

Schneewind, J. B. (1998). *The invention of autonomy: A history of modern moral philosophy.* New York: Cambridge University Press.

Shanahan, T., & Wang, R. (2003). Reason and insight: Western and Eastern perspectives on the pursuit of moral wisdom (2nd ed.). Belmont, CA: Wadsworth.

Chapter 3

Natural Law Ethics and Counselor Decision-Making

Ideas about natural laws can be traced to Aristotelian philosophy and virtue ethics (see Chapter 2). Natural law ethicists see the importance of virtues, especially prudence (exercising good judgment), in living a moral life (Vacek, 1996). People follow natural law in what they *do by nature,* as the result of the law written on their hearts, that is, the law of conscience. In natural law ethics, something is right because it fulfills human nature and the task is to discover and realize that nature.

Natural law is considered universal and unchangeable, and as such has been used as a standard to evaluate human conduct and civil laws. The concept of natural law is embodied in English and American common law. Thomas Jefferson referred to the philosophy of John Locke to justify the three "inalienable rights" of life, liberty, and the pursuit of happiness expressed in the U.S. Declaration of Independence in 1776 (Almond, 1993). Because natural law derives from nature, it is believed to be binding upon human behavior even beyond the laws established by humans. Hence, natural law stands in opposition to legal positivism, which maintains that legal validity has no connection with morality or justice and implies that law is separate from ethics (Marmor, 2001). However, since the time of the atrocities of Nazi Germany and the ensuing desire to hold officials responsible for their war crimes, there has been a revival of interest in setting higher standards than those of positive law, as evidenced by the United Nations adoption of a Universal Declaration of Human Rights (1948). Natural law asserts that there is an essential connection between law and justice, as in St. Augustine's dictum, "Unjust law is not law."

During the Middle Ages, St. Augustine in the fourth century CE and St. Thomas Aquinas in the thirteenth century CE offered a Christian version of Aristotle's ethics. Like Aristotle, Augustine's moral theory is eudaemonistic; that is, it implies that happiness is appropriate for human beings. However, in contrast to the beliefs of Aristotle, who was pagan, for Augustine true happiness could only be attained in relationship with God. He emphasized a supernatural union with God through love (Syse, 2001). Aquinas synthesized Aristotelianism and theology by adding the theological virtues of faith, hope, and charity to the cardinal virtues of the Greeks.

Natural law is also central to the moral theorizing of Thomas Aquinas, who articulated that position in his work, *Summa Theologiae,* a massive summary of Christian doctrine. He called the rational guidance of all of creation by God "eternal law" and called human participation in God's wisdom through eternal law "natural law." The moral philosophy of natural law is a tradition primarily associated with the Roman Catholic Church but embraced by other Christian religions as well. The Thomistic view (the view of Thomas Aquinas) involves a commitment to the existence of God as the giver of natural law. For Aquinas, natural law is natural because it is compatible with human nature and nature is rational. It follows that there is a natural foundation to moral beliefs, and morality can be rationally justified (Buckle, 1993). Natural laws are the principles that govern reason, so human beings know by rationality the *goods* that are to be pursued: life, procreation, knowledge, and society (Murphy, 2001). As matters of natural law, the killing of the innocent is always wrong, as is lying, adultery, sodomy, and blasphemy. Accordingly, those who disobey natural law go contrary to nature, and as a consequence they bring upon themselves the natural punishment they deserve for their sin (e.g., unwanted pregnancy, HIV/AIDS).

Christian religions, based on natural law and divine revelation, are strongly deontological (duty- or rule-bound). Actions are justified by showing that they are right, not by showing that the consequences of the actions are right. Thus, for example, abortion to save the mother's life cannot be justified because the act of abortion itself is not morally permissible if one believes that life begins at conception. God is the moral standard and one's ultimate duty is to obey God and his will. God reveals himself not only through nature but also in other ways, such as through the Bible. A biblical ethic is a blend of divine commands, natural law, virtues, and moral character.

Early Christian thought focused on the role of God in achieving good; willpower and intelligence were insufficient. The gospels as well as the books of the New Testament discuss various ethical issues such as lending and borrowing, forgiveness of debt, fair wages, submission to authority, greed, trustworthiness, etc. This Christian value system, derived from the Bible with a basis in the Old Testament, has had a major influence on Western civilization. The founding fathers of the United States believed in divine guidance in human affairs, and the Bible's moral revelations provided the ethical and legal framework for their organization of U.S. society. However, natural law need not be given a religious interpretation. There are contemporary nontheistic writers, notably Moore (1996) and Foot (2000), who do not invoke a divinity and argue that natural laws are discoverable by experience and reason alone.

MAJOR CONCEPTS

Natural law is a *free will position* that holds that *human beings can decide how they should act.* This free will position creates tension between Christianity and psychology, which holds an empirical deterministic philosophy (Fair, 1959). Empirical determinism maintains that all human behavior will be ultimately determinable, once the laws of behavior are fully revealed by science.

The *standard of truth in natural law is human nature:* People should do whatever promotes the fulfillment of human nature. To find out about human nature, one observes behavior to identify the goals that humans seek because those goals reflect the structure of our human nature. Thus, for Aquinas, the goals are the "natural inclinations" that all human beings have in common. Present-day psychological studies are also informative about basic human "inclinations."

Human inclinations are divided into two groups: the *biological values of life and procreation* and the characteristically *human values of knowledge and sociability.* A basic natural inclination is to preserve one's own existence. Individuals have an obligation to promote their health and a right to self-defense. By implication, suicide and murder are wrong. Procreation is a value so it is implied that artificial contraception and homosexuality are wrong. Because humans have a natural tendency to seek knowledge of the world and God, any stifling of the pursuit of knowledge in general or knowledge of God is wrong. Notable about this position is the implication that a lack of religion is wrong. Humans have a tendency to seek relationships with others and to form societies, so friendship and love are good. Anything that interferes with this inclination, such as lies and slander, is wrong. Thus, natural law leads to a personal ethic—a duty to oneself—and a social ethic—a duty to others.

Christian religions use a natural law ethic as a guide for their members on sex, contraception, and homosexuality. The teaching is that humans have natural sexual urges, and because offspring are the natural result of sexual activity, procreation is a natural value. Many Christians hold the view that if something is *"unnatural," it is also immoral,* especially with regard to sexual behavior. Contemporary debates about homosexuality, for example, center on the question of whether homosexual behavior is natural or unnatural in humans: Are some people "born" homosexual or are they rebelling against their "normal" heterosexual urges? Aquinas's natural law ethic argues that homosexuality is unnatural because it does not lead to procreation. But the issue can be quite complex, and what is "natural" can depend on the circumstances. The expression of sexuality, without the biological goal of procreation, can strengthen relationships between people by deepening love and purpose in life, fulfilling characteristically human goals.

Natural law theory is morally absolute, not relativistic, connecting human nature and ethical life. Theorists believe that there are objective standards of morality that exist independent of the individual. Ethical laws are natural; that is, they apply to all human beings regardless of the customs or beliefs of a particular society. Another aspect of the natural law perspective is that it is *nonconsequential. The consequences of an act do not enter into the ethical analysis.* An absolute value, according to natural law, is that of human life; therefore, a single life cannot be sacrificed to save several lives. This perspective stands in sharp contrast to a utilitarian view (see Chapter 4) with its cost/benefit concerns and doctrine of "utility," that is, the greatest good for the greatest number of people (Glover, 1990). Also, according to natural law, moral judgments must include an *evaluation of the intentions of the person performing an act.* For example, a person can volunteer at a church food pantry to be seen by neighbors and gain a good reputation in the community. Even though the consequences of the volunteer work are good, the work is not morally praiseworthy because of the person's intentions.

The basic concept of natural law is that a person should promote values that are compatible with human inclinations. According to natural law theorists, these include biological values and human values of knowledge and sociability. Because natural law says no action can violate these fundamental values, an ethical dilemma arises when situations force individuals to violate values no matter what action is taken. As a remedy, two principles guide moral decision-making from a natural law perspective (Harris, 1997): *the principle of forfeiture* and *the principle of double effect.* In the former case, people forfeit their own rights when they threaten the rights of others. Any person who threatens the life of an innocent person (one who has not threatened anyone's life) forfeits his or her own right to life. This principle justifies acts of self-defense for individuals and for state actions, such as capital punishment or defensive war.

The *principle of double effect* states that four criteria are required for an action to be considered an indirect violation of a fundamental value under the principle of double effect. It is morally permissible to perform an action that has *two effects, one good and one bad,* if the following criteria are met: (a) the act itself must be morally permissible; (b) the bad effect of the act must be unavoidable to achieve the good effect; (c) the bad effect must not be the means of producing the good effect but only a side effect; (d) the good effect must be at least as morally desirable as the bad effect is morally undesirable.

There are some concerns that natural law theories place too much emphasis on biological values, such as reproduction, over characteristically human values, such as love and commitment. This tendency is known as *physicalism.* For example, the sexual urge is a given in human nature and procreation is an effect of sexual relations; therefore, homosexuality is wrong because it does not follow natural biological processes. Some theologians argued that the Catholic church's position on human sexuality commits a naturalistic fallacy by deducing a moral "ought" from what "is" (Najim, 1999). The problems of inconsistency with natural law theory have implications for counselors because of the claim that fundamental values must not be weighed against each other and that consequences are not crucial in ethical analysis. For instance, one might view natural law theory as inconsistent in using the principle of forfeiture to justify taking a life in capital punishment. Also, one might argue that the obligation to produce children does not take priority over the characteristically human value of love (sociability).

ADDITIONAL READINGS: NATURAL LAW ETHICS

Buckle, S. (1993). Natural law. In P. Singer (Ed.), *A companion to ethics* (pp. 161–174). Malden, MA: Blackwell.

Finnis, J. (1998). *Aquinas: Moral, political and legal theory.* New York: Oxford University Press.

Freeman, S. J. (2000). *Ethics: An introduction to philosophy and practice.* Belmont, CA: Wadsworth/Thomson Learning.

Harris, C. E. (2002). *Applying moral theories* (4th ed.). Belmont, CA: Wadsworth.

Murphy, M. (2002). The natural law tradition in ethics. In E. N. Zalta (Ed.), *The Stanford encyclopedia of philosophy.* Retrieved February 23, 2006, from http://plato.stanford.edu/archives/fall2003/entries/natural-law-ethics/

Porter, J. (1999). *Natural and divine law: Reclaiming the tradition for Christian ethics.* Ottawa: Novalis.

Shanahan, T., & Wang, R. (2003). *Reason and insight: Western and Eastern perspectives on the pursuit of moral wisdom* (2nd ed.). Belmont, CA: Wadsworth.

Chapter 4

Utilitarian Ethics and Counselor Decision-Making

Utilitarianism is a Western theory that has a history dating back to the late 1700s (Harris, 2002; Shanahan & Wang, 2003). It has influenced the ethical decision-making in many facets of our lives including state and federal laws as well as professional codes of ethics. Harris stated that "utilitarianism is one of the most powerful and persuasive traditions of moral thought in our culture" (p. 119). Quinton (1973) suggested that "Utilitarianism can be understood as a movement for legal, political and social reform that flourished in the first half of the nineteenth century" (p. 1). Rachels (1998) described utilitarian theory as based in social reform in human behavior, offering an alternative to natural law.

The earliest proponent of utilitarian theory was David Hume in the mid-1700s (Rachels, 1998). Hume introduced many of the basic concepts of utilitarian theory and he believed morals guided human behavior (Quinton, 1973). Hume's basic beliefs included a perception that humans are naturally kind (Quinton). According to Quinton, a second belief proposed by Hume was that humans sympathize with others and seek common ground.

Jeremy Bentham followed Hume and was the first to formally write down ideas about utilitarian theory (Shanahan & Wang, 2003). Bentham's original views were influenced by his background in economics and government. Several key assumptions are characteristic of Bentham's views. First, he believed that pleasure and pain influenced human behavior and human decision-making. Consequently, what is good or bad is related to what is pleasurable or painful, the hedonist principle (Quinton, 1973). His simple view of ethics was that good or bad is a function of differences in the amount of pleasure or pain between courses of action for all individuals involved (Shanahan & Wang). Second, Bentham believed that good or pleasure as an outcome for all affected by a circumstance could be quantified. Specific amounts of pleasure could be attached to an action for an individual affected by the decision, and a total amount of pleasure could be calculated by summing values attached to everyone affected (Shanahan & Wang). Bentham proposed the *principle of utility,* which states that whenever there is a choice between several options the ethical choice is the one that has the best overall outcome for all involved (Rachels, 1998).

John Stuart Mill was a second proponent of utilitarian theory and studied Bentham's views. Mill received only informal training at home but studied Greek and Latin. He additionally studied logic and read Bentham's work at an early age. Mill wrote in the same vein as Bentham on such topics as government, economics, and ethics (Shanahan & Wang, 2003).

MAJOR CONCEPTS

Mill expanded Bentham's views, going beyond the simple concept of pleasure versus pain to introduce the idea that certain pleasures are higher than others. A criticism of utilitarianism was that there was no difference morally between animals and humans if an ethical decision was based upon simply identifying pleasure versus pain. Mill proposed that some human pleasures could be categorized as higher pleasures than others. An example of a higher pleasure is the intellect. Therefore, taking a stimulating class that benefits individuals and enlightens them, and that then may result in distribution of this new knowledge, would be more ethical than the satisfaction of sexual or physical desires that benefit only a few.

The ultimate decision as to whether *an action is ethical is determined by the outcome;* this is the *consequentialist principle* (Quinton, 1973). Intentions are not considered important in the ethical decision-making in utilitarian theory (Knapp, 1999). Rachels (1998) noted that Bentham and Mill believed there are *basic propositions* in utilitarian theory. "First, actions are to be judged right or wrong solely by virtue of their consequences, nothing else matters" (p. 102). He further stated, "In assessing consequences, the only thing that matters is the amount of happiness or unhappiness that is created; everything else is irrelevant" (p. 102). Moldoveanu and Stevenson (1998) noted one of the most important characteristics of utilitarian theory is the *greatest happiness principle,* or GHP. Knapp best described the ultimate goal of utilitarian theory thus: "The purpose of ethics is to engender the greatest amount of happiness for the greatest number of people. The sole moral duty is to produce as much pleasure as possible (positive utilitarianism) or to decrease as much pain as possible (negative utilitarianism)" (p. 11). Finally, Rachels stated, "Each person's happiness counts the same" (p. 102). Curiously, utilitarian theory also holds that the needs of nonhumans or animals are relevant in considering ethical decisions.

Harris (2002) noted that utility may be associated with happiness. Utility is defined as "preference or desire satisfaction" (p. 121). He further proposed that preferences or desires can be arranged hierarchically. For example, the hierarchy may include the following: "1) preferences whose satisfaction contributes to the preferences of others; 2) preferences whose satisfaction is neutral with respect to the preference satisfaction of others; 3) preferences whose satisfaction decreases the preference satisfaction of others." In other words, utilitarian theory holds that promoting the happiness of others is most important, while at the same time promoting the satisfaction or happiness of the self. Next is happiness for the self that has no impact on others. Finally, happiness for the self that decreases the satisfaction of others has the least utility.

Harris (2002) has suggested an approach to quantifying the utility of an act. In this model Harris suggests assigning values to, first, the number of persons affected by an act. Second, values are assigned to units of utility per person. Table 4.1 is an example.

Harris (2002) explains the distribution of units of utility as the amount of happiness that does not affect the happiness of others in a negative way. In the example above, Act 1 has one hundred units of utility per person, whereas Act 2 has only two units of utility per person because Act 2 decreases the happiness of others. Consequently, the more ethical choice is Act 1, even though Act 2 affects more people.

Utilitarian theorists have differentiated between two types of utilitarian theory: *act utilitarianism* and *rule utilitarianism* (Harris, 2002). *Act utilitarianism is based solely on evaluation of the specific circumstance(s).* The above example from Harris is consistent with act utilitarianism. The determination of the more ethical action is based solely on the circumstances of the two acts considered. The *outcome has little impact on future ethical decisions.* Moldoveanu and Stevenson

Table 4.1   A Method for Calculating Utility

Action	Number of people affected	Units of utility per person	Total
Act 1	2	100	200
Act 2	50	2	100

Source: Harris, C. (2002). *Applying moral theories.* Belmont, CA: Wadsworth.

(1998), in referring to act utilitarianism and the GHP, stated, "The Greatest Happiness Principle focuses on individual actions, and considers them independently of any rules that may be embodied in them" (p. 723).

Rule utilitarianism is founded on the belief that general rules govern ethical behavior. There are choices of actions that in general produce the most utility across many circumstances. Harris (2002), in describing rule utilitarianism, stated: "*Rules or actions are right insofar as they promote utility and wrong insofar as they promote disutility*" (p. 126). Moldoveanu and Stevenson (1998) wrote that rule utilitarianism based upon GHP is "the rule embodied by an action, and asks about the global utility consequences of acting in accordance with that rule, given what we know about how everyone else usually acts" (p. 723). Knapp (1999) described a benefit of rule utilitarianism being that rules for protection of minorities can be developed; this contrasts with an assessment based upon act utilitarianism, which may conclude that protecting minorities in a particular situation does not represent benefiting the greatest number with the most good. Another indication of the utility of a rule is whether others obey the rule.

There are circumstances under which act utilitarianism and rule utilitarianism would come to different ethical conclusions about the same situation. Colby, Gibbs, Kohlberg, Speicher-Dubin, and Candee (1979) developed methods of assessing moral development. One dilemma they used in their assessment may illustrate the possible different outcomes with act versus rule utilitarianism. The dilemma is described thus:

> In Europe, a woman was near death from a special kind of cancer. There was one drug that the doctors thought might save her. It was a form of radium that a druggist in the same town had recently discovered. The drug was expensive to make, but the druggist was charging ten times what the drug cost him to make. He paid $200 for the radium and charged $2,000 for a small dose of the drug. The sick woman's husband, Heinz, went to everyone he knew to borrow the money, but he could only get together about $1,000, which is half of what it cost. He told the druggist that his wife was dying, and asked him to sell it cheaper or let him pay later. But the druggist said, "No, I discovered the drug and I'm going to make money from it." So Heinz got desperate and considered breaking into the man's store to steal the drug for his wife. (p. 1)

Based upon the act utilitarianism, one would calculate the utility of Heinz's two choices: (a) stealing the drug and saving his wife's life, or (b) not stealing the drug and having his spouse die of cancer. The first step is the identification of those affected by the decision. Three individuals are immediately identified: Heinz, his

Table 4.2   Example of Calculation of Utility

Action	Number affected	Units of utility	Total
Act 1: steal drug	Heinz	100	100
	Heinz's spouse	100	100
	Druggist	1	1
		Total	201
Act 2: do not steal drug and let spouse die	Heinz	1	1
	Heinz's spouse	1	1
	Druggist	1	1
		(does not know Heinz's spouse)	
		Total	3

Source: Adapted from Harris, C. (2002). *Applying moral theories*. Belmont, CA: Wadsworth.

spouse, and the druggist. So, based upon Harris's (2002) format the calculations shown in Table 4.2 would be made.

If Heinz steals the drug, as in Act 1, the act will have high utility for both him and his spouse. The druggist will experience low utility and even possibly be harmed, to the degree that he is affected by losing $200. Act 2 results in minimal happiness and utility. Thus the person using act utilitarianism would choose Act 1; Heinz would be acting ethically to steal the drug for his ill spouse and save her life based upon utilitarian theory and the greatest good.

Rule utilitarianism would involve a review of general principles surrounding stealing. Would most people benefit and experience high utility if it is okay to steal when the situation warrants it? An answer to how rule utilitarianism would interpret the situation may be found in state and federal laws, which frequently are based upon utilitarian principles. There are no exceptions to laws against stealing. If people do steal under unique circumstances such as those described in the Heinz dilemma, they may receive reduced sentences, but their thefts are still considered illegal. Under rule utilitarianism it would be determined to be unethical to steal the drug from the druggist. So the ethical decision using rule utilitarianism is to choose Act 2, not steal the drug.

The common use of utilitarian ethics is noted by Knapp (1999), who stated, "On one level, many lay persons and psychologists are more or less utilitarian, although they might not have reflected in depth as to the foundations of their ethical beliefs" (p. 383). Utilitarian ethics has permeated much of our thinking and societal practices (De Keijser, Van der lendeen, & Jackson, 2002).

ADDITIONAL READINGS: UTILITARIAN ETHICS

Brandt, R. B. (1992). *Morality, utilitarianism, and rights.* New York: Cambridge University Press.

Goodin, R. E. (1993). Utility and the good. In P. Singer (Ed.), *A companion to ethics* (pp. 241–248). Malden, MA: Blackwell.

Hare, R. M. (1982). Ethical theory and utilitarianism. In A. K. Sen & B. Williams (Eds.), *Utilitarianism and beyond* (pp. 23–38). New York: Cambridge University Press.

Harris, C. E. (2002). *Applying moral theories* (4th ed.). Belmont, CA: Wadsworth.

Mill, J. S. (1987). *Utilitarianism and other essays.* New York: Penguin Putnam.

Pettit, P. (1993). Consequentialism. In P. Singer (Ed.), *A companion to ethics* (pp. 230–240). Malden, MA: Blackwell.

Rosen, F. (2003). *Classical utilitarianism from Hume to Mill.* New York: Routledge.

Shanahan, T., & Wang, R. (2003). *Reason and insight: Western and Eastern perspectives on the pursuit of moral wisdom* (2nd ed.). Belmont, CA: Wadsworth.

Chapter 5

Respect for Persons Ethics and Counselor Decision-Making

Although the contributions from the philosopher Immanuel Kant (1724–1804), the brilliant thinker from the German Enlightenment, provide the theoretical foundation for the ethical positions of respect for persons, it is the refinements and critiques of Kant's work that have consolidated the current ethics of respect for persons that is applicable to counseling.

The central theme of the ethics of respect for persons is that equal respect must be paid to the personhood of all humans. This theme is fundamental to Western ethical insights taken from Hebraic-Christian moral values and noted in the Talmud and Bible (Harris, 2002). At the root of rabbinic teaching was the understanding that humankind was created in the image of God. Thus, humans formed in the divine image and must recognize their importance in relationships with one another; an affront to a fellow human is *ipso facto* an affront to God (Cohen, 1975). One of the rabbinic teachings was the text, "Thou shalt love thy neighbor as thyself" (Leviticus 19:18); this was considered an important basic principle of the Torah (Cohen). As noted by Harris, in the New Testament of Christianity, we find Jesus saying, "In everything do to others as you would have them do to you" (Matthew 7:12).

From what is known in Western ethical philosophy as the *continental tradition,* which includes the work of the Dutch-Jewish philosopher Benedict Spinoza (1632–1677) and the French writer and philosopher Jean-Jacques Rousseau (1712–1778), we find a key idea in the ethics of respect for persons that suggests our everyday nature may not be our true nature. Instead, we are part of a larger entity, and most importantly freedom is found in following reason. Thus, if we are to do what is right and good, we use our reason to develop moral principles to guide our actions (Nell, 1975). From this perspective, we seek answers to ethical and moral questions. What are these principles; how are they determined; how can we know and act upon them; and how can our actions conform to these principles? Perhaps the most influential and penetrating analysis of these questions was proposed by Kant. Like other philosophers from the continental tradition, primarily Spinoza and Rousseau, Kant was firm in his belief that freedom could only be found in rational action, and his writings emphasize how reason is the foundation for ethical decision-making.

The primary axiom is that whatever is demanded by reason must be demanded of all rational beings. Its corollary is that rational action cannot be based on a single individual's personal desires, but must be in accordance with something an individual determines should become a universal law (Singer, 1993). This corollary is an imperative to emphasize a framework of formal principles rather than the actual content of specific rules. The implication of this primary axiom and corollary is that individuals, lacking direct insight into the world of values or the power to intuit the rightness of any action, can only ask themselves whether the action they are proposing has the formal character of law, and therefore is the same for all individuals. However, Kant recognized that a dilemma existed by taking this stance: Morality appeared to take the form of a law that demanded to be obeyed for its own sake, yet a moral law, not issued by some alien authority, represented the voice of reason, which any moral subject could recognize as his own (Singer). Kant was influenced by scientific knowledge expressed in the worldview of the British mathematician and scientist Isaac Newton (1642–1727), which provided his philosophical reliance on reason and his insistence on the need for an empirical component in knowledge.

However, Kant's theory is a complex discussion of how to have both coexist, that is, the emerging scientific knowledge and the possibility of human freedom. Kant transformed Western thought: Individuals had to acknowledge that they had input into the world, and to recognize the possibility that they were not the passive receptors of external truths or reality (Guyer, 1992). From this Kantian position emerges the ethics of respect for persons, a modern adaptation of recognizing our legislative power in both science and morals. Our own contribution to scientific and moral theory has to be reconciled with the practice of these theories (Guyer).

MAJOR CONCEPTS

At the core of Kant's ethical theory is his claim that normal adults are autonomous and capable of being fully self-governing in moral decisions (Schneewind, 1992).

Schneewind's interpretations of Kant's use and meaning of the concept of *autonomy* emphasize how, in Kant's vision of morality, each of us must be allowed a social space, "within which we may *freely determine our own action*" (p. 310). First of all, we do not need to be informed by some external authority about the conditions or the demands for being moral beings, and second, we can effectively control ourselves. What is central to his argument for autonomy is the rise of *obligation* when we impose a moral law on ourselves. The law itself calls to mind our obligation *to act in a certain way*. Obligation in the context created by Kant was a duty. In fact, Kant's most distinct contribution to ethics was his insistence that our actions possess moral worth only when we do our duty for its own sake. He attributed our actions to our common moral consciousness, which is an essential element of any rational morality (Singer, 1993).

In his firm stance that our actions possess moral worth only when we do our duty for its own sake, he did not consider morality evolving from a virtuous disposition or human virtuousness. Instead, Kant saw virtue in terms of struggles, that is, as a "moral strength of will in overcoming temptations to transgress the law" (Schneewind, 1992, p. 310). Several Kantian scholars (Freeman, 2003; Schneewind; Singer, 1993) have pointed out that the "moral strength of will" was not an authoritarian stance but rather a firm position against universal injustice. Included in his idea of injustice was his opposition to those who saw benevolent or sympathetic feelings as the basis of morality (Kant 1785/1953). Schneewind's interpretation of Kant's ideas about benevolence emphasize the relationship between the loss of autonomy and universal injustice:

> If nothing is properly mine except what someone graciously gives me, I am forever dependent on how the donor feels toward me. My independence as an autonomous being is threatened. Only if I can claim that the others *have* to give me what is mine by right, can this be avoided. (p. 311)

Among Kantian scholars (Freeman, 2003; Schneewind, 1992; Singer, 1993), there is consensus that Kant did not deny the moral importance of beneficent actions; rather, his rejection of benevolent paternalism and servility reflects the centrality of autonomy in his theory and his aim of limiting religious and political control of our lives.

The actions of the *moral agent* become crucial in Kant's ethics, because as agents who are autonomous, we engage in *actions that have true moral worth* when we perform an action out of duty, not from our preference (Dancy, 1993; O'Neill, 2003). To elaborate upon the meaning of duty, Schneewind (1992) drew from Kant's discussion about the relationship between means and ends. He surmised that Kant argued *against* the position where moral worth can be attained by using the *means* to further an *end*. The implication is that if an agent's preference is not to achieve the end, then she or he does not have to engage in any act (the means) that leads to achieving the end. Kant, however, held that true moral necessity makes an act necessary regardless of what the agent wants. Even when we know the compelling reason for carrying out an action, which we do not want to do and actually may not do, we admit to ourselves that we *ought* to do it. Kant claims such "ought" actions are conditional. "You ought to do a certain act if you want to attain a certain end . . . [a person] who wills an end, should also will the means which are indispensably necessary and in his power" (Kant, 1785/1953, p. 88).

Kant's meaning of autonomy, obligation, and virtue as they influence the means-end principle establishes the foundation of his central moral concepts, which are based on his distinction between hypothetical and categorical imperatives (Singer, 1993). A *hypothetical imperative* is any *plan of action that is personal or subjective,* and it applies only if we *desire the goal, the end point.* The imperative is hypothetical because "the necessity of action it imposes is conditional. You ought to do a certain act if you will [attain] a certain end" (Schneewind, 1992, p. 319). The imperative is personalized; for example, if you are helpful to people, they will think you are a caring and empathic person (Singer). However, Kant claims the means-end necessity is inadequate for moral law. He maintains that in order to assure the autonomy of a person as a moral agent, the person has to be freed from her or his subjective opinion about a situation, thus, a moral law must be a *categorical imperative*. The basis of Kant's concept of the categorical imperative begins with his insistence that our actions possess moral worth only when we do our duty.

The categorical imperative must be formal; it must be an "ought" that does not depend on a person's (the moral agent's) ends arising from the moral law (Paton, 1958; Schneewind, 1992). This point is key to Kant's ethics: A categorical imperative must *apply to all rational beings, regardless of their wants and feelings:*

> Act only according to that maxim [subjective plan of action] through which you can at the same time will that it should become a universal law. . . . Act as if the maxim of your action were to become through your will a universal law of nature. (Kant, 1785/1953, pp. 88–89)

Kant writes these statements as a formulation from the moral agent's point of view and considers the moral agent the primary focus of what he calls the first formulation.

However, he includes two other formulations. The second formulation addresses those who are affected by our actions: "Act in such a way that you always treat humanity, whether in your own person or in the person of another, never simply as a means, but always at the same time as an end" (Kant, 1785/1953, p. 96). This statement was interpreted by Schneewind (1992) as meaning that the ends of others, if morally permissible, set limits to the ends we may pursue because we must respect the permissible ends of others. The third formulation has us think of ourselves as members of a society where the categorical imperative respects the society's laws and natural laws and the actions of the moral agent are seen in relationship to the person who is the recipient of the actions: "All maxims . . . proceeding from our own law-making ought to harmonize with a possible kingdom of ends as a kingdom of nature" (Schneewind, p. 104). Singer (1993) interpreted this latter formulation as choosing a plan of action so that in accordance with the *principle of universal law, we respect others and ourselves as an end and never merely as the means.* In summary, it is important to recognize that Kant was firmly opposed to judging every action by its consequences. More specifically, the rightness of an action depends on whether it follows a rule irrespective of its consequences (Scheffler, 2003).

Modern Kantians have questioned whether Kant's theory can be of practical use. Some have thought his theory was insufficient to guide action, while others believed the theory led directly to a senseless uniformity of action that disregards the subtle diversity of human circumstances (Nell, 1975). In her analysis of Kant, Nell concluded that neither of these charges could be upheld because Kant's concept of the categorical imperative could guide action and help us make moral choices without leading to rigorism. Although modern critiques of Kant have carefully examined the usefulness of Kant's categorical imperative as an ethical guide because of its many contradictions, modern philosophers (Hare, 1963; Harris, 2002; Nell; Singer, 1993) have come up with proposals for universality tests (Harris; Nell; Paton, 1958). Nell used Kant's universality tests from the principle of universal law to argue that the following tests can be effective guides for ethical behavior:

- Act only on that maxim through which you can at the same time will that it should become a universal law.

- Act as if the maxim of your action were to become through your will a universal law of nature. (p. 32)

Harris (2002) took these Kantian tests and directed us to evaluate the *universal principle* as a moral standard, and then to determine whether we can consent to others following it:

- Moral standard: An action is right if you can consent to everyone's adopting the moral rule presupposed by the action.

- Self-defeating test: Can I consent to others' acting simultaneously according to the same rule I use without undermining my own ability to act in accordance with it? (p. 158)

One problem with implementing the universal principle and with applying the self-defeating test to it is that we have no quantitative method for determining whether a universal principle can be consistently and simultaneously adopted. To apply a universal principle requires determining how broad or narrow to make the rule for which you are applying the self-defeating test (Harris, 2002). Nell (1975) explained broad and narrow rules as those determined by Kant's division of human duties into duties of justice and duties of virtue. Duties of justice are narrow obligations because of the sorts of acts and behaviors they command; duties of virtue are broad obligations because of the sort of ends they require us to pursue (Nell, p. 57). Harris pursued this explanation even further by pointing out that the universalization of your action or behavior could undermine or at least seriously weaken the goal you have in mind for your actions. Thus, he continued, if both a rule and its alternative are self-defeating when actions of each are followed, then both the rule and the alternative will be morally impermissible.

If this is the case we must turn to the *means-end principle* (Harris, 2002; Nell, 1975). In this principle Nell (p. 110) found that the discussion of motives and ends in Kant's theory are a simpler definition of morally worthy actions, and a definition not dependent on the notion of an obligatory act: "For an act to be morally worthy it is not necessary or sufficient that it result in the promotion of an objective end. The objective end must be aimed for, but it need not be realized" (p. 111). Moreover, an action is right that treats human beings, whether you or someone else, as ends and not simply as means (Harris). To determine whether we are treating a person as an end and not merely as a means, Harris used two tests: the negative test and the positive test. In using the negative test, we are determining whether an action overrides the freedom or well-being of someone else or ourselves. However, in using the positive we do more than not interfere with freedoms and well-being of others and ourselves; we also contribute positively to someone's—ours or others'—capability to act as a moral agent.

ADDITIONAL READINGS: RESPECT FOR PERSONS ETHICS

Almond, B. (1993). Rights. In P. Singer (Ed.), *A companion to ethics* (pp. 259–269). Malden, MA: Blackwell.

Andersen, W. E., Mason, M., & Hurley, J. (1989). Respect for persons: Kant reconstructed, mistranslated, and deserted. *Journal of Christian Education, 94*(2), 23–32.

Downey, R., & Telfer, E. (1969). *Respect for persons.* London: George Allen and Unwin.

Harris, C. E. (2002). *Applying moral theories* (4th ed.). Belmont, CA: Wadsworth.

Hill, T. E. (2000). *Respect, pluralism, and justice: Kantian perspectives.* New York: Oxford.

Ilesanmi, S. O. (2005). Human rights. In W. Schweiker (Ed.), *The Blackwell companion to religious ethics* (pp. 501–510). Malden, MA: Blackwell.

Kellenberger, J. (1995). *Relationship morality.* University Park, PA: The Penn State University Press.

O'Neill, O. (1993). Kantian ethics. In P. Singer (Ed.), *A companion to ethics* (pp. 175–185). Malden, MA: Blackwell.

Orkar, M. M. (1999, August). The ethics of justice and care in the respect for persons principle: Implications for education. *Educational Insights, 5*(1). Retrieved February 23, 2006, from http://www.ccfi.educ.ubc.ca/publication/insights/online/v05n01/orkar.html

Rawls, J. (1967). The sense of justice. In J. Feinberg (Ed.), *Moral concepts* (pp. 135–146). New York: Oxford University Press.

Roberts, L. W., & Dyer, A. R. (2004). *Concise guide to ethics in mental health care.* Arlington, VA: American Psychiatric Publishing.

Sullivan, R. J. (1994). *An introduction to Kant's ethics.* New York: Cambridge University Press.

Chapter 6

Feminine and Feminist Ethics and Counselor Decision-Making

Until recently, ethical discourse in the United States was dominated by males and reflected an exclusively masculine perspective. With the rise of the women's liberation movement during the 1960s, feminism challenged Western ethical thinking that neglected or depreciated women (Friedan, 1963, 1981; Jaggar, 1992) and was applied to other misrepresented, oppressed, or minority populations as well (Brabeck & Ting, 2000).

The idea that morality is gender-based (i.e., there are different virtues for males and females) emerges in the ethical thinking of many philosophers, and, in particular, is central to the philosophy of Rousseau. In *Emile* (1763/1979), Rousseau contended that what are virtues for women are faults for men. He thought that women could only be virtuous by becoming wives and mothers, and, consequently, dependent and subordinate in marriage. In Rousseau's view, women who pursued goals outside of the family were less desirable. In what is considered the first great feminist treatise, Wollstonecraft (1792/1999) attacked Rousseau's position and argued that virtue should mean the same thing for men and women. Since that time, there have been passionate debates about the idea of a "female ethic" and whether there are specifically female virtues. The arguments have questioned "essentialist" beliefs about the nature of males and females. For example, Daly (1978/1990) took the radical view that violence and destruction in the world are the consequences of activities dominated by men (war, politics, economics). According to Daly, this havoc is due to the unchanging nature of masculinity and the male psyche, whereas females are "naturally" less aggressive and more nurturing. Most feminist thinking rejects an essentialist position, instead viewing the "nature" of males and females as changeable and socially constructed (Grimshaw, 1993).

MAJOR CONCEPTS

Feminism is not a singular ideology and there are two major streams of "woman-centered" approaches to ethics: *feminine* and *feminist*. Despite the similarity of those two terms, they represent different theoretical approaches. *"Feminine" refers to a search for women's unique voice and advocates for an ethic of care. "Feminist" refers to an argument against male domination and advocates for equal rights.* Both approaches seek to validate women's moral experiences, to understand women's oppression, and to eliminate gender inequality.

Feminine ethics addresses itself to aspects of traditional Western ethics that devalue female moral experiences, in particular, the contractual moral theories and justice ethics of Kant. Traditional ethics deal with contractual relations as a model for human relations: A relationship is moral to the extent that it serves the separate interests of autonomous individuals—as in a business contract. The current controversy centers on two fundamental aspects of human relationships, care and justice, and is similar to the virtues versus principles debate, which was considered in Chapter 2. An ethic of care concerns itself with questions of attachment to others, in contrast to an ethic of justice, which is concerned with questions of equality with others.

A feminist approach to ethics asks questions about power, that is, domination and subordination, before it considers questions of care and justice, or maternal and paternal thinking. The feminist position, more than the feminine approach, is political in that feminist ethicists are committed to eliminating the subordination of women and any other oppressed persons. Because feminists are interested in patterns of oppression, their concerns extend to other patterns of domination and subordination, such as racism and classism. The focus on women and oppression is what makes an ethic feminist, as opposed to feminine. The aim of feminist ethics is to create a gender-equal ethic that is based on nonsexist moral principles.

The feminine position is exemplified in the work of Carol Gilligan (1982). She criticized moral reasoning based on a justice perspective as an inherently biased male view. She argued that traditional Western ethical theories ignore or denigrate the virtues that are culturally associated with women. In opposition to Kohlberg's (1984) contention that moral behavior emanates from the construct of justice, Gilligan suggested that moral behavior focuses more on responsibilities within a context, often within the context of special relationships. In particular, Gilligan criticized the moral development theory of Lawrence Kohlberg (1981) as being centered in a Western ethical tradition that uses a language of justice, emphasizing rights and rules. Kohlberg's studies of moral reasoning favored males whom he thought were better able to discern moral principles. Gilligan insists that this Kantian definition of ethics, which emphasizes justice and rationality in moral judgments, obscures a female moral language of care, which emphasizes relationships and responsibilities. Rather than seeing women as morally inferior to men, Gilligan sought to reframe the issue as a moral difference.

Care is the key concept from the feminine perspective. Care reasoning can be differentiated from justice reasoning; the former emphasizes relational understanding (Gilligan, 2004; Gilligan & Attanucci, 1988) whereas the latter emphasizes logic. *Care is a compassionate determination of how to meet a person's needs* whereas *justice is an objective weighing of principles to determine moral rights and responsibilities* (Peterson & Seligman, 2004). Care and justice are distinct ethical approaches: (1) care takes a contextual approach whereas justice takes an abstract approach; (2) care assumes human connectedness whereas justice assumes autonomy; (3) care focuses on the maintenance of relationships whereas justice focuses on equality; (4) care is most applicable in the private domain whereas justice is most applicable in the public sphere; (5) care stresses the role of emotions in *good* character whereas justice stresses the role of reason in performing *right* actions; and (6) care is female whereas justice is male (Clement, 1996; Tong, 1998). Debates have ensued concerning an ethic of care versus an ethic of justice: Do men and women actually have different moral voices? Do the affective (care) and rational (justice) perspectives conflict, or are both needed for moral and ethical conduct? Are the virtues of care (benevolence) and justice (fairness) incompatible so that a single individual could not possess both? There is the view that women do not act on principle but are influenced by intuition and personal considerations. Grimshaw (1993) suggested that it might not be the case that women and men reason differently about moral issues, but that they have different ethical priorities: What is regarded as an important moral principle by women (maintaining relationships) is seen as a failure of principle by men.

Like Gilligan's, Noddings's (2003) relational ethics approach is feminine, but unlike Gilligan, Noddings claims that an ethic of care is not only different but better than an ethic of justice. She is critical of traditional ethics because it undervalues caring, as if it is easy to care for people. For Noddings, ethics are not about rules to guide behavior. Rather, ethics are rooted in particular relationships, such as that of mother and child, and involve special interactions between a caretaker and the one receiving the care. From this relational perspective, the practices associated with parenting, as well as our memories of receiving care, are the expressions of moral life.

Accordingly, a gender-equal ethics should not use the "contract" model prevalent in men's experience because most relationships are between persons of unequal status (Baier, 1986, 1994). Contracts are only appropriate for those who have equal power and are capable of voluntary agreements. They are not appropriate in situations where one party is vulnerable because of limited power due to gender, sickness, or age. Women's life experiences often involve caring for those who are dependent (children, aging parents) and both Noddings and Baier agree that ethics should be built on those everyday life experiences. People do not interact as business people negotiating a deal but as two individuals with different strengths and weaknesses.

The psychoanalytic perspective of Chadrow (1978) supports the view that women may be more disposed than men to a care perspective and that this caring sentiment originates in the mother-child relationship. Girls can identify with the mother and maintain that identification throughout life. However, boys identify with their fathers and detach themselves from the primary caring relationship. The different male and female styles of moral reasoning come from these two gender-specific developmental trajectories (Gilligan, 2004; Gilligan & Attanucci, 1988).

Maternal ethics is a feminine point of view that is concerned with the preservation, growth, and acceptability of one's children. According to Held (1987), mothers know that relationships are about cooperation, community, and serving others' needs. Held suggests that because women spend so much time mothering, they should develop theories that fit relationships in the private rather than the public domain.

Care ethics are consonant with a virtue ethics point of view—a virtuous person is caring (Halwani, 2003; Meara, Schmidt, & Day, 1996; Solomon, 1993). Because an ethic of care is based on contextual decision-making, often in the context of special relationships, its application is consistent with the outlook in some multicultural communities where the concept of community and relatedness is emphasized over autonomy and individual rights (Vasquez, 1996).

Both nonfeminist and feminist writers have attacked the position of an ethics of care. Nonfeminist critics point out that both care (benevolence) and justice are ethical obligations derived from a traditional Western moral tradition (Scher, 1987). Ross (1989) argued that a feminine approach can reinforce a sexist division of roles where women are relegated to the private, nurturing, domestic sphere, and men to the impersonal, public, and power realms. Veatch (1998) criticized the ethic of care as having an incoherent definition. Moreover, not all women are mothers, and there are questions as to whether one human relationship, that of mother and child, can serve as a paradigm for all human relationships (Brennan, 1999).

Feminists caution that it may be ethically unwise to link women with care because it can promote the view that women should care no matter what the cost to themselves. Tong (1998) suggested that men may be all too willing to concede that women are more caring than men, thus leaving it to women to foster personal relationships and to deal with emotional issues. Mill (1970) pointed out that praising women for their virtue measured a woman's worth based on the extent of her willingness to sacrifice for others. Caretaking is more of what society demands of women rather than something women created. According to Mullett (1988), a woman cannot truly care for another if she is economically, socially, or psychologically forced to do so. An ethic of care may only serve to reinforce traditional stereotypic roles for women. Also, a feminine explanation of female ambivalence about attachment and autonomy ignores the political forces that have confined women to caretaking roles (Spohn, 1992).

Moreover, there is empirical research (Blasi, 1980; Rest, 1986; Stewart & Sprinthall, 1994) to indicate that women actually use a justice perspective in ethical thinking, which undermines the feminine argument that care is more important than justice in women's ethical decision-making.

There are several schools of feminist ethics: existential, postmodern, multicultural, and lesbian, among others (Tong, 2003). Proponents of these various schools of thought maintain that the destruction of all systems, institutions, and practices that support the power differentials between women and men is a necessary prerequisite for the creation of gender equality.

Oppression is the key concept from the feminist perspective. In *The Second Sex* (1953), existentialist feminist Simone de Beauvoir wrote that, from the beginning, man named himself the Self and woman the Other. If the Other is a threat to the Self, then woman is a threat to man, and if men wish to remain free, they must not only economically, politically, and sexually subordinate women to themselves, they must also convince women that they deserve no better treatment. Thus, if women are to become true Selves, they must recognize themselves as free and responsible moral agents who possess the capacity to perform in the public as well as the private world. Socialist feminist thinking affirms that women must be men's economic as well as educational and political equals before they can be as powerful as men.

Postmodernism is a complicated idea that arose in the 1980s. In contrast to *modern* thought, which equates knowledge with science, *postmodern* thought is concerned with the social construction of knowledge, which is always situational, conditional, and temporary, and which denies universal truths (Klages, 2003). Postmodernism, with its acknowledgement and acceptance of multiple meanings, attracts feminists who see that all attempts to provide a single explanation for women's oppression will fail and who see it as yet another instance of "male think-ing" in seeking one truth about reality. Because there is no one entity, "women," upon whom a label can be fixed, it is important to reveal the differences and resist the patriarchal tendency to rigid thought and "truths" (Tong, 2003).

Historically, feminism has been influenced by white, heterosexual, middle- to upper-class women. Minority women criticize feminism for failing to incorporate the experiences of more diverse groups, such as racial and ethnic minorities, les-bians, and poor or working-class women (Espin & Gawelek, 1992). Multicultural feminists believe that feminist thought is inattentive to issues of race and ethnic-ity. Because Western culture values "white" ideals of beauty, for example, African American women are doubly oppressed—subject both to gender and racial dis-crimination. Feminists also address the life experiences of disabled women (Wendell, 1996), challenging the accounts of universal female bodily experiences. In response to these criticisms, feminism has broadened its scope.

Many cultures around the world are patriarchal, and sex discrimination often has cultural roots. Although multiculturalism includes worthy goals of tolerance, flexi-bility, and respect for diversity, protecting the rights of minority groups may also serve to reinforce practices that facilitate the control of men over women while women remain hidden in the domestic or private sphere. Multiculturalism has raised questions about the danger of moral relativism for feminist ethics (Brennan, 1999; Jaggar, 1991). Nussbaum and Glover (1995) stated the dilemma thus:

> To say that a practice endorsed by tradition is bad is to risk erring by imposing one's own way on others who surely have their own idea of what is right and good. To say that a practice is all right wherever local tradition endorses it as right is to risk erring by withholding critical judgment where real evil and oppression are surely present. (p. 1)

Okin's (1997) work is a reminder of the problem of moral relativism and how the multicultural movement may oppress women. For example, she cites cases where a successful "cultural defense" (p. 6) resulted in reduced charges for kidnap and rape by Hmong men who claim their actions were part of the cultural practice of *zij poj niam* or "marriage by capture." Those types of cultural defenses do not afford women equal protection under the law.

Lesbian ethicists (Hoagland, 1989) believe that feminine and maternal approaches reinforce female oppression. They also go beyond feminists, who affirm some relationships with men, by taking a radical position in claiming that what is good for lesbians is not necessarily good for heterosexual women or men. Heterosexuality is seen as patriarchy. Lesbian ethics is not just a sexual orientation; it is a refusal to be defined either sexually or morally by men. Instead of a "mother" ethic, lesbian ethicists prefer a "daughter" ethic because all women are daughters but not all women are mothers. The daughter ethic does not presume that all women should care for children or be trapped by caring duties as an obligation from which there is no escape.

Feminists have been particularly concerned about issues of reproductive technology, such as in vitro fertilization. Mullett (1988) points out that bioethicists use utilitarian arguments stressing the good of reproductive technology in offering infertile couples an opportunity to be biological parents. However, this technology may be contributing to women's continuing oppression because it suggests that now that women can, they *should* fulfill their destiny as biological mothers. Even though feminists are concerned about reproductive technology and want to raise the consciousness of women about these issues, they are not opposed to the development of technology because those technological advances also offer women more choices in life.

Nonfeminist critics complained that feminist approaches are female-biased, and that ethics cannot proceed from a specific standpoint (Rawls, 2001). Feminists suggest that the traditional ethical principles, rules, and norms actually serve to support patterns of domination and subordination. Yet, feminists have not articulated a clear and unified position on key moral issues of interest to the widest possible range of women.

Baier (1985, 1986, 1994) responded to the call for a clearer ethical theory that incorporates the moral perspectives of both men and women. Central to her concept is the idea of *trust* as the *bond in human relationships*. As Baier (1985) explained, trust rather than control is embedded in the caring relationships. *Trust is defined as the "reliance on others' competence and willingness to look after, rather than harm, things one cares about which are entrusted to their care"* (p. 59). This raises the issue of symmetric and asymmetric relationships. For example, reason-guided justice perspectives emphasize symmetric relationships among equals, who determine the rules and enforce sanctions on those who break them. However, Baier noted that most trust relationships are asymmetrical, with unequal responsibilities borne by each party.

This notion of a trust ethic is important in counseling, which is inherently an asymmetric relationship, because the counselor is in a position to affect the well-being of the client. There is even greater asymmetry in counseling situations that involve minority clients or those with physical or psychological disabilities, who do not experience equal status in society at large (Nicki, 2002). Counselors need to acknowledge the vulnerability of clients and the potential for abuse of power in relationships.

Feminist counseling grew out of dissatisfaction with male-centered theories, deficits in knowledge about female psychology, sex-role stereotyping, and general neglect of women's mental health concerns (Worrell & Remer, 1992). Radov, Masnick, and Hauser (1977) noted that behaviors considered indicative of psychopathology in women were often those that did not fit with the feminine stereotype. Martin (2001) also suggested that the medicalization of women's psychological distress, by medicating socially induced depression, for example, serves to further oppression and ignore the social injustice. Cummings (2000) noted that many of the problems that women bring to counseling are the result of their limited power in society (e.g., abuse, harassment) and their internalization of societal oppression (e.g., lookism, eating disorders).

ADDITIONAL READINGS: FEMININE AND FEMINIST ETHICS

Bader, K. M., & Allen, K. R. (1992). *Women and families: Feminist reconstructions.* New York: Guilford Press.

Cannon, K. (1988). *Black womanist ethics.* Atlanta, GA: Scholars Press.

Clement, G. (1996). *Care, autonomy, and justice.* Boulder, CO: Westview Press.

Collins, P. (1990). *Black feminist thought: Knowledge, consciousness, and the politics of empowerment.* Boston: Unwin Hyman.

Freeman, S. J. (2000). *Ethics: An introduction to philosophy and practice.* Belmont, CA: Wadsworth/Thomson Learning.

Grimshaw, J. (1993). The idea of a female ethic. In P. Singer (Ed.), *A companion to ethics* (pp. 491–499). Malden, MA: Blackwell.

Houser, R., & Ham, M. (2004). *Gaining power and control through diversity and group affiliation.* Westport, CT: Prager.

Moore, M. (1999). The ethics of care and justice. *Women and Politics, 20*(2), 1–16.

Prindeville, D. M., & Gomez, T. B. (1999). American Indian women leaders, public policy, and the importance of gender and ethnic identity. *Women and Politics, 20*(2), 17–32.

Sherwin, S. (1992). *No longer patient: Feminist ethics and health care.* Philadelphia, PA: Temple University Press.

Tong, R. (1993). *Feminine and feminist ethics.* Belmont, CA: Wadsworth.

Tong, R. (2003). Feminist ethics. In E. Zalta (Ed.), *The Stanford encyclopedia of philosophy.* Retrieved May 4, 2005, from http://plato.stanford.edu/archives/win2003/entries/feminism-ethics/

Wolf, D. (1991). Development, demography and family decision-making: The status of women in rural Java. *Journal of Asian Studies, 50,* 752–753.

Chapter 7

Native American Ethics and Counselor Decision-Making

Native Americans are those indigenous people that were residents of the United States. prior to Europeans entering this country. This includes indigenous people of Hawaii and Alaska. Current estimates of those who identify themselves as Native American, American Indian, Alaskan Native, and Hawaiian Native range from 2.5 million to 5 million (Gone, 2004; Sioui, 1995; U.S. Census Bureau, 2000). This compares with over 112 million Native Americans prior to the entrance of Europeans into the Native Americans' world in 1492 (Gone; Sioui). Diseases were primarily responsible for the significant loss of the Native American population both on the U.S. mainland and in Hawaii.

American Indians, Alaskan Natives, and Hawaiian Natives share similar histories even though they never crossed paths and were separated by several thousand miles of ocean. American Indians have a long history of over 10,000 years (Freuchen, 1957; Taylor, 1997). Half of this time was spent without European settlers and whites. However, approximately 500 years ago Americans Indians were confronted with the invasion of the Americas by whites.

Alaskan Natives supposedly crossed the Bering Strait from Europe between 5000 and 3500 BCE. The Vikings were believed to be the first Europeans to come in contact with Alaskan Natives beginning in the tenth century CE. More frequent and lasting contact began in the 1800s with the entrance of missionaries and whaling ships (Freuchen, 1957).

Like American Indians on the continents, Hawaiian Natives had lived on the islands for over 1,400 years before foreigners entered their world (Kuykendall &

Day, 1967). Hawaiians are thought to have originated from the western islands of Indonesia. Hawaii was discovered by European explorers in the late 1700s; Captain Cook is the most noted explorer of the Hawaiian Islands, and he initially named them the Sandwich Islands. Over the next several hundred years, the natives of Hawaii lost control of their islands, with foreigners taking over land and the political control of the islands (Kuykendall & Day). Native Hawaiians were similar to American Indians in that they respected and lived in concert with nature.

A place to begin understanding Native American ethics is a view that everything in the universe is connected. Several methods have been offered to represent this connection. For example, one is a view of the universe as a great circle that is continuous (Lombardi & Lombardi, 1982; Marshall, 2001). Lombardi and Lombardi stated,

> The perspective of the universe as the Great Circle becomes charged with a truth that is more than a physical fact, yet not merely a metaphysical concept. The chain of interdependence becomes sacred. The exchange of life-giving power transforms every commonplace act into a ritual and faith and solidarity. (p. 11)

Bopp, Bopp, Brown, and Lane (1985) suggested "the Sacred Tree" as a symbol of connections within the universe. They described the "Sacred Tree" as

> For all people on the earth, the Creator has planted a Sacred Tree under which they may gather, and there find healing, power, wisdom and security. The roots of this tree spread deep into the body of Mother Earth. Its branches reach upward like hands praying to Father Sky. The fruits of this tree are the good things the Creator has given to the people; teachings that show the path to love, compassion, generosity, patience, wisdom, justice, courage, respect, humility and many other wonderful gifts. (p. 7)

Another key in understanding Native Americans ethics is the strong connection to the environment. Note the comments by Bopp et al. (1985) referring to "Mother Earth" and "Father Sky." They further use the symbol of a wheel, which is round, or a circle to illustrate the connections in the universe. Specifically, the "Medicine Wheel" represents the universe. There are several examples of how the Medicine Wheel shows connections in the universe. One model includes four aspects of human nature (Bopp et al.). The four components of human nature represented on the Medicine Wheel include the mental, physical, emotional, and spiritual (see Figure 7.1). Humans strive to find a balance of these four dimensions of human nature.

Figure 7.1   Four Components of a Native American Medicine Wheel

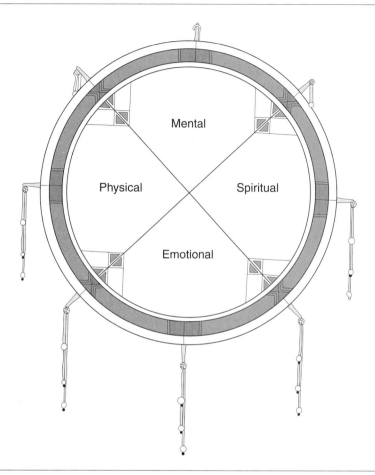

Another illustration of use of the Medicine Wheel is the "Gifts of the Four Directions." These directions provide for the development of the person's nature, e.g., mental, emotional, physical, and spiritual. The four directions are east, south, west, and north (see Figure 7.2). The movement around the wheel or the universe is an indication of the patterns exhibited in nature (Bopp et al., 1985). Bopp et al. stated, "The East is the direction from which the new day comes into the world. It is the direction of renewal, it is the place of innocence, guilelessness, spontaneity, joy and the capacity to believe in the unseen" (p. 42). Symbolically, the east also is seen as the direction from which illumination comes (Bopp et al.).

Figure 7.2 Gifts of the Four Directions and Movement in the Universe

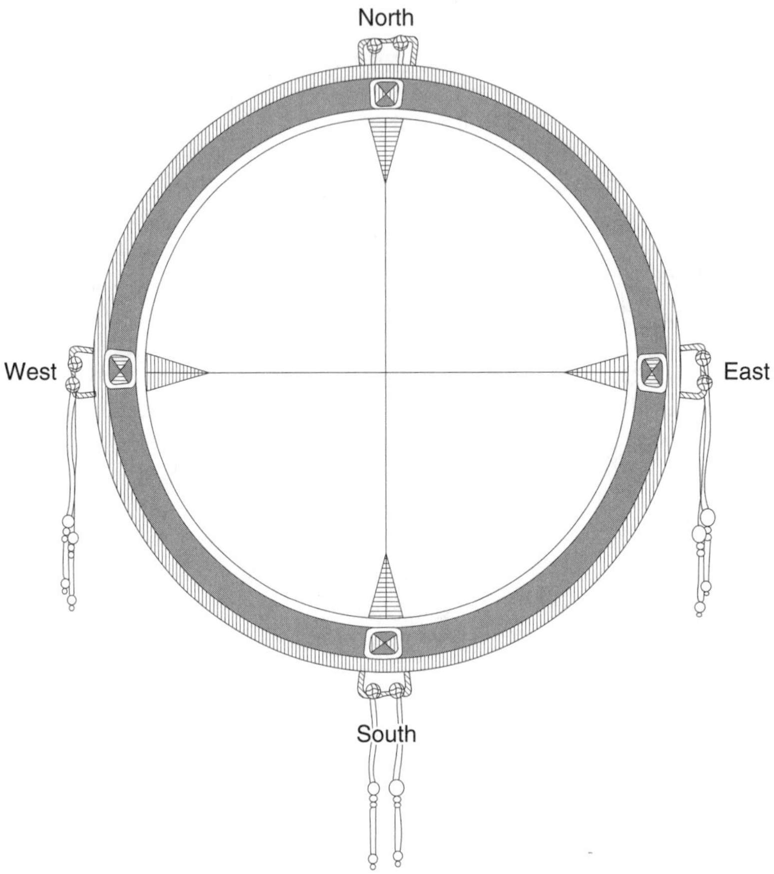

Source: Reproduced with permission from *The Sacred Tree* by Four Worlds International Institute for Human and Community Development, published in the USA by Lotus Press, PO Box 325, Twin Lakes, WI 51381. ©1984 All rights reserved.

The next place on the wheel is south, which represents the fullness of youth and physical strength. For example, emotional strength can be developed through contact with the south. This is where the individual begins to learn control over his or her emotions and physical nature.

Bopp et al. (1985) described the west as "the direction from which darkness comes. It is the direction of the unknown, of going within, of dreams, of prayer, and of meditation" (p. 53). The west also is considered the location of power for the individual. Symbolically, the west is where lightning originates, thus a symbol for power (Bopp et al.). The west additionally is a place of sacrifice; nothing can be removed from the world and nature without sacrificing something.

The north represents maturity or a place of winter with snow. Symbolically it may be denoted as snow on the rooftop, e.g., an elderly person's white hair. This is a place of wisdom. The north, according to Bopp et al. (1985), also represents completion and fulfillment, e.g., fulfillment of one's life. A final component of the north is the development of balance in a person's life. There needs to be a balance between excesses and deficits as in the balance of nature.

MAJOR CONCEPTS

Native American ethics is not as coherent a structure as some other ethical theories because there are so many groups represented. However, several sources that address Native American ethics provide insight into common basic concepts (Bopp et al., 1985; Bopp, Lane, Brown, and Bopp, 1989; Lombardi & Lombardi, 1982). We will address the most common concepts that represent Native American ethics.

A major concept or view is that of *respect or esteem for another person or nature* (Bopp et al., 1985; Cooper, 1998). Cooper described this concept as not putting anyone down, not taking another's possessions, protecting the natural environment, and not speaking ill of others. Another component of the concept of respect and honoring all human life is *respect for elders* (Cooper). One should not offend or be disrespectful to an elder. This includes following the advice of elders. Bopp et al. (1985) described respect as "treat every person, from the tiniest child to the oldest elder with respect at all times" (p. 76). They also stated, "Special respect should be given to elders, parents, teachers and community leaders" (p. 76). Marshall (2001) described the attitude of the Lakota, an American Indian tribe, in regard to respect for elders as: "Among us the old ones are the best models for how we should live our lives" (p. 1). Respect for all races fits into this concept also (Cooper).

A second major concept is to *be truthful* at all times (Bopp et al., 1985; Cooper, 1998). The person is admonished not to tell mistruths, even socially acceptable mistruths, such as saying you like something so as to not offend another. The intent is to be respectful and to tell the truth. Truth is sought through life experiences. As Marshall (2001) described it, truth is it not something that is easily identified. He stated,

Truth can, at times, hide so well that we can't find it to save ourselves, or it disguises itself so skillfully that we walk over it without knowing. And in the next instance it becomes plain as day, whether we want it to or not. (p. 119)

There is a consistent perspective on truth founded in the environment and physical world. Marshall succinctly described truth in the following way:

> We can see the sun come up over the eastern horizon in the morning and then disappear behind the western horizon in the evening. From the perspective of our existence on a spinning sphere, the sun appears to "rise" and "set." In reality the sun does neither. (p. 120)

Marshall (2001) further described truth based upon physical reality as "Reality is what is, first and foremost in our physical world. . . . Truth is the result of trials and errors of life, the lessons we have learned" (p. 120). Truth can be misunderstood as an illusion, and it is the person's responsibility to discover the truth and not be fooled by the illusion. This requires an openness to the realities of the physical world and openness to discovery.

Another major concept is *serving others* and not focusing solely on one's own personal needs. Bopp et al. (1989) described this concept as follows: "Do not fill yourself with personal affairs, but remember the meaning of life is only known in serving others" (p. 21). Also, serving others may be seen as including two components: sacrifice and generosity. The Native American view is that responsibility to others and the community is essential. Marshall described sacrifice:

> A rich man who writes a check to a hospital to build a new research facility is certainly an epitome of generosity. Generosity is a necessary virtue, but unless that man has given away all of his money he has not performed an act of sacrifice. (p. 106)

A fourth major concept is to achieve *moderation* in one's life (Bopp et al., 1989). Extremes of overindulgence are considered undesirable. Bopp et al. (1985), in describing the interaction of connections within the universe, use the medicine wheel as a symbol and state,

> The Medicine Wheel teaches us that we have four aspects to our nature: the physical, the mental, the emotional, and the spiritual. Each of these aspects must be equally developed in a healthy well-balanced individual through the development of volition (i.e., will). (p. 12)

Thus, the belief is that humans have free will to control and find balance in their lives.

Waters (2004) identified another ethical concept, and it is based upon the view that humans continuously affect each other and the environment. Consequently, humans must *take responsibility for their actions.*

ADDITIONAL READINGS: NATIVE AMERICAN ETHICS

Arvizu, D. R. (1995). The care voice and American Indian college students: An alternative perspective for student development professionals [Electronic version]. *Journal of American Indian Education, 34*(3). Retrieved April 25, 2005, from http://jaie.asu.edu/v34/V34S3car.htm

Code of Ethics. Retrieved April 15, 2005, from http://www.angelfire.com/biz2/turquoise butterfly/roadintro.html

Cordova, V. F. (2003). Ethics: From an artist's point of view. In A. Waters (Ed.), *American Indian thought: Philosophical essays* (pp. 251–255). Malden, MA: Blackwell.

Cordova, V. F. (2003). Ethics: The we and the I. In A. Waters (Ed.), *American Indian thought: Philosophical essays* (pp. 173–181). Malden, MA: Blackwell.

Davis, M. B. (Ed.). (1994). *Native Americans in the twentieth century: An encyclopedia.* New York: Garland.

Deloria, V. (2005). Indigenous peoples. In W. Schweiker (Ed.), *The Blackwell companion to religious ethics* (pp. 552–559). Malden, MA: Blackwell.

DuFour, J. (2003). Ethics and understanding. In A. Waters (Ed.), *American Indian thought: Philosophical essays* (pp. 34–42). Malden, MA: Blackwell.

Kidwell, C. S., Noley, H., & Tinker, G. E. (2001). *A Native American theology.* Maryknoll, NY: Orbis.

Nerburn, K. (Ed.). (1999). *The wisdom of the Native American.* Novato, CA: New World Library.

Waters, A. (Ed.) (2003). *American Indian thought: Philosophical essays.* Malden, MA: Blackwell.

SECTION II

Eastern Theories of Ethics

The second section focuses on Eastern ethical theories. We include in our discussion the following theories: Confucianism, Taoism, Hinduism, and Buddhism.

Chapter 8 is a presentation of Confucian ethics. Confucius is the primary originator of this theory, which began in China centuries ago. The theory is based upon ethical guidance from ancient rituals and practices.

The next chapter, Chapter 9, is a discussion of Taoism (Daoism). The primary contributor of this theory is Lao Zi, a Chinese contemporary of Confucius (Shanahan & Wang, 2003). The foundation of the theory is an intuitive seeking of balance in one's life.

Chapter 10 is a presentation of Hinduism and ethics (Shanahan & Wang, 2003). Shanahan and Wang noted that Hinduism is the oldest historically recorded philosophical view, dating back to 2500 BCE, and that the authors of major Hindu books are generally not known. A search for "truth" is a major focus of this view. Also, ethics in Hinduism may be understood as including virtues such as humility, patience, and honoring others. Additionally, it means avoiding vices such as greed and anger.

In Chapter 11, we discuss Buddhism, which is founded on the primary belief in finding the "middle way." Buddhism, an older philosophy founded around 500 BCE, was developed in response to the perceived limitations of Hinduism (Shanahan & Wang, 2003). Siddhartha Gautama, later called Buddha, was a major contributor to this theory. A key feature of the theory is the belief in suffering as a natural and expected human experience. The focus is on understanding suffering and achieving the "middle way."

Chapter 8

Confucian Ethics and Counselor Decision-Making

Confucianism has a long history, dating back over 2,000 years, and it is one of the three major sources of ethical thinking in Asian cultures. Similar to Greek ethics, Confucianism has a goal of developing desired virtues; however, a major difference is a focus on obligations to others (Shanahan & Wang, 2003). Confucius lived from 551 to 479 BCE during the Zhou dynasty. *Confucius* is Latin for the Chinese name Kong Fuzi or Master Kong (Yao, 2000). Confucius was raised by his mother after his father died when he was three years old (Shanahan & Wang). Chinese view Confucius as the "first teacher" in China (Hansen, 1992; Smith, 1991). After holding several unskilled jobs, Confucius became a teacher and flourished in this role; it is estimated he had over 3,000 students (Yao). Smith noted that Confucius sought positions in government, but because of his honesty and questioning of governmental officials' actions, he only achieved lower-level positions. He traveled to other regions of China seeking to consult with leaders and provide direction; however, he was not hired in any significant position. This history is relevant because Confucius strongly supported a positive respectful relationship between rulers and the common people. In fact, he believed that not following traditions and rituals resulted in confusion and chaos.

Smith (1991) stated, "Confucius was undoubtedly one of the world's greatest teachers. Prepared to instruct in history, poetry, government, propriety, mathematics, music, divination, and sports, he was, in the manner of Socrates, a one-man university" (p. 156). The interesting point about Confucius's method of teaching is the communication that he shared in the learning experience, rather than being the only source of information. He was open to student feedback and encouraged it. Key underlying principles in Confucianism are rituals, tradition, and respect for social order. Therefore, he promoted adherence to respect for political rulers, but as Smith noted he also promoted democratic attitudes and supported fair treatment of common people by totalitarian rulers.

During his lifetime, he was a well respected teacher, but he did not receive much recognition beyond this role. Several generations after his death, he was still perceived to be the mentor (Smith, 1991). Smith suggested that it is unclear as to exactly what contributed to the dramatic increase in his influence after his death. However, Smith hypothesized that Confucianism highlighted the importance of family, as well as a process or structure to bring individuals together and develop a society that is predictable and reduces chaos. Consequently, Chinese society embraced Confucianism because of its simplicity and its functional nature.

Yum (1988) noted that Confucianism was accepted to an extensive degree in both Korea and Japan. In regard to acceptance in those countries, Yum stated, "Confucianism was institutionalized and propagated both through formal curricula of the educational system and through the selection process of government officials" (p. 376). Oldstone-Moore (2002) included Vietnam as a country that also was greatly influenced by Confucianism.

The essence of this theory is that we learn social roles through life and literature, i.e., life through models (Yao, 2000). Confucius proposed that humans seek a well-ordered society. This may be accomplished in part through well-established social roles (Hansen, 1992). One's social role is essential to understanding one's position and subsequently one's actions. Yao stated that "the vitality of Confucianism can be generated through learning and education" (p. 30).

MAJOR CONCEPTS

Several major concepts are important to understanding and interpreting Confucian ethics (Smith, 1991). *Li* is an important concept in Confucian ethics and is described as *standards of acceptable social behavior* (Oldstone-Moore, 2002). Translation of Li includes ritual, etiquette, manners, and ceremonies. Development of Li is achieved through having models that provide information about acceptable social behavior, elders typically. Included in the concept of Li is seeking *the "mean" (chun yung) or the "middle way"* or a balance of extremes (Smith). So, for example, engaging in overindulging actions is a violation of the mean. Confucius suggested that there are five basic relationships or social roles in which Li is demonstrated: parents and children, husband and wife, elder sibling and younger sibling, elder friend and younger friend, and ruler and subject (Smith). For example, the ideal social role behavior for a parent and child is to show closeness and love. Children alternatively should show respect and obedience for the parent, which would be the correct Li. The Li for elder siblings is to be gentle toward younger siblings, whereas younger siblings should be respectful of elder siblings. Husbands should be good to their wives and wives should be good at listening to their husbands based upon Li. Elder friends, according to Li, should be considerate, and younger friends should defer to elder friends. Accordingly, rulers should be benevolent to subjects and subjects should respond with loyalty. Smith noted that Confucius believed that the young should be respectful of elders; there was a special position in society for elders and this should be expressed through appropriate Li. Tweed and Lehman (2002) quoted Confucius as saying "to honor those higher than ourselves is the highest expression of a sense of justice" (p. 95). Confucius believed that virtue is achieved primarily by observing and learning from people who provide models of virtue. Another way to understand and express Li is through accepted rituals of a society. Rituals provide clarity for Li in a society and the expected social behaviors.

Another concept is *Ren*, which is defined as *the ideal relationship between human beings* (Oldstone-Moore, 2002; Smith, 1991). This includes concepts of goodness, benevolence, and love between humans. Smith suggested that Ren may be described as "human heartedness." Smith also noted that Ren is "simultaneously a feeling of humanity toward others and respect for oneself, an indivisible sense of the dignity of human life wherever it appears. It is the effort of the individual to engage in actions that involve respect for others." Smith concluded that Ren is founded on the "silver rule" (the reciprocal of the Confucian golden rule) and described it as "Do not do unto others what you would not want others to do unto you" (p. 173). We can apply Ren through our own actions or through guiding others.

Two ways to manifest Ren are through *reciprocity (shu)* and *sincerity (zhong)*. Reciprocity is expressed through the silver rule. Consideration of the other person's reaction to a situation or action is the foundation of reciprocity (Oldstone-Moore, 2002). *Zhong* refers specifically to sincerity in feeling to be congruent with one's actions (Oldstone-Moore).

Another proponent of Confucian thought was Mencius (Shanahan & Wang, 2003). He lived several hundred years after Confucius and was disturbed that other schools of thought had moved away from Confucius's original theory. Mencius believed, more so than Confucius, that each of us is born with an instinctive morality and seeds of wisdom for growth. He further believed that through living without major deprivation, such as poverty or wars, a person would develop a sage-like wisdom. Instinctive morality is found through inclinations to behave, which are found in the *Xin* or heart mind. It is similar to Western views of conscience. Mencius identified *seeds of instinctive morality: empathy and sympathy* (commiseration) or the virtue of humanity; *ability to feel shame; respect and deference to superiors and modesty;* and *the ability to know right from wrong* (Shanahan & Wang). The development of these seeds can be thwarted through deprivation and events that interfere with normal development; these include political, social, economic, and psychological conditions. The seeds also may not develop if we do not attend to their development.

ADDITIONAL READINGS: CONFUCIAN ETHICS

Berling, J. A. (Fall, 1982). Confucianism. *Focus on Asian Studies, 2*(1), 5–7. Retrieved July 2, 2005, from http://www.askasia.org/frclasrm/readings/r000004.htm

Confucianism. Retrieved May 2, 2005, from http://en.wikipedia.org/wiki/Confucianism

Csikszentmihalyi, M. (2005). Differentiations in Chinese ethics. In W. Schweiker (Ed.), *The Blackwell companion to religious ethics* (pp. 381–394). Malden, MA: Blackwell.

DeBary, W. T., & Weiming, T. (1998). *Confucianism and human rights.* New York: Columbia University Press.

Hansen, C. (1993). Classical Chinese ethics. In P. Singer (Ed.), *A companion to ethics* (pp. 69–81). Malden, MA: Blackwell.

Ivanhoe, P. J. (2002). *Ethics in the Confucian tradition.* Indianapolis, IN: Hackett.

Mollgaard, E. (2005). Chinese ethics? In W. Schweiker (Ed.), *The Blackwell companion to religious ethics* (pp. 368–373). Malden, MA: Blackwell.

Shanahan, T., & Wang, R. (2003). *Reason and insight: Western and eastern perspectives on the pursuit of moral wisdom* (2nd ed.). Belmont, CA: Wadsworth.

Chapter 9

Taoist Ethics and Counselor Decision-Making

Taoism is one of three major philosophical thoughts in China; Buddhism and Confucianism are the other two (Robinet, 1997). The origins of Taoism may be traced to about 500 BCE with Laozi. Many philosophers have concluded that Taoism developed as a reaction against Confucianism (Kohn, 2001). Taoists believe that the introduction of Confucian ways of living produced a disruption in the natural order of human nature and the natural order of things. For example, the model for early Taoists was the farmer and his life. It was perceived to be simple and based on following nature. Farmers, according to Taoism, are aware of the natural rhythms of nature. Taoism is considered to be a religious orientation and is founded to some degree on goals of immortality.

There have been several contributors to Taoism (Creel, 1970; Miller, 2003) but the first was Laozi or the "old master." His major contributions were communicated in the Tao Te Ching, which may be interpreted as The Classic of the Way and Its Power. A problem with finding major concepts in Taoism is that the writings about Taoism were presented as disjointed commentaries consisting of short writings. There were other contributors to Taoist writings, but they have not been clearly identified (Kohn, 2001).

MAJOR CONCEPTS

Shanahan and Wang (2003) noted there are several important concepts in understanding Taoism and these include *Tao, yin-yang, the harmony of opposites and relativity, simplicity, reversal and cyclicity,* and *nonaction. Tao* is defined as *a way or a path that is true and desirable to follow.* However, an actual concrete definition of Tao is theoretically impossible because it can only be known through analogies and metaphors (Shanahan & Wang). The Way or Tao must be experienced to understand it. It may be similar to a common experience, for example, when you are trying to get to somewhere you have been before, but you cannot remember the exact direction. You search for clues and inevitably go in the right direction. You have the "feeling" of finding your way and "knowing" it is the right way. Another example may be an issue that you are attempting to address. After "sleeping" on the issue or taking time away from thinking about the issue, the conclusion becomes clear or the direction of your action becomes clear.

Two other concepts are the *yin* and *yang*. This refers to the interaction of two opposites. The opposites include the yin, which is considered to be the receptive and weaker aspect of the union and may be negative and destructive, and its opposite, the yang, which has been referred to as strong, positive, and constructive. In Taoism neither the yin nor the yang is considered good or bad by itself. Actually good and bad occur when there is too much of one expressed. There needs to be a balance between the two. The yin has been linked to female characteristics and the yang with the male.

Harmony of opposites and *relativity* are other important concepts and refer to understanding that life and events need opposites. One can only understand something by seeing or understanding the opposite. So if we say something is done fast, then we must have seen something that was done slowly. However, the second part of this concept is relativity. Relativity suggests that the conception of opposites is influenced by relativity, which is based on the person's perceptions and on the context. For example, a student from the Northeast went to Florida for a vacation during the winter. She went to the beach and the water temperature was in the low 70s and upper 60s. She went into the water and she heard people who were local saying she must be a tourist because the water was too cold for swimming. It was too cold for someone who was used to warm weather, but to someone who was used to colder weather the water was warm. The concept of relativity in Tao concludes there are no absolutes, but everything is relative including morals and ethics.

Simplicity, according to the I Ching or the Book of Changes (several writers over the centuries have contributed to the readings in the Book of Changes), states that the way of heaven and earth is simple. Therefore, the individual should realize simplicity or keep life simple.

Reversal refers to processes that occur when two competing forces interact and the perceived weaker force overcomes the stronger force, typically through persistence. A component of this reversal process is that the weak force overcomes the strong force, thus becoming the strong force. However, the new weak force then overcomes the new strong force through persistence, and then the new weak force becomes the strong force again. This process is called *cyclicity*. Shanahan and Wang (2003) stated that water and stone are examples of reversal and cyclicity. Water may be initially considered weak and a stone hard, but with persistence the pressure of water wears away stone. However, the water may not maintain its force, and the stone then becomes stronger again. Key in this process is the view that change, not stability, is inherent in nature.

Another important concept in Taoism is *nonaction* or w*u wei*. Nonaction does not really mean doing nothing. It refers to following nature and being natural, spontaneous, and harmonious with nature (Shanahan & Wang, 2003). Nonaction further means doing nothing to disrupt the natural course of events. Nonaction is only accomplished through not seeking knowledge or pursuing desires beyond what is necessary for living. Knowledge gives people information about what could be different, and that leads to an analysis of what could be, rather than letting nature take its course. Desires that go beyond meeting one's needs violate the concept of nonaction. An example of a violation of wu wei is an extravagant meal with numerous courses. The ultimate goal of nonaction is to act spontaneously without forethought.

The primary goal of Taoism is long life and immortality. There are certain things that need to be done to achieve this goal. The starting point of long life is the nourishment of energy. Accordingly, human beings receive energy from heaven and earth. The yin and yang harmonize the energy. There are various ways and techniques to harmonize the body and promote the goal of immortality and long life. All people are born with the energy of emptiness (Kohn, 1993). To achieve spirit immortality you must practice the energy of emptiness. This means do not let the world impact you in a significant way. For example, it is stated that seven perversions of emotions are joy, happiness, anger, sadness, love, hate, and desires. These should be controlled.

Shanahan and Wang (2003) noted that there are five ways to Tao: fasting and abstention, seclusion, visualization and imagination, oblivion, and spirit liberation. Fasting and abstention refer to living on simple foods such as fresh vegetables. Also, the person must regulate food so the body is perfectly balanced. The second way of the Tao includes other extremes such as refraining from long sitting, long standing, or long exhaustive labor. It also means living within the balance of the yin and yang. An example is the right balance of light and dark. Visualization and imagination are the third way to Tao. This refers to visualizing one's spirit. People have a tendency to focus on others and never attend to themselves. They need to see themselves in tranquility. The fourth way to Tao is oblivion (Kohn, 1993). Sitting in oblivion is the perfection of visualization and imagination. The intent is for the body to be completely obliterated. This refers to a quieting of the body and particularly the mind. Overconcern by the mind interferes with following Tao. Spirit liberation is achieved when the criteria of the other four ways have been met (fasting, seclusion, etc.).

ADDITIONAL READINGS: TAOIST ETHICS

Berkson, M. (2005). Trajectories of Chinese religious ethics. In W. Schweiker (Ed.), *The Blackwell companion to religious ethics* (pp. 395–405). Malden, MA: Blackwell.

Berling, J. A. (Fall, 1982). Taoism, or the way. *Focus on Asian Studies, 2*(1), 9–11. Retrieved February 23, 2006, from http://www.askasia.org/frclasrm/readings/r000005 .htm

Creel, H. G. (1970). *What is Taoism?: And other studies in Chinese cultural history.* Chicago: The University of Chicago Press.

Kleeman, T. (1991). Taoist ethics. In J. Carman & M. Juergensmayer (Eds.), *A bibliographic guide to the comparative study of ethics* (pp. 162–195). Cambridge, UK: Cambridge University Press.

Kohn, L. (2001). *Daoism and Chinese culture.* Cambridge, MA: Three Pines Press.

Lagerwey, J. (1987). *Taoist ritual in Chinese society and history.* New York: Macmillan.

Miller, J. (2003). *Daoism: A short introduction.* Oxford, UK: Oneworld.

Shanahan, T., & Wang, R. (2003). *Reason and insight: Western and Eastern perspectives on the pursuit of moral wisdom* (2nd ed.). Belmont, CA: Wadsworth.

Taoism. Retrieved May 1, 2005, from http://en.wikipedia.org/wiki/Taoism

Wong, E. (Ed. and Trans.) (1997). *Teachings of the Tao: Readings from the Taoist spiritual tradition.* Boston: Shambhala.

Chapter 10

Hindu Ethics and Counselor Decision-Making

Hindu tradition concerns itself with the quest for a moral life and the principles by which that goal is attained. *Vedanta* is an ancient religious Hindu philosophy emphasizing the unity of existence. It consists of three documents, the Upanishads, Bhagavad Gita, and Brahma Sutra. Of these documents, the Upanishads and Bhagavad Gita address morality in a practical way that all Hindus are expected to follow. In India, ethics are part of a complex spiritual system set in the context of its social and political structures.

Hindu philosophical thinking dates back to about 2500 BCE. During the earliest period, the Vedic, from around 2500 to 600 BCE, religious concerns emerged in the context of philosophy. The Upanishads, which belong to this period, proclaim salvation by knowledge rather than faith and works. The moral doctrines of the Hindus are based on spiritual concepts included in the teachings of the Upanishads, which derive their authority from divine revelation included in the Vedas, the sacred scriptures of India.

The second period of philosophical development in India extends from about 600 BCE to 200 CE. Philosophical doctrines were presented through great epic poems, and Hindu moral ideals were discerned through the personalities of the epics' characters. One of those poems, the Mahabharata, elaborates the social code and contains the Bhagavad Gita (Song of God), which is the central religious classic of India. The Gita teaches pantheism, i.e., God is in all things and all things are in God, and reincarnation, i.e., every soul evolves through a series of births and deaths. The divine core of the self is everywhere, in oneself as in all others—no matter whether the other is a saint, sinner, dog, ant, tree, or something else. All fear and misery arise from our sense of being separate from this cosmic unity; happiness is the understanding of this oneness with the universe.

According to the Gita, there are four great aims of life (doctrine of the *purusarthas*): the secular values of *artha* or wealth and *kama* or pleasure, and the spiritual values of *dharma* or virtue and *moksha* or spiritual liberation/ self-perfection. There are also four stages of life (doctrine of *asramas*): the student or *brahmacharya,* requiring discipline and dedication to the teacher; the house- holder or *grihastya,* entailing the obligations of marriage and family; the semi- retired individual gradually detaching from the material world or *vanaprastha;* and the individual breaking patterns of family and society to search for God in preparation for the next life or *sanyasa.* The four castes and their hierarchy are also set out in the Gita (doctrine of the *varnas*): the priest/teacher or *Brahmin,* the warrior or *Kshatriya,* the merchant or *Vaishya,* and the worker or *Shudra.* The hier- archy in the caste system is determined by the degree of voluntary renunciation, poverty, and self-control the role requires, and also by the degree of intellectual and spiritual attainments by the caste member.

The Gita describes the virtues and duties of the castes. People must do their duties according to their nature, and duty is determined by their place in the larger society. Each caste has its own ideas of perfection. The Brahmin, or educated class, has to suppress the impulse for physical enjoyment. The Kshatriya enjoys power and pleasure, but must be ready to lay down his life for the protection of his country. The Vaishya, whose moral code and intellectual attainments are not as rigorous or high as those of the two upper castes, amasses wealth, both for his own enjoyment and for the welfare of society. Not much is expected of the Shudra in terms of spiritual, intellectual, or moral perfection, but they are seen as fit for manual labor. The basis of the caste system, according to the Hindu view, is the self-evident inborn physical, intellectual, and spiritual inequalities among humans. An individual is born into a higher or lower caste as a result of actions performed in the previous life, and therefore individuals are responsible for their positions.

Heredity was the principle for determining caste. Higher positions in the caste system entail greater obligations to members of the lower castes. In the Vedas, the four castes are described as four important parts of the body of the cosmos person: head, arms, thighs (or stomach), and feet. The analogy suggests the interdepen- dence of the four castes for the common welfare of all; it also suggests that the exploitation of one individual by another undermines the strength of the whole society. Since India attained political freedom, laws have been enacted eliminat- ing taboos about marriage, dining, and social exchanges among the castes. The lower castes are now given greater opportunities for education and openings in government jobs.

MAJOR CONCEPTS

Ethics is a Western term developed as a discipline in Western philosophy. In Sanskrit, there is no clear distinction between religion and ethics or between philosophy and ethics, as there is in Western languages (Creel, 1977), so questions have been raised as to whether the term *ethics* can be applied to Hinduism. Because of the stratified societal structure, it has been argued that Hinduism offers no coherent ethical theory or universal principles (Albert Schweitzer, 1936, and John McKenzie, 1922, as cited in Miller, 1981). I. C. Sharma (1965) and A. Sharma (1999) attributed this criticism to a lack of knowledge of Indian philosophy and ethics, which is the main theme of the Vedas.

Dhand (2002) explained the challenges of interpreting Hinduism because of the immense literature ranging over 3,000 years, the diversity of the tradition, the varying degrees of authority, and the multiple genres, including biographies and autobiographies (e.g., Gandhi, 1927). In Hinduism, law, ethics, and soteriology (theology dealing with salvation) are tied together. Common to all Hindus is the belief in dharma (reincarnation), karma, and moksha (liberation) through a variety of moral, action-based, and meditative *yogas* (spiritual practices). Absolute happiness is oneness with the universe through the attainment of moksha or liberation from the cycle of life, death, and existential duality (separation of self and others).

The desire for the well-being of all beings and benevolence in the form of almsgiving is encouraged especially when done with no expectation of rewards, at least in this life. Hindu ethics prescribes behavior for a spiritual life. In that regard, it differs from secular ethics such as Utilitarianism, whose purpose is to obtain the greatest good for society. The Gita's model of an ethical person is one who is

> without hatred of any creature, friendly, and compassionate without possessiveness and self-pride, equable in happiness and unhappiness . . . who is dependent on nothing, disinterested, unworried . . . and who neither hates nor rejoices, does not mourn or hanker, and relinquishes both good and evil. (Bhagavad Gita 12:13–17, van Buitenen, 1985)

According to the Gita, the "three gateways of hell" leading to the ruin of the soul are lust, wrath, and greed, and the five cardinal virtues are purity, self-control, detachment, truth, and nonviolence. The virtues are universals across all castes. Hindus are advised to restrain all emotions that may lead to sin, such as *kama* (lust), *krodha* (anger), *mada* (egoism), and *matsara* (jealousy), because these strong emotions disrupt a harmonious society.

The Hindu concept of *dharma,* which refers to *virtue, duty, and righteousness,* is a code of conduct that the Mahabharata says applies to all persons but is complicated by an individual's level of knowledge, spiritual insight, and particular station in life (Dhand, 2002). Hinduism openly acknowledges psychological and social differences among people and, therefore, the need for different dharmas to guide them. Hence, there is a dharma that tells one how to conduct oneself as a woman or man, how to conduct oneself professionally, how to conduct oneself as a child, parent, brother, sister, friend, etc. Thus, it is possible to have numerous interrelationships and conflicting dharmas. The task is to determine which dharma is most pressing in the situation and to make a moral judgment about the right course of action given the circumstances.

Nine principles, similar to the Ten Commandments, are detailed in the Mahabharata that concern human beings, but primarily men, irrespective of their position in society or stage of life—a common *dharma* that includes *restraint of anger, truthfulness of speech, an agreeable nature, forgiveness, purity of conduct,* and *avoidance of conflict* (Dhand, 2002; O'Flaherty, 1978). Simpson (1997) suggested that the perspective of Hindu ethics, with its emphasis on the character of the person over the action, is essentially a virtue ethics perspective, which Western philosophers trace back to Aristotle.

Hindu ethics is mainly subjective or personal, the purpose being to eliminate such mental impurities as greed and egoism to attain the highest goods—spiritual liberation and self-perfection. Personal ethics have been emphasized over social ethics because it is reasoned that if individuals are virtuous, social service will follow. Kindness and tolerance in all human relations, along with nonviolence, are part of Hindu life.

Ahimsa, which refers to *noninjury and nonviolent action,* is a distinctive quality emphasized in Hindu ethics—it is the highest dharma. Ahimsa *implies not killing,* but its comprehensive meaning is *not to cause pain or harm* to any living creature, either in thought, word, or deed. Although not required, many Hindus practice vegetarianism as the natural way to live to minimize hurt to other beings. Hindus oppose killing because of the belief in reincarnation, i.e., what a person does in this life will return, if not in this life, then in the next. To do harm to others is to do harm to oneself.

Mahatma Gandhi (1869–1948) cited the Bhagavad Gita as an infallible guide of behavior. His nonviolent means of political resistance was largely responsible for India winning independence from the British in 1947. In practicing nonviolence according to Gandhian ethics, a person's motives must be pure. An individual cannot use nonviolence against oppression if in fear one hates the oppressors. Gandhi's guiding principle was to return good for evil. Genuine love for one's enemies effects a moral change in the enemies' hearts, such that they voluntarily do what is right. In his autobiography, *The Story of My Experiments With Truth* (1927), Gandhi recounted his commitment to the ideals of nonattachment or nonpossession of material goods and how his struggle for personal freedom became the freedom to serve others. According to Gandhi, total renunciation frees the body to serve others. Dr. Martin Luther King Jr. (1929–1968) also studied Hinduism and followed Gandhi's example of nonviolent political resistance in leading the civil rights movement in the United States during the 1960s. In his "Drum Major Instinct" sermon delivered in 1968, Dr. King also echoed Gandhi's call for service to others (King, 1968).

In considering the compelling religious problem of misery in the world, Vedanta does not blame God or the devil for evil—nothing happens by outside forces. Human beings are responsible for what life brings. All people reap the results of their own actions in this life or in previous lives. This is explained through the "law of karma." In everyday language, the term *karma* is sometimes misused or misinterpreted as luck. However, *karma* is derived from the Sanskrit word meaning "to do," *referring to action and to the results of action*. All our actions and thoughts create an impression on our mind and in the universe. The universe will give back what we gave it. Good actions and thoughts create good effects, bad actions and thoughts create bad effects. When actions and thoughts are repeated, the impressions are more lasting and influence our subsequent actions and thoughts. Responding in an angry manner *predisposes* one to react with anger rather than patience and builds future experiences. The law of karma might imply that one can be indifferent to the needs of others because they are getting what they deserve. But helping a suffering person contributes good karma for oneself.

ADDITIONAL READINGS: HINDU ETHICS

Bilimoria, P. (1993). Indian ethics. In P. Singer (Ed.), *A companion to ethics* (pp. 43–57). Malden, MA: Blackwell.

Bilimoria, P., Prabhu, J., & Sharma, A. (Eds.). (2004). *Indian ethics: Classical traditions and contemporary challenges.* London: Ashgate Press.

Hebbar, N. H. (2002). *Ethics of Hinduism.* Retrieved February 23, 2006, from http://www.boloji.com/hinduism/032.htm

Hinduism (n.d.). Retrieved August 19, 2004, from http://en.wikipedia.org/wiki/Hinduism

Klostermaier, K. K. (2000). *Hinduism: A short introduction.* Oxford, UK: Oneworld.

Nikhilananda, S. (n.d.) *An essay on Hindu ethics.* Retrieved January 2, 2004, from http://www.hinduism.co.za/ethics.htm

Perrett, R. W. (2005). Hindu ethics? In W. Schweiker (Ed.), *The Blackwell companion to religious ethics* (pp. 323–329). Malden, MA: Blackwell.

Prabhu, J. (2005). Trajectories of Hindu ethics. In W. Schweiker (Ed.), *The Blackwell companion to religious ethics* (pp. 355–367). Malden, MA: Blackwell.

Shanahan, T., & Wang, R. (2003). *Reason and insight: Western and Eastern perspectives on the pursuit of moral wisdom* (2nd ed.). Belmont, CA: Wadsworth.

Chapter 11

Buddhist Ethics and Counselor Decision-Making

As a Pan-Asian religion and philosophy, Buddhism has had a central role in the spiritual, cultural, and social life of the Eastern world and of many living in the West. In the twentieth century, Buddhism began spreading to the West and subsequently has contributed to Western spiritual and philosophical thought (Goldstein & Kornfield, 1987; Mitchell, 2002; Ross, 1980; Smith & Novak, 2003; Tucci, Kitagawa, & Reynolds, 1993). The foundation of Buddhism took hold in northeastern India between the late sixth century and the early fourth century BCE, which was during a period of history where social changes and religious activity were taking place. For many in India, the sacrifice and ritualistic formalities of the Hindu high caste (Brahmins) were becoming intolerable. During this period of history, Buddhism began with the enlightenment of Siddhartha Gautama (in Pāli), known after his enlightenment as Buddha Gautama, who was thought to live from 563 to about 483 BCE.

The actual sequence of events in the Buddha Gautama's 80-year life paralleled a way of living that he taught to his followers (Goldstein & Kornfield, 1987; Mitchell, 2002). In virtually all Buddhist traditions, the Buddha lived many lives before his birth as Gautama, and then through his life as the Buddha, Gautama affirmed his own teachings. The life of Gautama began with his birth into a family of the warrior caste or ruling class. At age 29, he received four signs consisting of observations and events, of which one was the birth of his son. This event was a turning point in his life. Upon hearing the news of his son's birth, Gautama decided to give up his princely life and become an ascetic; this is known as the *great renunciation*. He took on the title of the Buddha, meaning the *awakened one* or *enlightened one.* This title, given to Gautama, is not a proper name, but is somewhat like the use of the title messiah, the Christ (Rāhula & Reynolds, 1993). From the tradition of Gautama's time, the prefix points to a belief that innumerable Buddhas will exist in the future as they have in the past.

In the next stage of Gautama's life, he went in search of teachers to instruct him in the way of truth. Once Gautama learned from his teachers how to attain the mystical state of no-thing, he began a quest for the absolute truth, *nirvana.* During this quest, Gautama at the age of 35 struggled and overcame Māra, the evil one and the tempter, the lord of the world's passion. In the night after the defeat, while Gautama was meditating, he realized the *four noble truths,* in which ignorance and darkness were dispelled. This was the moment he attained the *enlightenment* or *awakening.* Immediately following his enlightenment, he meditated on the various aspects of the *dharma* that he had realized, most notably the *doctrine of causal relations:* the view that there is no eternal, everlasting, unchanging permanence. After these reflections, the Buddha had to be convinced to accept his vocation as a teacher and to explain to the world the truth that he had just realized. In his first sermon, the substance of the Buddha's message was a tale about the middle path, known as the *noble eightfold path.* This tale was about a man who had left home and was faced with two extremes: to follow self-indulgence or to follow self-mortification. To avoid these two extremes, the man discovered the middle path leading to vision, to knowledge, to calmness, to awakening, to nirvana (Ross, 1980; Smith & Novak, 2003).

From this point on, the Buddha was described as a charismatic teacher who had an exceptional gift of converting people through his power and ability to convey his message through oral discourse. The historical development of Buddhism and Buddhist thought points to the power of the Buddha, as founder, to proclaim a religious message that became a distinctive religious community, which expanded throughout South Asia, Sri Lanka and Southeast Asia, Central Asia and China, Korea and Japan, Tibet, Mongolia, and the Himalayan Kingdoms. During the long Buddhist history, Buddhist influences have periodically reached the Western world (Pardue, 1971; Kitagawa, Tucci, & Reynolds, 1993).

MAJOR CONCEPTS

After the Buddha's death, his disciples and institutionalized Buddhist councils transmitted his teachings to others and attempted to determine and then establish the Buddha's original teachings. The followers of the Buddha said that *suffering, impermanence, and no-self* were the fundamental components of his teaching. The basic premise of these conditions is that *existence as a human involves pain* and *existence gives rise to suffering.* Impermanence was also considered a condition of human existence, which implies limitations and in turn gives rise to desire. Desire, inevitably, causes suffering, since desire is transitory, changing, and perishing (Goldstein & Kornfield, 1987; Mitchell, 2002; Smith & Novak, 2003; Tucci, Nakamura, & Reynolds, 1993).

Human existence is embedded in a context of impermanence, with human beings and all that surrounds human life being impermanent. To live with impermanence, human beings search for a way of deliverance, for enlightenment, which is beyond the transitoriness of human existence (Goldstein & Kornfield, 1987; Tucci, Nakamura, & Reynolds, 1993). The transitory nature of human beings clears the way to understand no-self, a condition which is not a self or soul. The implication is that a person is in a process of continuous change, with no fixed underlying entity (Tucci, Nakamura, & Reynolds).

Karma, the Buddhist's belief that *no intention is ever wasted* whether good or bad (Morgan, 1996, and Warren, 1976, as cited in Shanahan & Wang, 2003) teaches that "what you sow you shall reap, if not in this life then in future rebirths when the fruit of karma ripens" (Morgan, 1996, as cited in Shanahan & Wang, p. 55). The implication of a karmic belief does not mean there is no need for combining practical social action with good individual intentions. Rather, the Buddhist belief in karma considers that social issues and involvement in social causes arise from the right individual intention and not from responding to undue social pressure or manipulation to behave in certain ways. The right individual intention combined with appropriate karmic effects can develop into good mental attitudes (Morgan, 1996, as cited in Shanahan & Wang; Saddhatissa, 1970). A difficult problem arises for Buddhists in accepting the belief in karma and rebirth while recognizing the doctrine of no-self. The closest possible analogy Buddhist scholars can use is to think of fire, which maintains itself yet is different at every moment; this is considered to be the continuity of an ever-changing identity (Tucci, Nakamura, & Reynolds, 1993).

In addition, Buddha's insights about humanity's fundamental realities (suffering, permanence, and no-self) were the Buddhist formulation of the *Four Noble Truths:* (1) the truth of humanity, with misery and suffering a part of humanity; (2) the truth from recognizing what gives rise to suffering and from knowing that suffering originates within us from the craving for pleasure; (3) the truth that this craving can be eliminated; and (4) the truth that elimination is the result of a methodical way or path to be followed (Bowker, 1997).

The Four Noble Truths do not stand alone as a prescription for living; rather, they are related to the *law of dependent origination.* This concept in Buddhism emphasizes the importance of interdependence among all physical and mental expressions, which constitute each individual's unique humanity (Bowker, 1997; Kalupahana, 1975, as cited in Bowker, 1997). The law of dependent origination involves the belief that every method of expression is connected to and dependent on some other expression. This law is fundamental to all schools of Buddhism, even though diverse interpretations of it exist.

In formulating the Four Noble Truths the Buddha also envisioned a process by which to overcome the cause of suffering. The Buddha considered the liberating process toward purification to be the last of the Four Noble Truths, called the *Noble Eightfold Path,* which was the path to be followed as the way to escape the continuous cycle of birth, suffering, and death. Buddha's teachings promoted liberation from this renewed cycle by following the precepts of the Noble Eightfold Path: right understanding, right thought, right speech, right action, right livelihood, right effort, right mindfulness, and right concentration. These precepts or principles have been translated as being *right,* meaning *complete* or *perfect,* as opposed to meaning incorrect or wrong. In Buddhism the term *right* has distinct precepts *(sīla),* which are the basic obligations of a Buddhist. The practices of wisdom, morality, and meditation expand the meaning of the Noble Eightfold Path, and cluster the eight steps along the Noble Eightfold Path into the Buddhist perception of truth demonstrated by ethical behaviors, as noted in the following passage (Morgan, 1996, as cited in Shanahan & Wang, 2003, pp. 57–58):

Wisdom

Right understanding is the perception of the world as it really is, without delusions. This involves particularly understanding suffering, the law of cause and effect, and impermanence.

Right thought involves the purification of the mind and heart and the growth of thoughts of unselfishness and compassion, which will then be the roots of action.

Morality

Right speech means the discipline of not lying, and not gossiping or talking in any way that will encourage malice and hatred.

Right action is usually expanded into the five precepts: avoid taking life, stealing, committing sexual misconduct, lying and taking stimulants and intoxicants.

Right livelihood is a worthwhile job or way of life, which avoids causing harm or injustice to other beings.

Meditation

Right effort is the mental discipline which prevents evil arising, tries to stop evil that has arisen, and encourages what is good.

Right mindfulness involves total attention to the activities of the body, speech and mind.

Right concentration is the training of the mind in the stages of meditation.

The Noble Eightfold Path is not intended to be a series of sequential steps. Instead, each step is a component in the overall process, and enlightenment is greater than the summation of each component, "since in fact the perfected ways of behaviour precede all else" (Bowker, 1997, p. 101).

Enlightenment or *nirvana* is the point of perfection or completeness of the Noble Eightfold Path. The aim of religious practice is to be rid of the delusion of self and to free oneself of restraints of the ordinary world: illusion, passions, and cravings. Nirvana is a goal, not a paradise or a heavenly world. In Western culture, however, the word used to mean enlightenment has been nirvana, which is translated as *dying out:* the dying out of the fierce fires of lust, anger, and delusion. However, the Buddha repudiated the notion of nirvana as a state of extinction or a "release from suffering" (Mitchell, 2002; Tucci, Nakamura, & Reynolds, 1993). Instead, nirvana was salvation as an ultimate goal to be sought and cherished. In his teaching, the Buddha asserted that nirvana can be experienced in our present existence by those who, knowing the Buddhist truth, practice the Buddhist path. This was the last of the Four Noble Truths learned along the Noble Eightfold Path, which was to be *a liberating process* toward purification. To follow the *path* was to acquire the knowledge of the *middle way,* and thus to *avoid extremes* in order to escape the continuous cycle of birth, suffering, and death (Mitchell; Tucci, Nakamura, & Reynolds).

ADDITIONAL READINGS: BUDDHIST ETHICS

Buddhism. Retrieved June 3, 2005, from http://en.wikipedia.org/wiki/Buddhism

Carter, J. R. (2005). Buddhist ethics? In W. Schweiker (Ed.), *The Blackwell companion to religious ethics* (pp. 278–285). Malden, MA: Blackwell.

Dalai Lama (1999). *Ethics for the new millennium.* New York: Penguin Putnam.

DeSilva, P. (1993). Buddhist ethics. In P. Singer (Ed.), *A companion to ethics* (pp. 58–68). Malden, MA: Blackwell.

Harvey, P. (2000). *An introduction to Buddhist ethics: Foundations, values, and issues.* New York: Cambridge University Press.

Kasulis, T. P. (2005). Cultural differentiation in Buddhist ethics. In W. Schweiker (Ed.), *The Blackwell companion to religious ethics* (pp. 297–312). Malden, MA: Blackwell.

Keown, D. (1995). *Buddhism & bioethics.* New York: St. Martins.

Keown, D. (2000). *Contemporary Buddhist ethics.* London: Curzon Press.

Keown, D. (2005). Origins of Buddhist ethics. In W. Schweiker (Ed.), *The Blackwell companion to religious ethics* (pp. 286–296). Malden, MA: Blackwell.

Shanahan, T., & Wang, R. (2003). *Reason and insight: Western and Eastern perspectives on the pursuit of moral wisdom* (2nd ed.). Belmont, CA: Wadsworth.

SECTION III

Middle Eastern Theories of Ethics

The third section of this book is focused on Middle Eastern theories of ethics; it includes discussions of Judaism and Islam. Chapter 12 is a discussion of Judaism and ethics. As with many of the other ethical theories, there is a connection between Jewish ethical behavior and Judaic religious beliefs. Dorff (2000) noted the key foundation in Judaism and its ethics is a linkage between the individual, family, and community. Ultimately, those practicing Judaism and its ethics hold that humans have responsibility to repair the world. Repair of the world is accomplished through finding cures for disease; promoting of peace; and taking responsibility for the care of others in the family, the community, and all of humanity.

Chapter 13 is a discussion of Islam and ethics. Muhammad was the founder of Islam and he proposed his ideas in approximately 500 CE. The underlying principles of Islam focus on the importance of truth. Other important qualities of Islamic ethical behavior include trust, honesty, gentleness, and purity.

Chapter 12

Jewish Ethics and Counselor Decision-Making

J udaism is a diverse culture with its own history, language, homeland, philosophy, religion, and ethics. Definitions of Judaism (Kellner, 1993) can be both secular (i.e., Zionist, calling for the resettlement of Jews in their ancient homeland, or non-Zionist) and religious (i.e., Orthodox, Conservative, or Reform). Judaism is oriented toward practical perfection in the world and its behavioral norms are codified in the *Halakhah* or Jewish Law. Academic achievements and financial success, not for the sake of possessing knowledge or material wealth but rather for the sake of doing, are recurrent themes in Judaism (Rosen & Weltman, 1996). In contrast to the predominant Christian orientation of Western religions, which are primarily concerned with questions of faith and correct beliefs, Jewish teachings are concerned with regulating behavior and correct actions (Jospe, 1995).

For Jews, moral behavior is guided by the Judaic religion. Judaism does not have a creed, dogma, or set of beliefs; rather, its tenets are spelled out in the commandments of Mosaic law in Leviticus and Deuteronomy, two books in the Old Testament (Bakon, 2004). The moral teachings of the Torah are the bases of Jewish ethics. Many of the proverbs in the Torah deal with business ethics such as competition, profits, selling, saving, obedience to the law, honesty, integrity, greed, deception, and conflicts of interest. Members of Hebrew society are expected to follow these standards without question. The Talmud, another authoritative source of Jewish laws and traditions, goes beyond the Torah in denouncing as fraud the taking advantage of a person's ignorance, fraudulent dealings, and gains obtained by gambling. The primary contribution of Judaism to Western religion is that one worships God through decent, humane, and moral relationships with others (Kellner, 1993).

The literature of Jewish ethics can be divided into four main periods: biblical, Talmudic, medieval, and modern. The Torah and the Talmud are primary sources of Jewish ethics but do not specifically address the subject. One influential outgrowth of the medieval period was the Musar movement (Kellner, 1995), a Jewish ethics education movement developed in the nineteenth century that still exists today. *Musar*—literally meaning *tradition,* but the Hebrew term for ethics—has its focus on character traits and how actions mark the soul. Serving, caring, and helping are qualities that move one closer to holy perfection (Morinis, 2002). This movement began as an ethical reproof in eastern European Orthodox Jewish communities, specifically in Poland and Russia, as a response to social changes. At that time, anti-Semitism, the assimilation of Jews into the Christian world, poverty, and poor living conditions caused emotional turmoil and the break-up of many Jewish institutions. Traditional Jewish law and customs were declining and many Jews felt that they had lost touch with their ethical core. The Musar movement is still accepted today in much of Jewish orthodoxy.

Modern Jewish ethics is distinguished from its medieval equivalent by its division into separate branches (Kellner, 1995). There are no significant theological differences within Judaism, but rather different positions, i.e., the Orthodox, Reform, and Conservative branches. The three branches share the same belief system, but the degree of observance differs among them. One ethical question has revolved around the relationship between moral norms and God's word. And the further question: If God's will defines that which is morally right and good, how can God's will be discerned? Orthodox theorists follow the Torah and maintain that Jewish law is the sole authoritative source of God's will. Literal interpretation of that source assures the most accurate understanding of God's will. By contrast, Reform theories allow the individual to make decisions about God's will. Conservative theorists follow Jewish law not only to know God's will but also interpret those sources in terms of their historical context and relevance in contemporary life.

Reconstructionism, the fourth denomination of Judaism developed by Rabbi Mordecai Kaplan in the 1920s (Kaplan, 1962/1994), held that in light of advances in science, philosophy, and history, it is impossible for modern Jews to adhere to traditional theology. For Kaplan, God is not personal, but the sum of all natural processes that allow human beings to become self-fulfilled. Reconstructionist Jews believe that personal autonomy overrides traditional Jewish laws. They reject the idea that the Jews are a chosen people and disavow all traditional forms of theism. Other followers of Judaism reject Kaplan's theology as incompatible with classical interpretations of Judaism.

MAJOR CONCEPTS

Jewish ethics differs from secular ethics because its morality is compatible with Jewish religious heritage. Jewish ethics are based on the fundamental concepts of Judaism, which holds that ethical duties are derived from the Hebrew Bible (Torah), i.e., divine or biblical revelation. This position assumes a belief in God. Life is sacred because humans are made in the image of God, and to live ethically Jews are called upon to imitate God here on earth. Sherwin (2000) viewed this theological assumption as endemic to Jewish ethics: Because the human being is created in God's image, certain actions against another person—for example, murder—are morally wrong; thus, an immoral act against another person is an affront to God, both to God's will and to God's person. The basic truths of Western civilization had their basis in the Old Testament and were explicitly stated in the Ten Commandments. Classical Judaism defines what is moral in terms of God's will as articulated in God's commandments. From this deontological (duty- or rule-bound) perspective, it is one's duty to obey God and the commandments. Samuelson (2001) sees modern Judaism returning to an emphasis on its scriptural and communal roots.

Major concepts in Judaic ethics center on *family and community.* The family is a critical unit in Jewish ideology and practice (Dorff, 2000; Liebman & Fishman, 2000). Both psychological and physical needs are met through marriage; sex in marriage serves two purposes: companionship and procreation. The family is the context in which to *provide for the education of children,* and parents have a duty to teach their children the Judaic tradition. Community is also important in Jewish life because *only in a community can all the duties of Judaism be carried out: justice, care for the poor, education,* etc.

Social action is part of the Jewish identity (Dorff, 2000; Semans & Fish, 2000). Community is not voluntary and the sense of community is a covenant with God. People are to help God in the ongoing repair of a global community (*tikkun olam*). This includes research into preventing or curing disease, political steps to avoid war and promote peace, political and economic measures to prevent hunger, legal methods to ensure justice, and educational efforts to teach morality and understanding. The *commitment to repair the world* stems from the religious belief that the world has not been redeemed, and that humans must help God bring about the Messianic hope for the future.

Humility is a key concept in Judaic ethics. Biblical prophets exhorted all people to *live humble and righteous lives.* In Jewish literature, humility is not counted as merely one of a number of virtues, each with equal status. Rather, it is the central virtue. Due to its moral status and because of its practical consequences, humility is a necessary precursor of any other virtues (Roth, 1995).

Honesty and truthfulness are absolute requisites, and a person's reputation is sacred. Hatred, quarreling, revenge, and anger are condemned as unethical, and potentially leading to murder. The Jewish idea of righteousness includes benevolence and charity. Because human life is considered infinitely valuable, people are duty-bound to preserve their life and health (Rosner, 2002).

In terms of ethical principles for professional conduct, *beneficence* is a major goal as is *nonmaleficence*. Clarfield, Gordon, Markwell, and Alibhai (2003) suggested that the latter is even a greater imperative because of the Holocaust and the harm done by medical professionals to individuals without their consent.

The Holocaust was not only a historical event but also a symbol of ultimate political evil. Dubiel (2003) suggested that the Holocaust's unthinkable and inhuman acts of cruelty toward Jews, which violated fundamental norms of civilized societies, should serve as a catalyst for an *ethic of responsibility* that transcends the bounds of any single country or culture. Dubiel contended that the Holocaust highlighted the need for solidarity among all human beings, including immigrants and prisoners of war. Accordingly, this solidarity rests on the improbable foundation of solidarity among strangers, and the ethical *responsibility of all people to reduce the pain of even total strangers.* The idea that Jews are the "chosen" people confers a sense of privilege but also imparts a profound sense of responsibility to others. For these reasons, Judaism is particularly sensitive to professional ethics, especially nonmaleficence, because of the medical profession's complacency with Nazi medical experimentation during the Holocaust. An ethic of responsibility also has important repercussions for individuals working in other professional settings (McKie, 2004). For example, counselors have an ethical responsibility to society to speak out against inappropriate or unethical therapeutic practices because they are accountable for the care of people who are vulnerable and in need of help.

ADDITIONAL READINGS: JEWISH ETHICS

Dorff, E. N. (2002). *To do the right and the good: A Jewish approach to modern social ethics.* Philadelphia, PA: Jewish Publication Society.

Dorff, E. N., & Newman, L. E. (1995). *Contemporary Jewish ethics and morality: A reader.* New York: Oxford University Press.

Gibbs, R. (2000). *Why ethics? Signs of responsibility.* Princeton, NJ: Princeton University Press.

Green, R. M. (2005). Foundations of Jewish ethics. In W. Schweiker (Ed.), *The Blackwell companion to religious ethics* (pp. 166–175). Malden, MA: Blackwell.

Jewish ethics. Retrieved March 3, 2004, from http://en.wikipedia.org/wiki/Jewish_ethics

Kellner, M. (1993). Jewish ethics. In P. Singer (Ed.), *A companion to ethics* (pp. 82–90). Malden, MA: Blackwell.

Novak, D. (1998). *Natural law in Judaism.* New York: Cambridge University Press.

Putnam, H. (2005). Jewish ethics? In W. Schweiker (Ed.), *The Blackwell companion to religious ethics* (pp. 159–165). Malden, MA: Blackwell.

Sherwin, B. L. (2000). *Jewish ethics for the twenty-first century: Living in the image of God.* Syracuse, NY: Syracuse University Press.

Chapter 13

Islamic Ethics and Counselor Decision-Making

Islam has a long history dating back over 1,400 years. The term *Islam* is Arabic, meaning "submission to God," and it is supported by derivatives of earlier interpretations of the meaning of Islam including concepts of "peace" (Belt, 2002). The primary contributor to Islam was the Prophet Muhammad ibu Abd Allah, who was born in Mecca in 570 CE. After his father died when he was six years old, he lived with his grandfather until the grandfather passed away, then went to live with his uncle. Belt described the first insight Muhammad experienced:

> At about age 40 Muhammad retreated to a cave in the mountains outside Mecca to meditate. There, Muslims believe, he was visited by the archangel Gabriel, who began reciting to him the Word of God. Until his death 23 years later, Muhammad passed along these revelations to a growing band of followers, including many who wrote down the words or committed them to memory. (p. 78)

After Muhammad's death these writings were used in the composition of the Qur'an (it is frequently referred to as the Koran in English).

Initially, Muhammad experienced considerable struggle to gain acceptance. He introduced his ideas in Mecca and after ten years moved to Medina. He had been invited to Medina and eventually governed this city. Consequently, he acquired numerous followers in Medina. After several years, he decided to return to Mecca with a small army and he successfully conquered Mecca after three battles (Gale Group, 2002). Muhammad died in 632 CE. Belt (2002) noted that Islam was well established at the time of his death in the Arabian peninsula. After Muhammad's death, several caliphs further consolidated followers of Islam (Esposito, 1999). Islam's influence expanded but, at times, also contracted in some geographic locations due to wars and peoples being conquered (Haddad, 1999). Islam continued in the Middle East, parts of North Africa, and eastern Europe, e.g., Romania, Bulgaria, etc. Also, the prevalence of Islam more recently has increased in the West. In the United States, the practice of Islam has increased significantly in the past twenty years both from immigration and conversion. For example, there has been a significant increase by African Americans in adopting Islamic thought, belief, and religion in the United States (Carter & Rashidi, 2003; Gomez, 1994; Haddad, 1991). It has been projected that Islam will become the second-largest religious group in the United States (U.S. Department of State, n.d.).

MAJOR CONCEPTS

One of the major writers on Muslim ethics was Abd al-Jabbar (Hourani, 1971). A first step in understanding Islamic ethics is the consideration of *knowledge,* which is defined as *"an intellectual content corresponding to reality in the manner of truth, and an emotional state of satisfaction and tranquility"* (Hourani, p. 13). Knowledge can be achieved through introspection, or finding knowledge and truth within oneself. Referring to introspection, Hourani stated, "There is no clearer or stronger evidence of truth than what is learned in this way" (p. 21). Knowledge or knowing, according to Hourani, is based upon the following general truths: that doing wrong is always evil, that humans usually act in their own interest, and that humans believe what they perceive. Hourani concludes in referring to knowledge that

> the knowledge of general truths is not innate, prior to any evidence; it is drawn out from particular experiences, in which it is learned by a direct apprehension like that of geometry, where we learn through but not from physical diagrams. (p. 22)

So, the conclusion is that Islamic ethics and knowledge, or knowing what is ethical, is clear and specific. Islam is not a theory based upon moral relativism but is based upon moral absolutism; there is a right way to interpret an ethical issue. Hourani noted that truths are generally acknowledged by every rational person.

Islamic ethics differentiates five major classes of ethics and/or acts: *evil or forbidden acts, undesirable acts, neutral acts, desirable acts, and good or required acts.* Forbidden acts may be defined as disgraceful, shameful or bad acts (Hourani, 1971).

Essentially, *forbidden acts cause harm to others or oneself.* Hourani stated, "Pain is evil in itself, that is, when it is simply useless suffering" (p. 32); pain is considered evil. The exception is an act that is based upon retribution or is deserved by the recipient; then it is not evil. Forbidden acts may be defined as an outcome that causes pain regardless of the individual's intent. One may not intentionally try to inflict pain, but it does occur and if the person experiencing the pain does not deserve the pain, then it is considered *undesirable. Undesirable acts* are those that *can be avoided* if one attends to them, but they generally do not involve a direct action on the part of the individual. An act is also *undesirable* if a person acts to hurt others or self, or if a person lets an event happen that injures others.

Neutral acts are those that have no impact on others. Someone can go into the woods and scream loudly and it does not harm anyone. It is considered a neutral act as long as it does not harm others or there is not a positive outcome. If someone screams in a department store and it upsets others, than it becomes an undesirable act.

Desirable acts are those that create a positive outcome and thus are considered to be good. Such acts are *not obligations* on the part of the actor but can improve or promote happiness. If a worker enters the office and says hello to others with a smile, this may promote good feelings and may be considered good. It is not required, but is a desirable act.

Good or required acts are those that *potentially help* others or remove harm. For example, not killing others (unless there is a good reason) is considered a required act. Hourani (1971) stated, "Good is objective, like evil; subjectivism is to be rejected" (p. 103). Again this is an illustration of a moral absolutist position. There are *four components of good: justice, benefit, truthfulness, and willing good* (Hourani). Justice concerns engaging in socially good actions to help or injure others. Injury may be just if the recipient is deserving of it. *Benefit* according to Hourani is whatever *brings pleasure. Truthfulness is considered good if such acts bring about pleasure and avoid pain.* However, if truthfulness hurts someone who is undeserving of pain, then it is considered evil. The solution is not to tell a mistruth but to remain silent or avoid stating such a mistruth (Hourani). The *will for good* is based upon the intent of the actor; it *refers to motivation or intent.* Having an intention of bringing about benefit is considered good, but not all intentions are good if pain and suffering occurs with an intended good act. So a counselor can have a good intent, e.g., wanting to help a client, but if the counselor does not have the skills to be helpful and tries to help anyway, the counselor's efforts become an undesirable act. The outcome may be harmful and therefore would be evil.

ADDITIONAL READINGS: ISLAMIC ETHICS

Amjad, M. (2000). *Principles of Islamic ethics: An introduction.* Retrieved August 4, 2005, from http://www.understanding-islam.com

Denny, F. M. (2005). Muslim ethical trajectories in the contemporary period. In W. Schweiker (Ed.), *The Blackwell companion to religious ethics* (pp. 268–277). Malden, MA: Blackwell.

Donner, F. (1999). Muhammad and the caliph: Political history of the Islamic empire up to the Mongol conquest. In J. Esposito (Ed.), *The Oxford history of Islam.* Oxford, UK: Oxford University Press.

Hourani, G. F. (1985). *Reason and tradition in Islamic ethics.* New York: Cambridge University Press.

Islam. Retrieved June 3, 2005, from http://en.wikipedia.org/wiki/Islam

Moosa, E. (2005). Muslim ethics? In W. Schweiker (Ed.), *The Blackwell companion to religious ethics* (pp. 237–243). Malden, MA: Blackwell.

Nanji, A. (1993). Islamic ethics. In P. Singer (Ed.), *A companion to ethics* (pp. 106–118). Malden, MA: Blackwell.

Reinhart, A. K. (1983). Islamic law as Islamic ethics? *Journal of Religious Ethics, 11,* 186–203.

Reinhart, A. K. (2005). Origins of Islamic ethics: Foundations and constructions. In W. Schweiker (Ed.), *The Blackwell companion to religious ethics* (pp. 244–253). Malden, MA: Blackwell.

Safi, O. (Ed.). (2003). *Progressive Muslims: On justice, gender, and pluralism.* Oxford, UK: Oneworld.

SECTION IV

Southern Hemisphere Theories of Ethics

The fourth section covers Southern Hemisphere theories of ethics, including Pan-African ethics and Hispanic or Latin American ethics. Latin American ethics is the focus of Chapter 14. There are numerous influences on Latin American ethics; these include natural law, African ethics, Judaism ethics, and the beliefs of indigenous people, e.g., Aztecs, Mayans, etc. (Zea, Mason, & Murguia, 2000). Despite the different views within Latin American ethics, an underlying principle is the balance between the individual, the family, the community, and the environment (Foster, 1960). Zea et al. (2000) noted that disharmony among these entities results in problems.

The last chapter addressing an ethical theory, Chapter 15, is on Pan-African ethics. Pan-African ethics may be understood initially in terms of philosophies that have developed as a consequence of domination, slavery, and political and physical domination (Adeleke, 1998; Cook & Wiley, 2000; Sanders, 1995). Inherent in the ethics from this orientation is the recognition of a joint struggle against such dominance. A foundation of Pan-African ethics is the concept of harmony and peace. Key in this theory of harmony and peace is the relationship between humans and nature. Decision-making is not focused on logical deductive reasoning but on such methods as imagination, intuitive experience, and personal feelings.

Chapter 14

Hispanic/Latino Ethics and Counselor Decision-Making

The Hispanic/Latino culture encompasses so many countries, customs, religions, values, and ethics that it is almost impossible to group them as one (Gracia, 2000). Often the term *Hispanic* is used imprecisely to refer to all people of the Spanish diaspora who share a broad cultural heritage. In its original usage, *Hispanic* specifically referred to a cultural heritage related to Spain. However, not all Spanish-speaking people trace their family lineages to Spain. Now, the term *Hispanic* identifies people whose cultural heritage is derived from Spain: They may be descendents of Spanish families, or they may be non-Europeans who claim individual Spanish cultural identities tied to different countries of origin. People with a *Latino* heritage are descendants of families from Mexico, Central America, or South America. Latinos from Mexico, Puerto Rico, and Cuba are now the largest U.S. minority (U.S. Census Bureau, 2001), and as a group they represent a mixture of several ethnic backgrounds including European, Native American, and African. The categories *Hispanic* and *Latino* are not accepted by all groups, but are commonly used classifications that indicate a background including varying degrees of Spanish language and customs.

Hispanic/Latino culture is an integral part of life in the United States. Starting in 1492 when Christopher Columbus arrived on the northeast shore of Cuba, and for the next fifty years, the Spanish circumnavigated the globe. Within a generation, the Spaniards discovered and explored the Western hemisphere and colonized over half of the present-day United States.

Catholicism was thrust upon the people of Latin America by the Spaniards, and that legacy is still evident in their everyday lives and culture. A key factor in the acceptance of the Catholic religion by the indigenous people of Mexico was the miracle of the Virgin of Guadalupe, whose story goes back to 1531 when the Virgin Mary reportedly appeared to Juan Diego, an Indian laborer. The Catholicism practiced by many Hispanics and Latinos today is infused with the beliefs and rituals of the indigenous people of Mexico (Aztec and Mayan) as well as African and Native American influences. In Hispanic/Latino cultures there is a strongly held belief in *spiritism,* or the idea that all people come to earth with a specific group of spirits to guide them (Zea et al., 2000). Practitioners of spiritism hold evil spirits responsible for difficulties in their lives and work to attract more positive spirits by purifying their thoughts and actions. These spiritual beliefs have been syncretized with Catholic beliefs. Due to the influence of Catholicism, there are strong elements of natural law perspectives in the moral and ethical values of Hispanic/Latino culture.

MAJOR CONCEPTS

There are several value conflicts between Hispanic/Latino and Anglo cultures. For example, *curanderismo,* a folk-medicine system blending ancient healing rituals and spiritual cleansings, is still practiced in Latin America and in different regions of the United States, especially the Southwest. Curanderismo teaches that humans are physical, emotional, mental, and spiritual beings. When all these aspects of a person are in harmony with the inner self and the universe, the soul is intact. Treatment of disharmony entails conciliating these systems in a holistic manner. Traditional Western medicine and psychology have not acknowledged many of the illnesses based on this notion of disharmony, which have strong psychosomatic or anxious qualities, and have dismissed treatments using herbs and prayer as superstitions. However, there is now increasing interest in including various spiritual traditions, such as spiritism, as counseling options for Hispanic/Latino clients (Baez & Hernandez, 2001; Koss-Chioino, 1995; Zea et al., 2000).

Another difference with Anglo culture is the time perspective held by Hispanics and Latinos. Because Hispanics/Latinos focus on the present rather than on the future, there is a fatalistic quality to their outlook. Fatalism does not allow an individual to confront fate, and therefore there is no choice but to accept and bear it (Shorris, 1992).

Also, in Hispanic/Latino culture, the needs of the family and community always take precedence over the needs of the individual. In fact, family unity is a significant ethnic marker (Reese, 2001). Respectfulness and conformity to parental and extended family members' authority is a central value (Harrison, Wilson, Pine, Chan, & Buriel, 1990). Older children are expected to help care for the younger ones, and the generations are interdependent socially and economically. From an Anglo perspective, children might be viewed as being raised to be very dependent on their parents. A strong sense of ethnic identity is also fostered through close relationships with extended family and community. Although their culture is patriarchal, Hispanic and Latino families are "matrifocal" in the sense that it is the mother who manages the household.

One ethical concept in this theory is *machismo,* which has been a strong theme in Latin American politics and society. In its original form, machismo, as described by the Aztecs, prescribed a competition among men with the goal of dying a famous death through exploits as a warrior (Shorris, 1992). In machismo, traditional *masculine cultural characteristics are valued* whereas feminine characteristics are denigrated. Loosely defined, *machismo is the standard by which men measure their virility.* Today in the United States, the term has a negative connotation as hypervirility, or an exaggerated pride in aggressive masculinity, coupled with a disregard of the consequences. This perverted form of machismo is a distorted view of manhood synonymous with being a philanderer, wife-beater, and drunk. However, *machismo actually requires that a man be honorable, keep his word, have an effect in the world, and bear responsibility for his actions* (Shorris).

Marianismo is the stereotypic female role characterized by hyperfeminine behavior (Stevens, 1994). The ideal is a "Mariana" who is someone like the Virgin Mary—*chaste, nurturing, self-sacrificing, and submissive to men.* A woman's reputation is based on how well she lives up to this ideal of feminine virtue. Since the women's movement, marianismo has evolved into a cult of spiritual superiority, which elevates women as morally and spiritually superior to men.

Hispanic/Latino moral life is the practice of love and justice in the community. Liberation theology and ethics arose out of indignation over the serious moral problems of poverty and inequality in Latin American countries. According to Brackley and Schubeck (2002), *solidarity* has been the collective response of the victims to oppression. *Solidarity is located at the center of Hispanic/Latino ethics,* challenging the ethic of individualism prevalent in U.S. culture as well as opposing systems of social and economic exclusion, such as capitalism. *Solidarity* gives a social dimension to the *concepts of love and justice compatible with the Hispanic/Latino cultural values of honoring God, family, and community.*

ADDITIONAL READINGS: HISPANIC/LATINO ETHICS

Brackley, D., & Schubeck, T. L. (2002). Moral theology in Latin America. *Theological Studies, 63,* 123–160.

Deloria, V. (2005). Indigenous peoples. In W. Schweiker (Ed.), *The Blackwell companion to religious ethics* (pp. 552–559). Malden, MA: Blackwell.

Garcia, I. (1997). *Dignidad: Ethics through Hispanic eyes.* Nashville, TN: Abingdon Press.

Gracia, J. J. E. (2000). *Hispanic/Latino identity: A philosophical perspective.* Malden, MA: Blackwell.

Hispanics. Retrieved November 15, 2004, from http://en.wikipedia.org/wiki/Hispanic

Shorris, E. (1992). *Latinos: A biography of the people.* New York: W.W. Norton.

Zea, L. (1949/1963). *The Latin-American mind.* (J. H. Abbott & L. Dunham, Trans.). Norman, OK: University of Oklahoma Press.

Chapter 15

Pan-African Ethics and Counselor Decision-Making

Pan-Africanism is a relatively new term coined within the past century to promote the unity of Africans and people of the African diaspora; that is, the scattering of language and culture of those of African ancestry who live in other parts of the world such as the United States and the Caribbean (Adeleke, 1997). Adeleke (1998) stated, "Pan-Africanism emphasizes the unity of Africans and black diasporans in a joint struggle, a struggle ordained by the pains of the deep historical wounds inflicted by slavery, racism, colonialism and neo-colonialism" (p. 182). Prior to the 1900s there was little discussion of a connection between Africa and those who had ancestry in the continent, who more than likely were victims of the slave trade.

The first Pan-African Congress was held in Paris in 1919 (Adeleke, 1997). The original intention was to promote more autonomy for African countries in the context of expansive colonialism on the continent. There have been a number of additional meetings throughout the world but not on a consistent basis. More recently the focus has been on promoting African unity with an intent of promoting social, economic, and political advances.

In an effort to understand the recency of the efforts to create African unity for diasporans and those living in Africa, it is necessary to briefly review how so many became disporans, almost all as a consequence of forced exile (through the slave trade). Morel (1920) traced the slave trade from the mid-1500s to the early 1900s. The slave trade was begun by the Portuguese in the mid-1500s and resulted in slaves transported back to Europe. The discovery and populating of the Americas expanded the slave trade and eventually the English dominated this activity

(Morel). Africans were brought to the Caribbean and America primarily, e.g., Jamaica and other English colonies. Most of the Africans were taken from West Africa. It has been estimated that well over ten million Africans were captured and sold into slavery (Becker, 1999). Also, a significant number of Africans died in the "middle passage" or transport to the Americas (Morel). The consequence of such diffusion and particularly forced exodus from Africa impacted the culture and values or ethics of those disaporans. For example, many were introduced to Christianity and Western values. However, it has been suggested that Africans and diasporans still share a common culture, problems, and identity as an oppressed group (Adeleke, 1998).

MAJOR CONCEPTS

As has been noted above, Pan-African ethics is not based upon one philosophical or religious orientation but likely has been influenced by several sources including Islam, Christianity, and tribal beliefs. However, there are commonly held views on what constitutes such ethics (Kirk-Greene, 2001; Mbiti, 1969). Kigongo (2005) addressed the potential coherence of African ethics and stated, "We can talk of the ethics of a specific ethnic group in Africa, there are different ethnic groups in Africa that are described as African, for they share commonalities (among then ethical) that gives them the collective identity of Africa" (p. 3). Omonzejele (2005) stated, "African ethics is based on communal living. It fuses the society into one big whole. In traditional African society there is no 'me' but 'us' no 'my' but 'ours'" (p. 1). Also, Pan-African ethics has been identified as a consequentialist approach. Omonzejele described what constitutes good among Africans as "those things that enhance positive human growth" (p. 2). Conversely, a key foundation of Pan-African ethics is *behaving in a way that is not harmful to others in the community* (Mbiti, 1969). Several characteristics that promote the communal nature of Pan-African ethics have been identified: truth; keeping one's word or fidelity; and trust, patience, generosity, and gentleness (Gbadegesin, 2001; Kigongo, 2005; Kirk-Greene, 2001).

Kirk-Greene (2001) noted that *truthfulness* in African morals is an essential characteristic of a "good person." The belief is that *a lie can harm others,* and since a key feature of Pan-African ethics is to avoid harming others, then one avoids a lie and is truthful. A concept similar to truthfulness is *trust or keeping one's word* (Kirk-Greene, 2001). Trust and keeping one's word goes beyond simply a verbal statement; it includes behavior that demonstrates addressing the best interests of others. If one is entrusted with another's care—for example, an adult with a developmental disability—then one must provide quality care if one initially agreed to do so.

Kirk-Greene (2001) noted that the concept of *patience* may have been an influence from Islam and in essence concerns submission of will to a higher power. Gbadegesin (2001) states that good people are also evaluated on their *generosity and gentleness*.

The last concept that potentially applies is the significance of *shame* and how shame is a result of *not fulfilling one's duty*. Kirk-Greene (2001) suggested that shame is a consequence of not fulfilling one's social role. Fulfilling one's social role is important because of the significance of community and unity of the group. One has obligations to the group.

ADDITIONAL READINGS: PAN-AFRICAN ETHICS

Barboza, S. (Ed.). (1998). *The African American book of values.* New York: Doubleday.

Becker, E. (1999). *Chronology on the history of slavery and racism.* Retrieved February 23, 2006, from http://innercity.org/holt/slavechron.html

Bujo, B. (2001). *Foundations of an African ethic: Beyond the universal claims of Western morality* (B. McNeil, Trans.). New York: Crossroad.

Bujo, B. (2005). Differentiation in African ethics. In W. Schweiker (Ed.), *The Blackwell companion to religious ethics* (pp. 423–437). Malden, MA: Blackwell.

Gyekye, K. (1996). *African cultural values.* Philadelphia, PA: Sankofa.

Hallen, B. (2002). *Short history of African philosophy.* Bloomington: Indiana University Press.

Hallen, B. (2005). African ethics? In W. Schweiker (Ed.), *The Blackwell companion to religious ethics* (pp. 406–412). Malden, MA: Blackwell.

Karenga, M. (2004). *MAAT, the moral ideal in ancient Egypt: A study in classical African ethics.* New York: Routledge.

Moore, A. (2002). African-American early childhood teachers' decisions to refer African-American students. *Qualitative Studies in Education, 15,* 631–652.

Walker, V. & Snarey, J. (Eds.). (2004). *Race-ing moral formation: African-American perspectives on care and justice.* New York: Teachers College Press.

SECTION V

Ethical Decision-Making Model

Section V focuses on an explanation of the hermeneutic model of ethical decision-making and illustrates applying the model. Chapter 16 describes a systematic model for ethical decision-making using a hermeneutic approach (Betan, 1997; Fowers & Richardson, 1996). Key in our ethical decision-making model is the view that understanding an ethical decision is what Gadamer (1975) described as an essential component of hermeneutics: understanding in terms of the metaphor of a horizon. According to Gadamer, human interpretation of situations is based on the range of vision seen from a "horizon" and furthermore may be understood as "everything that can be seen from a particular vantage point" (p. 269). We use a three-dimensional sphere to conceptualize our ethical decision-making model based upon hermeneutics. Where the counselor and client are on the sphere determines the factors and influences on the ethical decision-making processes.

For example, in the first step of developing ethical sensitivity, we discuss how counselors can become aware of contextual influences including worldviews (culturally sensitive theories). Training in different ethical orientations provides the practitioner with a basic understanding of relevant worldviews and how they impact daily decisions in clients' lives. Step two is a definition of the ethical dilemma based in part on the context. Thus, if a counselor is working with a Japanese client, then a review of Eastern philosophical and theoretical traditions may be warranted to help clarify the final definition of the issue. We propose other steps in ethical decision-making similar to previous models (Corey, Corey, & Callahan, 2003; Rest, 1994; Welfel, 2002), but in addition we offer a contextual perspective (Betan, 1997) based upon philosophical/theoretical views. We ask the question: What are the important elements of the horizon that should be considered in ethical decision-making?

Chapter 17 is a discussion of how to pragmatically use this hermeneutic model of ethical decision-making in counseling practice. We presented in earlier chapters complex and abstract theories that create a challenge for the professional counselor to interpret in actual practice. It is easy for counselors to react to this challenge day to day based upon personal values and gut reactions and not approach ethical decision-making in a systematic way. We attempt to provide an alternative approach by demonstrating "fusion of horizons" (Follesdal, 2001) and the application of the ethical theories presented in earlier chapters.

Chapter 16

Ethical Decision-Making
A Hermeneutic Model

$\mathbf{A}$s was stated in Chapter 1, ethical decision-making is a critical part of the training and practice of professional counselors (Cottone & Claus, 2000; Corey et al., 2003). In this chapter, we propose a model of ethical decision-making based upon a hermeneutic approach. The hermeneutic approach is a flexible culturally sensitive approach to ethical decision-making. A definition of hermeneutics is presented and then linked to ethical decision-making. Finally, there is a discussion of the hermeneutic circle and how it can be applied to ethics and counseling.

Follesdal (2001) stated that "hermeneutics is the study of interpretations" (p. 375). Furthermore, according to Follesdal, "The term hermeneutics (from the Greek *hermeneno,* to interpret) was first introduced in 1654" (p. 375). Initial definitions and use of hermeneutics focused on interpreting literature. Martin and Thompson (2003) stated, "Hermeneutics is the art of interpretation" (p. 2). Follesdal pointed out that the natural sciences have used a hypothetical-deductive reasoning approach, whereas the social sciences have employed a critical method approach; hermeneutics employs aspects of both the hypothetical-deductive reasoning and critical method approaches.

In a hermeneutic approach, this is accomplished by suggesting interpretational hypotheses and determining whether the interpretations are accurate. Martin and Thompson (2003) concluded that "human life involves a constant flow of interpretation and reinterpretation" (p. 2). Since the time of the early view that hermeneutics involves interpretation of text, particularly biblical text, the purpose and application of hermeneutics have expanded to include all human interpretation (Betan, 1997; Hathaway, 2002; Martin & Thompson). Dilthey (1978) expanded the application of hermeneutics to understanding human behavior or interpreting the meaning of behavior. More recently, hermeneutics has been used in understanding counseling process and psychological and social research (Chessick, 1986, 1990; Hathaway; Martin & Thompson; Zeddies, 2002).

Follesdal (2001) further described the origins of hermeneutics as interpreting text and then adjusting the interpretation once it is reread within a wider context. Also, the interpretation depends upon understanding the whole and its parts. Early writers on hermeneutics also suggested the idea of a hermeneutic circle to depict the circular process of going back and forth between parts and whole. Chessick (1990) described the hermeneutic circle as

> beginning with a preliminary notion of the whole, one then moves to an ever-more probing analysis and synthesis of the parts which in turn leads to an evolving ever-changing concept of the whole. This affords an increasingly internalized and thought-through understanding of the whole. (p. 257)

We will come back to this idea of a hermeneutic circle later in this chapter.

Several other important concepts were introduced in the early writings on hermeneutics. Follesdal (2001) stated,

> A main task of hermeneutics is to adapt our fore-meaning to the text. We must approach the text with openness, that is, with awareness that we have fore-meanings and that the text may have a meaning that is incompatible with our fore-meaning. (p. 377)

He further stated that

> we revise our anticipations of what is expressed in the text, until we find an interpretation that seems to us to be true or at least reasonable. That is, we adjust our opinions until we find that we can agree with the text. (p. 377)

The criterion of understanding has been termed a "fusion of horizons" (Follesdal, 2001). Hathaway (2002) defined a horizon as "the range of possible meanings available to a person at their moment and place in history. It is constituted by the dispositions the person brings to the present by virtue of their place in tradition(s) or culture" (p. 207).

Horizons and fusion of horizons are important concepts in hermeneutic theory. Fusion of horizons involves the integration of multiple horizons. For example, if a counselor and a client discuss a problem openly, their mutual understanding may result in a fusion of horizons. Specifically, the client and counselor enter the relationship with preunderstandings based upon their histories, culture, and traditions. Through open discussion, they both alter their original understanding of the problem to a "fused" similar understanding of the problem. In a sense the client and counselor are seeing from a similar horizon, a fused horizon, and focusing on similar aspects of the problem. Both the client and counselor go beyond the initial personal conception of the problem and develop a new revised view. Thus, changing preunderstandings may be accomplished through exposure to different sources of information. Also, because hermeneutics is circular, there may be dynamic change with the interaction of the preunderstandings, even ones that have been changed at one point by exposure to other horizons or information in a horizon. Gadamer (1975) suggested that preunderstandings can be changed through exposure to the horizon of a text or context (a different source of information). Also, Chessick (1990) described development of the horizon: "Meaning and understanding are subject to time and change. . . . We always survey the past from within our own horizon, a horizon which is always shifting" (p. 257). This is an important part of the hermeneutic process, e.g., meaning and interpretation are dynamic and change through interaction between parts and the whole, and the moment in time and change in time may alter the meaning of the situation. Furthermore, Chessick noted that a horizon "involves the customs, institutions, and language of a given culture" (p. 259).

Osborne (1991) suggested that fusion of horizons may be further explained by the process of one's changing understanding through a hermeneutic spiral. The hermeneutic spiral consisted of assimilation, productive tension, and expanded horizons. Hathaway (2002) defined assimilation as the initial understanding that individuals acquire when they try to assimilate a new horizon from the perspective of their preunderstandings. A second part of this process is productive tension, which involves an awareness of the relationship between preunderstandings and information in the other or new horizon (Hathaway, 2002).The third part of this process, a hermeneutic spiral, is expanded horizons involving the expansion and fusion of horizons from the original preunderstandings to a new horizon for the individual.

ELEMENTS OF THE HORIZON IN ETHICAL DECISION-MAKING

There are a number of elements that constitute the horizon in counseling ethics. Figure 16.1 depicts the hermeneutic circle, including the possible horizons in counseling ethics. In this model, the ethical dilemma is at the center, with component parts interacting with the dilemma. Keep in mind that hermeneutics and the interaction between parts and the whole influence each other in a continuous dynamic manner. Also, the whole is the total horizon for a particular ethical dilemma. Note in our model the interaction between parts, e.g., professional codes of ethics, and the ethical dilemma as well as the whole. Not only do the parts on the outer part of the circle influence the ethical dilemma, but the parts influence each other. The hermeneutic model of ethical decision-making is probably better represented by a sphere, a three-dimensional figure with the various components

Figure 16.1   Hermeneutic Model of Ethical Decision-Making in Counseling

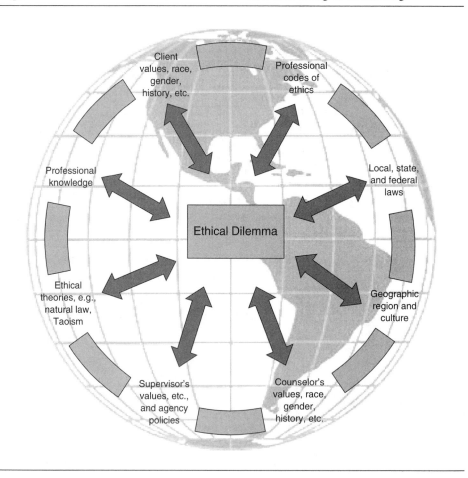

interacting simultaneously and influencing each other. For example, interpretation of professional codes is influenced by the personal values and characteristics of the counselor, which in turn may be influenced by the values and personal characteristics of the supervisor. Another point noted earlier in our discussion is that any interpretation of meaning of an ethical dilemma is based upon the time or historical context. A concrete example is the identification of child abuse, posttraumatic stress disorder, or an eating disorder. Forty years ago these examples for the most part did not exist as problems as they do today.

We are suggesting that the horizon of ethical decision-making, the whole, includes the following parts: an ethical dilemma; the counselor and his or her values, race, gender, personal history, etc.; the client and his or her values, race, gender, personal history, etc.; the supervisor's personal characteristics, values, etc.; agency policies; the geographic region and culture; local, state, and federal laws; professional codes of ethics; professional knowledge; and ethical theories such as natural law, Taoism, or Pan-African ethics. We want to note that ethical decision-making using a hermeneutic model may involve multiple ethical theories that may be relevant to consider. Before we explain the relevance of each of these parts, we want to note that there may be other parts of the horizon that are also relevant; however, we feel the horizons included in our model are the most relevant based upon the professional literature.

THE ETHICAL DILEMMA

The first part of the whole in the hermeneutic circle that we want to address is the ethical dilemma itself. In our model, the ethical dilemma is depicted as the innermost part of the process because it is the focus of the decision-making. Corey et al. (2003) and Welfel (2002) noted the importance of identifying an ethical dilemma in counseling practice. We identify several broad categories of ethical dilemmas but also want to note that not all ethical dilemmas will fall into one of these categories. Ethical complaints to state licensure boards can provide some insight into potential ethical dilemmas facing counselors, although not all ethical dilemmas come to the attention of such boards (Neukrug, Milliken, & Walden, 2001). Several investigators have identified major ethical dilemmas confronting practicing counselors (Bergeron & Gray, 2003; Merskey, 1996; Neukrug et al.; Scott, 2000). The major ethical dilemmas identified include the following issues: boundaries; competence of the counselor; confidentiality; informed consent; multicultural competence; and professional demeanor.

Ethical Dilemma: Boundary Issues

Boundary ethical issues may include dual relationships–nonsexual, counselor-client sexual relationships, bartering, and types of counselor self-disclosure (Burian, 2000; Lamb, Catanzaro, & Moorman, 2003). Burian noted that dual social relationships can result in loss of objectivity on the part of the counselor. Lamb and Catanzaro (1998) found that certain crossings of nonsexual boundaries were precursors to more serious problems such as sexual boundary violations. Somer (1999) suggested that boundary violations generally begin gradually and develop to be more severe over time.

Neukrug et al. (2001) contacted state licensure boards and requested information on complaints submitted against counselors. These researchers found that the most common complaint was a violation involving dual relationships: nonsexual relationships. Dual relationships may involve counseling a friend, neighbor, or relative. It also may involve receiving referrals from friends or coworkers who know the client and may be aware of the counseling process, e.g., referral from a coworker who may have access to records. Wherever the counselor has multiple roles with a client, there exists the potential for an ethical dilemma of dual relationships. Dual relationships have been found to be more prevalent as a problem in rural areas with smaller social networks (Perkins, Hudson, Gray, & Stewart, 1998). Dual relationships as ethical dilemmas have been categorized as boundary issues (Corey et al., 2003; Okamoto, 2003).

Another type of dual relationship involving boundary issues concerns self-disclosure: How much information should a counselor share with a client and what types of self-disclosures may be made (Kim, Hill, Gelso, Goates, Asay, & Harbin, 2003; Nyman and Daugherty, 2001)? Nyman and Daugherty noted that the professional literature suggests that a counselor's personal self-disclosure may burden a client and potentially take away the focus on client issues. For example, disclosure about marital and family activities by the counselor to the client may be an ethical issue, particularly if the talk time and information interferes with focusing on client issues. Shapiro and Ginsberg (2003) proposed that accepting referrals from current clients creates a potential ethical dilemma and can be a boundary violation. The question that may arise is whether the counselor is using the client to further his or her financial gain. Other examples of boundary issues involve socializing with a client outside of the counseling session and bartering for payment (Corey et al., 2003).

Ethical Dilemma: Counselor Competence

Counselor competence and qualifications are a second major area of potential ethical dilemmas. Graduate-level training and professional credentials are ways to achieve a level of competence but they do not guarantee effective implementation of counseling techniques. The second-most common complaint to state licensure boards against counselors concerned competence (Neukrug et al., 2001). How do counselors develop and maintain counseling skills and competence? What level of professional training is necessary to be effective? A related question is: What is competence and what level of skill is necessary? McLeod (1992) stated that there is "an expectation that counselors will possess qualifications and certificates which validate their capacity to practice effectively" (p. 359). Researchers have found a relationship between counselor effectiveness and client satisfaction (Constantine, 2002; Jones & Markos, 1997). For example, there may be questions about whether it is unethical for a counselor to read a book about hypnosis and then begin using the technique with clients without any formal training. The counselor in this example probably has not acquired the expertise necessary to provide such a counseling service. Another ethical issue around counselor competence concerns continued updating of the counselor's skills after completing formal graduate training. A major area of competence concerns the use of assessments by the counselor. Ethical issues of assessment include the use of diagnostic tools such as the *Diagnostic and Statistical Manual (DSM)*. Problems here may center on making accurate diagnoses, having adequate experience, and holding appropriate qualifications.

Another relevant question to address in understanding ethical issues and counselor competence is: What level and type of continued training or updating is adequate to prepare the counselor for continued effective practice? State licensure and national certifications all require some amount of continuing education for counselors.

Ethical Dilemma: Confidentiality

Isaacs and Stone (2001) stated, "Confidentiality is one of the most critical aspects of any counseling relationship" (p. 342). Confidentiality refers to maintaining privacy and not disclosing information to others outside the counseling relationship unless there is approval or consent by the client. Clients come into the counseling relationship and expect that what is discussed will be kept confidential. Neukrug et al. (2001) found that violations of confidentiality were a frequent complaint made against counselors to state licensing boards. Confidentiality, however, is not absolute, and there are circumstances when counseling session information may be disclosed (Isaacs & Stone, 2001; Kermani & Drob, 1987). There are a number of potential ethical issues regarding confidentiality such as those involving minors, circumstances surrounding harm—harm to the client who is considering suicide or a client who is expressing thoughts of harming others—court-involved clients, mandated reporting of child abuse, and clients with medical conditions such as HIV who may engage in dangerous acts related to their condition, e.g., spreading the condition. Confidentiality is seen as such an important issue that federal legislation was passed recently to improve the confidentiality of patient records, the Health Insurance Portability and Accountability Act, HIPAA (U.S. Department of Health & Human Services, 2003).

Ethical Dilemma: Autonomy

Autonomy is another important element in ethical decision-making for counselors. There are two elements that comprise autonomy: freedom to choose a course of action and competence to make an informed choice. Beauchamp and Childress (2001) stated that informed consent is based upon full disclosure of information so an informed choice can be made, voluntary choice to choose a course of action, and competence to understand the choices. Competence concerns the capacity, intellectual and emotional, to make informed decisions. An individual who is cognitively impaired may not be able to make an informed choice, or an individual with a mental illness may not be thinking clearly enough to make an informed choice. An example may be someone who is severely depressed and who is expressing thoughts of suicide. The ethical dilemma may be whether to pursue hospitalization against the person's will to protect him or her. Autonomy may be taken away in this example if the client is hospitalized.

The concept of empowerment fits within the issue of autonomy in counseling. Empowerment began to permeate treatment in the counseling field over the past twenty years (Banja, 1990; Clark & Krupa, 2002; Fawcett et al., 1994; Houser, Hampton, & Carriker, 2000; Ozer & Bandura, 1990). In addition, federal disability legislation has attempted to incorporate the philosophical bases of empowerment. Fawcett et al. defined empowerment as "the process of gaining some control over events, outcomes, and resources of importance to an individual or group" (p. 472). The empowerment concept clearly fits within the view of autonomy and ethical dilemmas concerning control over decisions in the lives of individuals with mental health diagnoses, particularly more severe mental illness.

Ethical Dilemma: Multicultural Competency

Multicultural competency has recently been noted to be an important ethical issue in counseling (Bellini, 2002; Constantine, 2002; Kim & Lyons, 2003) and is separate from general counselor competence (Constantine). Multicultural competency refers to the counselor having the necessary awareness, knowledge, and skills to work with culturally diverse groups (Constantine; Sue, Arredondo, &

McDavis, 1992). Sue et al. proposed that multicultural competence include three general dimensions: being aware of one's own values, biases, and preconceived beliefs about culturally diverse groups; actively trying to understand the world-view and experiences of culturally diverse group members; and developing counseling skills appropriate for culturally diverse clients. Sue et al. suggested that lack of these competencies is unethical and stated, "A serious moral vacuum exists in the delivery of cross-cultural counseling and therapy services because the values of the dominant culture have been imposed on the culturally different consumer" (p. 68). There have been numerous attempts to define and measure multicultural counseling competencies with varied success (Fuertes, 2001; Fuertes & Brobst, 2002; Kocarek, Talbot, Batka, & Anderson, 2001). This lack of clarity about competencies creates ethical dilemmas for counselors who work with culturally diverse populations. What is the level of competence necessary before a counselor can ethically work with diverse populations? One answer has been to improve graduate-level training in this area (Constantine).

Ethical Dilemma: Professional Demeanor

Professional demeanor has not been a significant focus of research or ethics in counseling, but there are writings about these issues (Scheffler, Garrett, Zarin, & Pincus, 2000). Ethical dilemmas around fees for counseling services are potentially significant (Wolfson, 1999). Lanza (2001) stated, "Money is a taboo subject for many people" (p. 69). She further suggested that because of attitudes toward quantifying personal worth, setting counseling fees is generally difficult. The counselor may avoid discussing rates with clients and simply set the fees, either too high or too low. Wolfson concluded that "the fee is likely to evoke a range of ethical-clinical tensions and dilemmas for practitioners in private and agency practice settings insofar as it represents the practitioner's or the agency's income" (p. 270).

The client and the client's family may have different expectations than the counselor or agency and expect low fees because of a belief that counselors and social-service agencies are altruistic and do not seek financial gain. Another issue is that counselors may have access to client resources or may influence clients to give the counselor access to their finances. Fee structure in managed care is another ethical issue for counselors (Scheffler et al., 2000). Issues of reduced fees and making inappropriate diagnoses to gain access to services have been cited as major problems confronting counselors in managed care (Lakin, 1988).

Counselor dress can impact the client in a positive or negative way. Researchers have only minimally studied the impact of counselor dress on client outcomes (Littrell & Littrell, 1982). Littrell and Littrell studied the perceptions of Native

American adolescents and their counselor preference. They found that counselor dress did impact clients' perceptions. Counselors who were dressed more fashionably or currently were preferred by adolescent clients. Do counselors have a responsibility to dress more currently, particularly with certain populations such as adolescents who may prefer to work with such a counselor? Do they have an ethical responsibility to be fashionable and dress a certain way so that clients are more receptive? Another issue concerning counselor dress may be whether counselors have any responsibility to avoid dressing provocatively. For example, what impact may counselors who dress more sexually provocatively have on their clients and what are any ethical issues?

Another potential ethical dilemma related to counselor demeanor is the question of whether professionals should advertise their services (Hite & Fraser, 1988). Hite and Fraser noted that "advertising by professionals was restricted by professional associations. In the late 1970s, key rulings by the Supreme Court forced relaxation of historic advertising bans by professional associations" (p. 95). The major concern with advertising among professional associations is the maintenance of credibility and dignity.

Counseling is somewhat of a business, so how should professional counselors seek referrals and business for their practices? For example, how should they use advertising?

THE COUNSELOR'S PERSONAL VALUES, RACE, GENDER, AND PERSONAL HISTORY

Counselors' values, race, gender, and personal history are parts of the whole on the horizon of the hermeneutic circle (see Figure 16.1). Corey et al. (2003) noted potential ethical concerns involving counselors. Key in these ethical concerns is a level of self-awareness (Corey et al.). For example, one possible ethical issue is unresolved personal issues that may impact the counseling process.

Another possible concern in this part of the hermeneutic circle is countertransference. In the twenty-first century, we need to be aware that counseling involves two dissimilar participants in a therapeutic encounter. Counselors of diverse populations will need to begin identifying their own uniqueness in order to be accepting of what they bring to the therapeutic relationship. Counselors' assessment of their contribution to the relationship must include a commitment to knowledge of self. They, like all people, are shaped and influenced by many factors of importance, such as their cultural heritage(s) and various dimensions of identity, including ethnic and racial identity, gender socialization, socioeconomic experiences, and other dimensions of identity that lead to certain biases and assumptions about themselves and others (APA, 2003b). No longer can counselors be guided by moral and ethical relativism, which assumes that it is possible to be a "blank slate" with clients. Counselors are not neutral to dimensions of difference, and they are not immune from their own cultural uniqueness. In making this statement, we are stating that differences, which have traditionally been described as deficits, are no longer defined by the dominant and authoritarian group with power. Rather, a more accurate approach to ethical decision-making in a diverse society is to take a position that allows each group to articulate its own cultural identity but at the same time acknowledge the common ground of psychological principles that connect each group with other groups (Pedersen, 1995). While counselors will need to be culturally aware and knowledgeable about their clients' worldviews, it is equally important that they be informed about themselves. Ethical dilemmas arise when counselors' own personal values affect the treatment of clients.

Other countertransference issues that may affect the counseling relationship include the counselor's personal needs to be a caretaker. Also, the counselor may have a need to receive reinforcement and recognition by the client. Finally, another issue is the need for power by the counselor (Bargh & Alvarez, 2001; Duncan, 2003). Clients are typically vulnerable and open to influence; counselors who have a high need for power may unduly influence a client.

THE CLIENT'S PERSONAL VALUES, RACE, GENDER, AND PERSONAL HISTORY

Demographic and attitudinal changes in our society have created controversy, tension, and dissonance in how to apply professional ethical codes. Most evident is the changing profile of the population in the United States. The major shifts in demography have been noted by the U.S. Census Bureau (2004). In addition to noting current statistics of the population, their data and analyses include speculations about population demography in the year 2050.

The U.S. Census Bureau (2004) anticipated that, if demographic data follow current trends, during the period of 2000–2050, the white population will be the slowest-growing race group. The black population will grow at more than twice the white population's annual rate of change, while the Asian and Pacific Islander populations are projected through the year 2020 to continue to be the fastest-growing race or ethic group, with growth rates that will exceed 2.5 percent a year and account for 17 percent of the nation's growth from 2000 to 2020 and for 21 percent of growth from 2020 to 2050. The Hispanic population, a major factor in population growth, will contribute 44 percent of the nation's population growth from 2000 to 2020 and 62 percent from 2020 to 2050 (U.S. Census Bureau). The difficulties for counselors resulting from these current and anticipated changes lie in the divergent sets of philosophical assumptions and worldviews that clients and counselors will bring to the therapeutic relationship. Any single response to a client may be flawed and incomplete. As counselors we are instructed to adopt the ethical codes and the philosophical frameworks presented in our professional training programs. Without examining the philosophical assumptions of the current ethical codes we may unwittingly accept the perspective of the dominant culture and possibly minimize or trivialize the role of culture in ethical decision-making (Ibrahim, 1996).

The personal values of a client have been found to affect the counseling relationship (Vashon & Agresti, 1992). For example, it has been found that client outcomes in counseling are related to similarity between client and counselor values (Arizmendi, Beutler, Shantell, Crago, & Hageman, 1985; Beutler, 1979). Values have been defined as beliefs that guide actions across various situations (Connor & Becker, 2003). Family influence on the development of personal values has been found (Kasser, Koestner, & Lekes, 2002). Odell and Stewart (1993) stated that "the handling of values is an ethical issue of no little import" (p. 129). Furthermore, researchers have found that successful counseling outcomes result when clients alter their personal values and more closely resemble the values of the counselor (Odell & Stewart). An important ethical dilemma is how similar the client's values have to be to the counselor's for counseling to be successful. Also, another dilemma is whether promoting similarity between the client and counselor is ethical and best for the client. For the profession as a whole, the question becomes: Do counselors use those moral and ethical frameworks presented by their training programs—which reflect society's norms—as the sole basis for their ethical decision-making? Or can counselors come to an ethical decision while considering the values, morals, and ethical positions of their diverse client population?

Values are defined as beliefs that guide actions and behaviors. Also, family values impact the development of personal values. A client may enter counseling with certain values that may be in conflict with community values. For example, a client may have a sexual orientation that conflicts with the community's values, e.g., a gay or lesbian sexual orientation. Another example of client values that conflict with community values may be in child-rearing practices. A family may see value in corporal punishment whereas the community may see this as child abuse.

The literature of feminist ethics provides a unique contribution to understanding ethical psychological practice and is useful in resolving the dilemmas created by client diversity. Brabeck and Ting (2000) have identified the following five overlapping themes of feminist ethics that are also germane to the practice of ethical decision-making with any diverse population:

1. The assumption that [women] and their experiences have moral significance

2. The assertion that attentiveness, subjective knowledge, can illuminate moral issues

3. The claim that a [feminist critique] of male distortions must be accompanied by a critique of all discriminatory distortions

4. The admonition that [feminist ethics] engage in analysis of the context and attend to the power dynamics of that context

5. The injunction that [feminist ethics] require action directed at achieving social justice (p. 18)

In the brackets we can easily replace the word *women* or *feminist* with any population that has been misrepresented, distorted, and oppressed by the historically dominant, male perspective (Scaltsas, 1992).

Although clients bring immediate identifiers such as race, ethnicity, gender, and disabilities to the process of ethical decision-making, the cultural environment in which clients have grown up and lived is highly influential in their construction of moral reasoning. Boss (2004) discussed three levels of thinking that sharpen our analytical skills: experience, interpretation, and analysis. Each of these levels of thinking relies upon the events in clients' lives and in the social construction of their world order. Throughout their lives clients experience events by observing and listening to information given by others who have been affected by the same set of events. Interpretation involves the process of trying to give meaning and to make sense of life experiences. These interpretations are affected by the prevailing cultural interpretation at a point in history. Analysis demands that counselors raise their level of consciousness about their clients and refuse to accept biased interpretations of clients' experiences. Ethical dilemmas arise when the dissonance between clients' and counselors' experiences, interpretations, and analyses is not heard and respected.

THE SUPERVISOR'S PERSONAL VALUES, RACE, GENDER, AND PERSONAL HISTORY

Supervisors' values and personal characteristics, as well as agency policies, constitute another major component of the horizon for ethical decision-making for counselors. It is commonly accepted and recommended that supervisees consult with supervisors around ethical dilemmas (Herlihy, Gray, & McCollum, 2002; Welfel, 2002). Supervisors, like counselors and clients, bring their own personal values to the decision-making process. What does this mean for the counselor attempting to make an ethical decision? Two examples of supervisor values may be their multicultural sensitivity to clients and their multicultural sensitivity to counselors (Ladany, Lehman-Waterman, Molinaro, & Wolgast, 1999). Multicultural sensitivity concerns sensitivity to and understanding of issues of gender, race, culture, sexual orientation, disability, etc. The counselor has a responsibility to be aware of the supervisor's personal values. An important value is multicultural sensitivity because the supervisor's values with respect to multicultural sensitivity will impact his or her recommendations when giving feedback on an ethical issue. Welfel noted that counselors consult with supervisors and must ultimately decide for themselves the course of action in an ethical dilemma.

Expertise of the supervisor in the area addressed with the ethical dilemma is another consideration (Ladany et al., 1999). Just as counselors must continually engage in professional development activities, supervisors must maintain and update their knowledge through continuing education or seek feedback about their supervision (Wheeler & King, 2000). Also, the supervisors should acknowledge their limitations and/or the necessity to responsibly pursue information addressing the ethical dilemma presented by counselors. Supervisors may be held accountable for the actions of their supervisees (Herlihy et al., 2002) and part of this responsibility is to be knowledgeable in the area of the ethical dilemma, or to refer the counselor to someone who is (Magnuson, Norem, & Wilcoxon, 2000). Supervisors may or may not share with supervisees their levels of expertise in the area of an ethical dilemma, so the counselor responsible for making the ethical decision must decide the weight to give the advice given by the supervisor.

Another consideration is the training and background of the supervisor. The counselor may be supervised by someone who received training in a different social-service profession such as social work, psychology, or psychiatry. Consequently, the ethical codes followed by the supervisor and the counselor may be different; and not all professional codes share exactly the same views. The counselor likely will follow the codes of the American Counseling Association (ACA) and the supervisor may follow the codes of the National Association of Social Workers (NASW) or the American Psychological Association (APA). If the professional codes conflict, which is to be used in resolving the ethical dilemma? For example, the ACA includes a section under the confidentiality code that allows for disclosure of information to a third party if it involves a contagious fatal disease, whereas the APA codes do not provide direction for such a disclosure.

AGENCY POLICIES AND VALUES

Another consideration is the agency policies and values (Linzer, 1992; Watkins, 1989). The agency may embrace policies and practices that may or may not be consistent with the counselor's code of ethics. Linzer described a good example of how agency policy and values may impact counselor ethical decision-making in an agency that has religious origins, Jewish Family Services. In his example, staff are confronted with the agency's values around client sexual activities. Similarly, if a counselor works in an abortion clinic, the agency has certain values and the counselor needs to determine what they are and how they impact the counselor's ethical decision-making. Watkins discusses agency policy around client confidentiality and counselor values. Other examples of how agency policies may impact a counselor's ethical decision-making include diagnosing clients for eligibility of services. A counselor may feel pressured to use a more severe diagnosis to keep and maintain income for the agency and perhaps for himself or herself. The impact of managed care and how agencies respond to it is another source of ethical dilemmas (Cooper & Gottlieb, 2000). Austad and Berman (1991) concluded that managed care was based on the philosophy of "the least extensive, least expensive, least intrusive intervention" (p. 11). Agencies must adjust to the economic demands and requirements of those funding mental health services, and the counselor's code of ethics may be in conflict with such values when the counselor believes more services are needed than are allocated.

PROFESSIONAL CODES OF ETHICS

Professional codes are also a consideration in ethical decision-making and on the horizon for the counselor (see Figure 16.1). Different professional codes have been developed for the various counseling professions, such as school counseling, mental health counseling, rehabilitation counseling, and family therapy and counseling (American Association of Marriage and Family Therapy [AAMFT], 1998; American Mental Health Counselors Association [AMHCA], 2000; Commission on Rehabilitation Counselor Certification [CRCC], 1997). (See Appendix A for links to professional codes.) Professional codes are only relatively recent additions to the profession and practice of counseling, first introduced forty years ago (Neukrug and Lovell, 1996). Typically, ethical codes have been developed based on certain Western ethical theories such as utilitarianism and respect for persons (Kantian ethics; Harris, 2002; Henry, 1996).

Neukrug and Lovell (1996) cited the strengths and limitations of professional codes of ethics. Some of the benefits or strengths include standards that protect consumers, a framework for ethical decision-making, and a reference for defense in judicial proceedings. Neukrug and Lovell also provide insight into why ethical decision-making is limited if only professional codes are used. The limitations include concerns that many ethical dilemmas are not covered by professional codes, the client's view is not considered, and conflicts exist among different professional codes (Hadjistavropoulos, Malloy, Sharpe, Green, & Fuchs-Lacelle, 2002; Neukrug and Lovell, 1996).

PROFESSIONAL KNOWLEDGE

Another variable to consider on the ethical decision-making horizon is the professional knowledge of the counselor (see Figure 16.1). A counselor's professional knowledge base requires commitment, understanding, and competent practice. A counselor must acquire a professional identity that encompasses all aspects of counselor roles and functions, including knowing standards for ethical practice and advocating for equity and social justice. Counselors must understand the cultural contexts of relationships, issues, and trends in a multicultural and diverse society. They must consider factors such as culture, ethnicity, nationality, age, gender, sexual orientation, mental and physical characteristics, education, family values, religious and spiritual values, and socioeconomic status, as well as the unique characteristics of individuals, couples, families, ethnic groups, and communities. They must be aware of the nature and needs of individuals at all developmental levels and be knowledgeable about career development and other work-related life factors. Counselors must be competent in counseling, consultation, and helping processes, as well as in the theory and process of group work. They must understand basic measurement concepts, norm- and criterion-referenced testing, and individual and group assessment skills. Counselors must also acquire research skills to evaluate the effectiveness of counseling (Council for Accreditation of Counseling and Related Educational Programs [CACREP], 2001).

Continuing professional development to update skills and keep abreast of new developments in the field is also required. One area of increasing importance is the area of psychopharmacology. In the past, mental and emotional disorders were conceptualized as psychogenic, with treatment consisting of counseling and psychotherapy. Today, however, the biological bases of behavior are emphasized, with treatment involving psychotropic medications. Ingersoll (2000) recommended at least introductory psychopharmacological education for all counselors. Counselors need to know how medications may affect a client's progress in counseling. Ingersoll also considers the legal and ethical questions as to whether counselors with psychopharmacology training should discuss or advocate the use of psychotropic medications with their clients. The legal concern is the issue of practicing medicine without a license. The ethical concern is the issue of practicing within the bounds of competence. But counselors are also ethically bound to advocate for the best interests of the client, which might mean informing clients of all treatment possibilities. Clear guidelines for ethical behavior have not been developed for counselors to follow when working with clients taking psychotropic medications.

GEOGRAPHIC REGION AND CULTURE

Geographic region and culture are other important variables on the horizon of ethical decision-making for counselors (Sue et al., 1992; Welfel, 2002). Geographic region issues generally involve discussion of rural versus urban counseling practice (Campbell & Fox, 2003; Schank & Skovholt, 1997). Those practicing in rural settings are faced with issues of dual relationships and have more frequent contact outside of counseling. A counselor in a small rural setting (generally defined as an area with less than 50,000 residents) may be asked to see the client of a friend or relative because of the limited number of counselors available. Problems with such dual relationships have been identified and may include issues of trust, e.g., can the client know for sure that the counselor will not share information with people in the community with whom the client has personal relationships (Campbell & Fox)? Another problem cited by Campbell and Fox concerns impairment in the counselor's objectivity by the close associations with those in the community.

Additionally, geographic region can include the location where counseling takes place, and recently there have been major changes in the location where counseling occurs (Ganote, 1990; Kuntze, Stoermer, Mueller-Spahn, & Bullinger, 2002; Lawrence & Robinson Kurpius, 2000). For example, there has been a significant increase in online or virtual counseling (Kuntze et al., 2002). Kuntze et al. cited potential ethical concerns arising out of online counseling, which is a different medium than the traditional office setting and in a sense goes beyond geographical regions. It includes issues of competence and confidentiality. In regard to competence, who or what entity monitors the qualifications of those providing online counseling? It is quite different than geographic regions where the state licenses qualified professionals. The possibility that someone can hack into electronic files and access client information with online counseling creates new issues of confidentiality.

Other nontraditional counseling settings that have become more frequently used and create potential ethical concerns include long-term care facilities

(Ganote, 1990), correctional settings, and client homes (home-based counseling; Evans et al., 2003; Harris & Mertlich, 2003). Each of these settings provides additional challenges for the counselor; for example, home-based counseling may create issues around dual relationships because seeing someone in his or her home may suggest a more friendly nonprofessional relationship. Also, there may be problems with privacy in all of these settings.

Culture is another issue that fits under this part of the horizon of ethical decision-making. Pedersen (1995) stated, "Counselors have a responsibility to interact meaningfully with cultures of clients so that the methods used reflect ethical standards both explicitly and implicitly" (p. 47). To find and to choose a dependable standard of ethical judgment requires grappling with several questions (Ruggiero, 2004): (1) Are moral judgments appropriate outside of one's own culture? (2) How does one interpret differences between moral standards of one culture and another? (3) What values, morals, and ethics do different cultures have in common? The answers to these questions are affected by the current social movement of *multiculturalism* and the attention given to the effects of globalization (Ruggiero). In response to both multicultural and global awareness, Pedersen suggests a more culture-centered ethical guideline for the future and challenges counselors to become responsible for interpreting and applying ethical standards with their clients in a way that encourages equity among all participants in the counseling enterprise. The professional codes of ethics followed by counselors in the United States are intended to provide a guide to professionals in the right and proper conduct for their work. These codes are based upon ideals to be considered when arriving at ethical decisions, and reflect the prevailing social values and normative rules of the culture in the United States (Meara, Schmidt, & Day, 1996). As clinicians, our experiences with diverse clients often reveal to us our own confusion and tension when we are confronted with norms and values for living that may be contradictory to those principles and values from our prevailing society and from professional codes of ethics. This tension highlights the choices, and the dilemmas, we have in coming to a fair and equitable ethical decision.

The first question, "Are moral judgments appropriate outside of one's own culture?" requires awareness and knowledge of *cultural relativity,* a principle that anthropologists have acknowledged is complex and controversial. From their observations of cultures, they have come to important realizations (Kluckhohn, 1949; Kluckhohn & Leighton, 1974; Ruggiero, 2004). A culture's values reflect its geography, history, and socioeconomic circumstances, and, therefore, hasty comparisons of other cultures with our own often produce erroneous conclusions (Ruggiero). *Cultural relativity* is a theory of philosophical ethics and is concerned with what ought to be. This is in contrast to *sociological relativism,* which is descriptive and aims to describe the moral beliefs of a given society (Boss, 2004). The argument of cultural relativity, according to Kluckhohn, is not that behavior acceptable in one culture is allowed in any culture:

> Cultural relativity means, on the contrary, that the appropriateness of any positive or negative custom must be evaluated with regard to how this habit fits with other group habits. . . . Whatever a group decides is moral will be moral as long as it is consistent with other behaviors of the group. (p. 41)

However, when this position is applied to professional counseling, clinical experience provides evidence that "ethical principles generated in one cultural context cannot be applied to other substantially different cultural contexts without modification" (Pedersen, 1995, p. 34). The task of promoting social and moral responsibility cannot be compromised and diluted by maintaining a relativistic position, where accountability for fairness and justice for clients is determined by common practices of a community and society (Kierstead & Wagner, 1993; Pedersen). To ensure that ethical judgments are fair and reasonable, Ruggiero (2004) recommended caution in resolving three important dilemmas:

> (1) Understanding is no substitute for moral judgment. Because speaking from ignorance is irresponsible, we should refrain from judging any act until we understand the context in which it occurred. However, we should also avoid the mistake of ending our inquiry when we reach that understanding. (2) The essential moral quality of an action does not change from time to time or place to place. On one hand, we can't classify the acts in the distant past as ethical or morally neutral, even though people thought them so. On the other hand, it does not seem reasonable to say the acts were unethical, because the people who performed them had no way of knowing the harm that would result. (3) Culpability for immoral acts may vary widely. We can separate the act, for example cannibalism, from the person who performs it by acknowledging that those who performed the act lacked moral insight, or we can evaluate the outcome of the act itself. (pp. 58–60)

The second question, "How does one interpret differences between moral standards of one culture and another?" requires knowledge about a culture's expectations for ethical conduct. Shweder (1991), a cultural anthropologist, identified three distinct cultural orientations for determining acceptable behavior: individual rights, communal duty, and social justice. *Individual rights* refers to the protection and value of individual thought and choice. This focus is found in professional ethical codes used by Western-trained counselors (see Section I). Historically, this orientation has been articulated primarily by four influential Western moral theories: egoism, natural law, utilitarianism, and respect for persons (Harris, 2002). The ethics of egoism, represented by such philosophers as Aristotle and Thomas Hobbes, maintains that individuals should pursue their own interests, welfare, well-being, or good. From an Aristotelian perspective, promoting one's own self-interest is to seek self-actualization as a means to develop character traits, such as rationality, self-discipline, and industry. Such actions enable individuals to pursue their well-being more effectively. Natural law, most clearly defined by Saint Thomas Aquinas, proposes that individuals should promote and protect those values fundamental to human dispositions. These values include the biological significance of life and procreation and the human importance of knowledge and sociability. Utilitarianism, brought to prominence by John Stuart Mill, considers equally the welfare (utility) of each individual. Moral actions and rules that lead to the greatest overall human welfare are the right actions, which ultimately protect the value of individual human thoughts and action. In the ethics of respect for persons, highly influenced by Kant's moral philosophy, an action is right if the equal dignity of each individual is respected.

Communal duty insists on the conformity of individual action to a code of proper conduct, which benefits a collective of individuals and is the foundation for many Asian cultures (see Section II). The Asian philosophies of Confucianism, Taoism, and Buddhism are comprehensive ethical systems encompassing all aspects of life, including interpersonal relationships, religion, and education (Smith, 1991). Their overall influences are embedded in the worldviews of many Asian cultures (Hong, 1993; Hong & Friedman, 1998). Common themes among these three philosophies have left their imprint on many core Asian cultural values, such as interpersonal harmony, moderation, compromise, mutual respect, modesty, nonassertiveness, and accepting of one's fate (Hong & Ham, 2001). Individuals are seen as the product of all the generations of their families. Because of this generational continuum, personal actions reflect not only on the individuals who perform them but also on their extended families and ancestors (Shon & Ja, 1982). These cultural values guide the ethical behavior of individuals, who, as individuals, are expected to function in clearly defined roles and positions in the family hierarchy, based on age, gender, and social class, in order to reinforce societal expectations (Lee, 1997).

Cultural orientation and *social justice* encompass the commitment to general human welfare and human rights. Shorris (1992) described countries with social histories that are "a painful mix of race, culture, and conquest with centuries of turmoil over the issue of social justice . . . for every human being wishes to be at

Chapter 16 ◆ *Ethical Decision-Making* 121

least equal in his (her) own mind" (p. 15). These countries have social justice as part of social ethics. One example is seen in the patterns of revolution in many Latin American countries, which reflect the people's struggle to attain economic equity and social justice (Shorris). Part of that struggle is seen in liberation theology, the power movement in the Catholic church, which contributed to the elevation of social justice as an ethical stance (Gutierrez, 1973).

The third question, "What values, morals, and ethics do different cultures have in common?" may be an acknowledgment that the values of humanity are universal. Kitchener (1984) suggested a deeper, more universal set of moral principles of professional ethics in her model, using five general principles: autonomy, beneficence, nonmaleficence, justice, and fidelity (Beauchamp & Childress, 1979). Even though the values of Western culture are apparent in these principles, we are also aware that some values may be subordinate to others, whereas other values may be given greater weight. For example, in a collectivist society, autonomy may be given almost no value, while beneficence may be dominant. In some cultures, a particular value may be considered inapplicable to the situation at hand (Ruggiero, 2004).

LOCAL, STATE, AND FEDERAL LAWS

The Committee on Professional Practice and Standards (2003) of the APA indicated that "law is defined as the body of rules governing the affairs of persons within a community, state or country." State, local, and federal laws are important issues in counselor ethical decision-making and are another issue on the ethical horizon as depicted in Figure 16.1. (See Appendix B for links to state laws and counseling.) Counselors must be aware of legislation that governs their practice. For example, as mandated by all 50 states, counselors must report incidents of abuse of children (Jankowski & Martin, 2003). Also, many states have mandated reporting abuse of the elderly or those with disabilities. However, reporting abuse of children, the elderly, or a disabled person may violate a professional code of maintaining confidentiality.

Confidentiality is a critical issue in all counseling professions and is the basis of trust in a counseling relationship. Counselors attempt to maintain confidential information to protect the rights of clients. The Health Insurance Portability and Accountability Act (HIPAA) created the first national standards to protect individuals' medical records and other personal health information. HIPAA affords therapy notes more protection—most notably from third-party payers—than they had been given in the past. Under HIPAA, disclosure of therapy notes requires more than just generalized consent; it requires a patient's specific permission to release this sensitive information. And, whereas in the past insurance companies have requested entire patient records—including psychotherapy notes—in making coverage decisions, now health plans cannot refuse to provide reimbursement if a patient does not agree to release information covered under the psychotherapy notes provision. However, HIPAA's definition of therapy notes explicitly states that these notes are kept separate from the rest of an individual's record. Therefore, if this type of information is in a patient's general chart, or if it is not distinguishable as separate from the rest of the record, access to the information does not require specific patient authorization (see www.apa.org).

There are exceptions to maintaining confidentiality (Kermani & Drob, 1987). For example, the Tarasoff decision (1976) set the precedent for requiring counselors to warn intended targets of potentially homicidal clients. Some states allow minors to seek abortions without parental consent (Lawrence & Robinson Kurpius, 2000). In such cases, the legal right of the minor client to an abortion may conflict with the personal values of the counselor who may want to breach confidentiality and inform the parents.

Another issue confronting a counselor is a decision to abide by the law versus following professional codes, personal values, or agency rules. For example, the court may subpoena the records of a counselor, but the counselor may decide that maintaining the confidentiality of the client is more important based on professional codes or personal values.

ETHICAL THEORIES

We live in a multicultural and diverse society. The U.S. Census Bureau (2002) reports increased diversity over the past thirty years. For example, the minority population in the United States now makes up thirty-one percent of the population versus only seventeen percent just over thirty years ago. We are suggesting that increasingly diverse ethical theories of this population are another part of the horizon for ethical decision-making. Cottone and Claus (2000) referred to the lack of inclusion of major philosophical and ethical theories in ethical decision-making models, stating that "it was surprising to find the number of practice-based models developed apparently without attention to underlying philosophical or theoretical tenets" (p. 384). Others also have recommended inclusion of major philosophical theories in developing ethical decision-making models (Hare, 1991; Rest, 1984). Many of the professional codes are founded on Western ethics and particularly virtue ethics and principle ethics (Freeman, 2000). This provides a limited view of ethical decision-making.

Shanahan and Wang (2003) discussed moral relativism, the attempt to find commonality among morals and ethical decision-making practices. They concluded that "if you look around the world, what you see is not moral unity but rather moral diversity. Each culture has its own peculiar (and sometimes very peculiar) moral perspective on the world, and these different moral perspectives frequently clash" (p. 12). Despite the acknowledgment of diversity of morals and ethics across the world, there has been criticism of moral relativism (Harris, 2002; Shanahan & Wang). With no universal ethical codes, how does one make an ethical decision? Shanahan and Wang clarified this dilemma somewhat and stated, "The ethical diversity among cultures may be at a fairly high level and may be grounded on more basic moral principles that cultures have in common" (p. 13).

Kinnier, Kernes, and Dautheribes (2000) suggested a core list of values and ethics that they believe transcend cultures. They used an ethnographic content analysis in reviewing both religious texts and nonreligious writings that address ethics, and attempted to identify a list of core ethics across cultures. The approaches they considered included those of Christianity, Islam, Judaism, Hinduism, Taoism, Confucianism, Hinduism, and the United Nations, among others. They came up with the following examples of universal values: to seek truth, to seek justice, and respect and caring for others. The authors concluded that a balance between moral relativism and objective moral values and ethics is warranted; a few common values may be found across ethical theories, but there remain cultural values that are unique to such theories.

The hermeneutic model is based in part on the fusion of horizons and includes consideration of such things as the cultural and ethical philosophies of the counselor, the supervisor, and the client and the geographic region and community. Consequently, an understanding and consideration of a wide range of ethical philosophies and theories is necessary for counselors, particularly in our diverse and multicultural society. In fact, multicultural competence is an important part of counselor competence (Bryan & Lyons, 2003; Constantine, 2002).

A hermeneutic model is not based upon moral relativity because the intent is to find the most accurate interpretation of the ethical dilemma and the best interpretation of an ethical decision. So a hermeneutic model incorporates a multiculturally sensitive interpretation, but still strives for an ethical decision that is an accurate interpretation based upon the fusion of horizons and the relevant variables in the ethical dilemma and ethical decision. Consequently, a counselor considering the fusion of horizons may consider one or several ethical theories as part of the decision-making process. For example, a counselor may decide to use a theory that is consistent with his or her own views *and* a theory that is consistent with the client's views and values. Additionally, the counselor may choose to use more than two theories, and to include the view of the supervisor or community.

SUMMARY

We are proposing a model of ethical decision-making based upon a hermeneutic approach. Hermeneutics is the accurate interpretation of a situation. Key in the interpretation is an understanding of the horizon and the elements to consider when making an interpretation of a problem and an ethical decision. We are suggesting that the whole horizon of ethical decision-making includes the following parts:

- an ethical dilemma;
- the counselor and his or her values, race, gender, personal history, etc.;
- the client and his or her values, race, gender, personal history, etc.;
- the supervisor's values, race, gender, personal history, etc.;
- agency policies;
- the geographic region and culture;
- local, state, and federal laws;
- professional codes of ethics;
- professional knowledge; and
- ethical theories.

Finally we are suggesting that an accurate interpretation of an ethical decision should be based on use of appropriate ethical theories that are consistent with the fusion of horizons, such as those of the counselor, the client, and the supervisor, etc. In the next chapter, Chapter 17, we demonstrate the use of hermeneutic ethical decision-making with a case example. The remaining chapters contain cases that can be used to develop a deeper understanding of the hermeneutic model of ethical decision-making and as an opportunity to practice applying the model.

Chapter 17

Application of the Hermeneutic Model

A key consideration in applying the hermeneutic ethical decision-making model is an identification and selection of relevant elements of the horizon, including use of various ethical theories. The practical application of a hermeneutic ethical decision-making model potentially involves the use of several ethical theories relevant to the situation along with other components of the horizon. We will use a case to illustrate the application of a hermeneutic model.

CASE OF HARRIET: ONLINE THERAPY

Harriet is a counselor who lives in a rural community, and she has been working in a community agency for five years. The agency is over forty-five minutes from her home, and she has decided it is time to start her private practice. She has had a goal of having a private practice since she entered her master's program over eight years ago. She feels she is knowledgeable, and she received her state license over two years ago. The community in which she lives has only about 2,000 residents within a thirty-mile range, and the pool of possible clients is limited, so she has decided to offer Web-based counseling in addition to her office counseling services. Harriet discussed setting up her online therapy with a colleague, Sarah, whom she met during her master's program in counseling. They had kept in contact over the years and her colleague had developed her own online therapy service.

Harriet decided to advertise online to recruit clients and was contacted by Kyon, a woman of Korean descent in her mid-fifties. Kyon expressed an interest in online therapy. Kyon also lived in a rural community in another state over two hours away, so office visits were not acceptable to her. Kyon stated she had lost her husband through death approximately three months earlier. She reported feeling anxious and sad and that she cried frequently.

Harriet and Kyon initially spoke by phone and agreed to online therapy with a primary approach of using asynchronous emails. They began online therapy and were in regular contact. Initially Kyon reported benefiting from the therapy. She felt Harriet understood her, she felt safe disclosing online, and she was able to be honest with her feelings. The therapy went on for three months. Then abruptly Kyon stopped her emails and Harriet did not hear from Kyon for a week. She attempted to contact Kyon by phone but she was unsuccessful. Finally Harriet reached Kyon's daughter, who was visiting her home. The daughter stated her mother had been hospitalized for a suicide attempt.

A month later, Harriet received a letter from the licensing board in the state where Kyon lived. The board requested that she attend an interview to discuss her online therapy with Kyon. They acknowledged that they had no jurisdiction over Harriet and her license but they wanted to discuss a complaint made by the daughter so they could understand online therapy and identify procedures to address it in the future. The complaint by the daughter was that Harriet provided online therapy and opened up strong emotions in her mother without any intervention or procedures to address associated crises. Kyon's daughter was alleging unprofessional conduct and violation of competence.

Harriet was upset by the charges and she wanted to attend an interview and explain her side. Consequently, Harriet agreed to a meeting time with licensure board members. Harriet had an initial meeting with the licensure board to discuss the review process. The licensure board and Harriet agreed to use a hermeneutic ethical decision-making model. They identified the elements of the horizon relevant to the case of Kyon. The elements of the horizon in this hermeneutic model include the ethical dilemma; the counselor's values, race, gender, personal history, etc; the client's values, race, gender, personal history, etc.; the supervisor's (in this case the consultant's; see below) values, race, gender, personal history, etc., and counseling agency policies; applicable local, state, and federal laws; professional knowledge; geographic region; professional codes of ethics; and ethical theories of Buddhism and virtue ethics (see Figure 17.1). They decided to use Buddhism because they were aware that Kyon was a practicing Buddhist. They also decided to use virtue ethics because many of the professional codes were based upon virtue ethics.

THE ETHICAL DILEMMA

Harriet decided to open a practice after five years of working in a counseling agency. She is licensed in her state and has received the appropriate supervision

Figure 17.1   Hermeneutic Model of Integrating Theories in Ethical Decision-Making

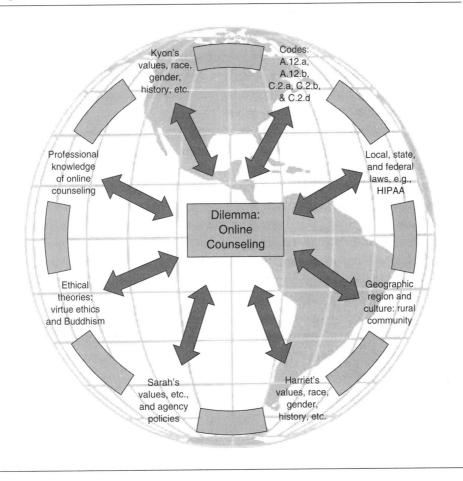

during her agency work. She has consulted with a former colleague, Sarah, who has a successful online therapy practice. Harriet met with Sarah for a couple of hours and discussed how she could set up her online practice. Sarah shared her experiences. Harriet accepted Kyon as a client and both agreed upon using asynchronous communication through emails. She informed Kyon of HIPAA guidelines and Kyon acknowledged she understood them. Harriet acknowledged that she had not informed Kyon that she was her first online client.

The licensure board noted that Harriet failed to establish a method to assess the severity of her client's problems and she failed to have a procedure for monitoring her client's mental status. She also failed to provide a format for accessing crisis services for her client. The questions for the licensure board were whether ethical violations occurred, and, if they did, whether the board could establish further guidelines if necessary to protect mental health clients in its state.

HARRIET: THE COUNSELOR'S PERSONAL VALUES, RACE, GENDER, AND PERSONAL HISTORY

Harriet grew up in the rural community in which she currently resides. She attended college at a university over 60 miles away and she also completed her master's degree in counseling there. Her family members also were long-time residents of the area; both her mother and father grew up there and were teachers in the local school district. She has an older brother who did move away from the area and he lives in a large urban area, 45 minutes from her home. Harriet grew up with traditional rural values of hard work and a strong sense of community.

Harriet lives with her spouse whom she married after completing her undergraduate degree. They met in high school and both had attended the same college. He is an insurance salesperson in this small rural community; he has his own agency. They have two young children, both boys.

After graduating with her master's degree, Harriet took a job as a counselor in a counseling center in a medium-size town of 38,000. She did not enjoy the long-distance drive each day to work and back, but felt it necessary to reach her goal of opening a private practice close to home.

KYON: THE CLIENT'S PERSONAL VALUES, RACE, GENDER, AND PERSONAL HISTORY

Kyon is a fifty-year-old female who was born in South Korea. She immigrated to the United States when she was in her early twenties. She was educated as a nurse and entered the United States with the intention of working as a nurse. She worked over twenty years as a nurse, always in a community hospital. She met and married a Korean male who was an x-ray technician. Kyon eventually found employment in a small community hospital in a relatively rural area, as did her spouse.

They had two children, a boy and a girl. The boy after age 18 moved away from the community, whereas the daughter remained in close proximity to her parents. Kyon was raised as Buddhist and she is an active practitioner of this religion. Her spouse was and her children also are practicing Buddhists.

Kyon's spouse died suddenly three months prior to her seeking counseling online. She continued working for a short time after her husband's death but decided to quit her job because she felt she was not performing well. She remained primarily at home, venturing out only for groceries and other necessities of living. She contacted Harriet after her daughter encouraged her to seek counseling. Kyon was embarrassed to seek counseling in her community and felt online counseling would allow her to maintain her privacy.

SARAH: THE SUPERVISOR'S PERSONAL VALUES, RACE, GENDER, AND PERSONAL HISTORY

Sarah is more of a consultant than supervisor in this case. She is a thirty-six-year-old white female. Sarah lives in a small town in the same state as Harriet, except she lives on the other side of the state over 100 miles away. Sarah, similar to Harriet, has worked in a community counseling center to gain the appropriate experience and supervision to achieve licensure. She has been licensed for a few years and has established a private practice including an online practice. Sarah has attended a few workshops at professional conferences addressing online therapy. However, when she established her practice online she did not seek out supervision. Sarah has had positive experiences with online therapy and generally has ten to fifteen clients online at any one time as part of her practice. Sarah met with Harriet for a few hours before Harriet started her online practice. They discussed how to set up an online practice and some clinical issues. Sarah volunteered to be available to answer questions as they arose. Harriet did contact Sarah to update her about her success and stated things were going well. Sarah provided no further consultation.

PROFESSIONAL CODES OF ETHICS

The following ACA (2005) professional codes appeared to be relevant:*

A.12. Technology Applications
A.12.a. Benefits and Limitations
Counselors inform clients of the benefits and limitations of using information technology applications in the counseling process and in business/billing procedures. Such technologies include but are not limited to computer hardware and software, telephones, the World Wide Web, the Internet, online assessment instruments and other communication devices.

Source: Reprinted with permission from the American Counseling Association, 2005, *ACA Code of Ethics,* Alexandria, VA.

A.12.b. Technology-Assisted Services

When providing technology-assisted distance counseling services, counselors determine that clients are intellectually, emotionally, and physically capable of using the application and that the application is appropriate for the needs of clients.

A.12.c Inappropriate Services

When technology-assisted distance counseling services are deemed inappropriate by the counselor or client, counselors consider delivering services face to face.

C.2. Professional Competence

C.2.a. Boundaries of Competence

Counselors practice only within the boundaries of their competence, based on their education, training, supervised experience, state and national professional credentials, and appropriate professional experience. Counselors gain knowledge, personal awareness, sensitivity, and skills pertinent to working with a diverse client population.

C.2.b. New Specialty Areas of Practice

Counselors practice in specialty areas new to them only after appropriate education, training, and supervised experience. While developing skills in new specialty areas, counselors take steps to ensure the competence of their work and to protect others from possible harm.

C.2.d. Monitor Effectiveness

Counselors continually monitor their effectiveness as professionals and take steps to improve when necessary. Counselors in private practice take reasonable steps to seek peer supervision as needed to evaluate their efficacy as counselors.

An important question for Harriet and the licensure board is whether Kyon was an appropriate client for online therapy. What effort did Harriet take to assess whether Kyon was appropriate for this medium of therapy (A.12.a)? The second question concerns whether Harriet clearly and adequately explained the strengths and limitations of online therapy (A.12.b). A third issue is whether Harriet is competent in providing therapy via an online format (C.2.a). Harriet was trained in traditional person-to-person counseling. She had consulted with a colleague who was practicing online therapy, but does this constitute adequate training and competence for conducting online therapy? A related code addresses the counselor's responsibility to develop procedures to ensure adequate care for the client and protection for the client while the counselor is developing expertise in a new specialty area (C.2.b). Harriet is developing skills in a new area, but she appears not to have developed procedures to ensure protection of her client, particularly in regard to any crisis and emergency needs. The last issue, and the professional code that may apply, is the importance of appropriate supervision (C.2.d). Harriet has not sought out supervision necessary to monitor her effectiveness in this new format.

PROFESSIONAL KNOWLEDGE

Harriet and the licensure board members reviewed the professional literature addressing online therapy. They discovered that online clinical therapy is growing (Elleven & Allen, 2004; Rassau & Arco, 2003; Rochlen, Zack, & Speyer, 2004) and potentially includes telepsychology and online therapy. Maheu (2003) defined online clinical practice as "the use of any technology to deliver therapeutic dialogue at a distance, whether conducted over a direct video link (e.g. telepsychology or telepsychiatry) or over a network such as the Internet (e.g. therapy online)" (p. 20). Rochlen et al. provided a definition of online therapy and they defined Internet therapy "as any type of professional interaction that makes use of the Internet to connect qualified mental health professionals and their clients" (p. 270). Online therapy can be asynchronous or synchronous. Asynchronous online therapy is generally conducted via email. Synchronous online therapy employs chat-based formats conducted in real time (Rochlen et al.). The vast majority of online therapy is conducted asynchronously through emails (Elleven & Allen).

Harriet and the licensure board discovered the benefits of online therapy cited in the professional literature (Castelnuovo, Gaggioli, Mantovani, & Riva, 2003; Rochlen, Zack, & Speyer, 2004). Benefits of online therapy include convenience and increased access to counseling services, disinhibition in expressing emotions, and the positive effects of writing as a therapeutic intervention (emails). Limitations of online therapy include the absence of nonverbal cues, which have been a foundation of counseling theory and intervention (Rochlen et al.). Another limitation is in the ability to identify and address crises, since the majority of online therapy takes place through emails, through which depression and suicidal behaviors may be less visible than in face-to-face counseling (Maheu, 2003; Rochlen et al.).

There has been a dearth of research addressing online therapy, primarily because it is a new intervention (Chang & Yeh, 2003; Lange & Rietdijk, 2003; Rochlen, Land, & Wong, 2004). The research to date supports the effectiveness of online therapy. For example, Rochlen et al. studied counseling with males both online and in person, and there were essentially no differences in preferences for both modalities. Lange and Rietdijk studied online therapy in the treatment of posttraumatic stress. Positive outcomes were noted. However, because of the limited amount of research conducted to date, researchers note the preliminary nature of the results (Rochlen et al.).

Harriet and the licensure board also discovered ethical concerns expressed about online therapy (Fisher & Fried, 2003; Maheu, 2003; Ragusea & VandeCreek, 2003; Skarderud, 2003). Fisher and Fried stated, "Questions about validity, efficacy, and safety of different Internet-mediated techniques for psychological assessment and therapy remain largely unanswered as the field rapidly evolves. Constant innovation in telehealth continues to outpace the development of specific guidelines for the delivery of services" (p. 103). Specific ethical concerns center around counselor competence in using online therapy and around protection of confidentiality (Barnett & Scheetz, 2003; Fisher & Fried). For example, Fisher and Fried cited the importance of having appropriate training and supervision in providing online therapy. The question for Harriet and the licensure board is whether she had received enough training and supervision in providing online therapy. Fisher and Fried also stated, "Harm to Internet clients/patients may be incurred when psychologists fail to appropriately diagnose a disorder, fail to identify suicidal or homicidal ideation, or reinforce maladaptive behavior" (p. 104). Another question is whether Harriet caused harm to her client by not detecting suicidal ideation. Maheu proposed that counselors need to establish adequate crisis procedures prior to beginning online therapy.

GEOGRAPHIC REGION AND CULTURE

Harriet and Kyon live in rural communities. They have limited ability to contact each other face-to-face; they live over two hours away from each other. Consequently they agree on counseling via the Internet. Both have access to email and know how to use it. Email has been found to be the primary format used in online therapy, which is an asynchronous interaction (Elleven & Allen, 2004).

Harriet and the licensure board also discovered that Asian Americans typically underutilize counseling services (Atkinson & Lowe, 1995; Chang & Yeh, 2003). Some researchers (Good, Dell, & Mintz, 1989) have suggested that women in general are more likely to seek out counseling services than men. However, Atkinson and Lowe found no difference between male and female Asian Americans seeking counseling services. Kyon's seeking counseling took a major effort on her part. Some have proposed that online therapy provides move confidentiality than face-to-face counseling and results in less of the stigma associated with mental illness (Ragusea & VandeCreek, 2003).

LOCAL, STATE, AND FEDERAL LAWS

There are no current local, state, or federal laws governing online therapy. A federal law that addresses the distribution of health information electronically may apply in this case, the Health Insurance Portability and Accountability Act (HIPAA). The intent of this legislation, as described in the previous chapter, is to protect and limit the disclosure of an individual's health care information, particularly disclosure electronically (Office for Civil Rights, 2003). Disclosure is permitted only with the fully informed consent of a client or patient. The question here is whether Harriet sought informed consent from Kyon and explained the limitations of protecting privacy on the Internet (Fisher & Fried, 2003; Ragusea & VandeCreek, 2003). Ragusea and VandeCreek discuss methods for protecting confidentiality when using the Internet such as employing firewalls.

ETHICAL THEORIES: VIRTUE ETHICS AND BUDDHIST ETHICS

Harriet and the licensure board agreed to use both virtue ethics and Buddhism in attempting to make an ethical decision based upon this case. They determined that four primary ethical principles of virtue ethics may apply to this case: nonmaleficence (the duty to do no harm), beneficence (the duty to do good or help), fidelity (the duty to be truthful, and to honor others, their rights, and their responsibilities), and autonomy (the duty to maximize the individual's right to make decisions).

Nonmaleficence may apply because the licensure board questioned whether Harriet should have known to have established a crisis procedure. That fact that she established her online therapy service without a clear, well-thought-out procedure for dealing with crises may be the result either of a lack of knowledge or of not caring about the possible crises of clients. Beneficence potentially applies as in most counseling relationships. The question becomes: What does the counselor do to promote the welfare of the client? Did Harriet act with beneficence in providing online therapy to Kyon, or was her interest in establishing her business? Another possible virtue ethic that may apply is fidelity, and the issue is whether Harriet clearly informed Kyon of the dangers and limitations of online therapy. Was she truthful in informing Kyon of such risks? The last principle that may apply in this case is autonomy. Kyon is an adult and should have the right to make autonomous decisions about her psychological care. If this is true, then Kyon was free to choose to pursue online counseling, but the associated risks must have been shared with her by Harriet.

Harriet and the licensure board also reviewed the concepts of Buddhism in an effort to understand the ethical issues in this case. They noted that the concepts of the Noble Eightfold Path potentially applied here (see Chapter 11). The specific concepts that possibly applied included right understanding, right thought, right livelihood, and right effort. Recall that right understanding refers to an accurate perception of the world and an understanding of suffering. Did Harriet have right understanding of Kyon's suffering? Could she have done anything to improve right understanding? Right thought concerns thoughts of compassion and unselfishness. Did Harriet have such thoughts? Or did she pursue online therapy without being fully prepared with the intent of promoting her private practice? Another Buddhist concept that may apply is right livelihood, which concerns pursuing a job that does not harm others. The question here is whether Harriet pursued a job and an activity that caused harm to others. The final concept that possibly applies is right effort, which concerns the use of mental discipline to promote good (potentially similar to beneficence). The issue for Harriet and the licensure board to consider is: What effort did Harriet take to promote the welfare and good of Kyon? Was the online counseling adequate and helpful to Kyon?

HERMENEUTIC ETHICAL DECISION-MAKING

The licensure board and Harriet met and reviewed the elements of the horizon in this ethical dilemma. The board noted that Harriet was highly motivated to pursue the use of online therapy to maintain her rural lifestyle. They also noted that Kyon, her client, was accustomed to maintaining a rural lifestyle based upon her personal history and values. Also, Kyon came from a culture that typically underutilizes counseling services and may prefer the more confidential and anonymous counseling format that online therapy provides. Finally, the board noted that Harriet had consulted with Sarah, who also values living in a rural community. They shared this value and shared a goal of establishing online therapy services.

Harriet did not meet with Kyon and assess her ability to use computer technology and her skills for online therapy. Consequently, Harriet violated the ACA's (2005) professional code addressing whether a client is appropriate for online therapy (A.12.a). A related code concerns informing clients of the limitations of computer technology (A.12.b). Harriet acknowledged to the licensure board that she did not provide information to Kyon about any limitations of computer technology, e.g., the extra efforts needed to monitor nonverbal cues that might reveal issues not revealed in online therapy, such as depression.

Another professional code (ACA, 2005) addresses the issue of counselors practicing outside the boundaries of their competence. Harriet did meet with Sarah, who had started her own online therapy business. However, Harriet did not establish a continuous long-term supervisory relationship to gain feedback and improve her skills. The licensure board concluded that Harriet violated this particular professional code (C.2.a). Another related code concerns counselors practicing in new areas after receiving appropriate training and supervision (C.2.b). Again, Harriet made minimal effort to gain additional skills in online therapy through further training or ongoing supervision. Last, Harriet did not seek appropriate supervision (C.2.d). Subsequently, Kyon was hospitalized for a suicide attempt. This may have been avoided if Harriet had been receiving supervision and received feedback and monitoring of Kyon's progress.

Researchers have noted the importance of having well-defined crisis intervention procedures in place prior to beginning online therapy (Fisher & Fried, 2003; Maheu, 2003). Harriet and the licensure board agreed that she should have established crisis intervention procedures and informed Kyon of what they were and how to use them. The professional literature also notes the importance of appropriate supervision, particularly with such a new form of therapy. As has been cited in our discussion of professional codes, Harriet omitted seeking ongoing supervision.

Harriet did provide Kyon with a written statement describing HIPAA guidelines and she was aware of the necessity of gaining consent before Harriet released any information, particularly any electronic release of information.

The licensure board and Harriet discussed the application of both virtue ethics and Buddhism to this case. The first concept that possibly applied from virtue ethics is nonmaleficence; Harriet explained to the licensure board that she intended to help Kyon. She acknowledged she was naive about the complexity of providing online counseling and neglected to set up crisis procedures. The board concluded that Harriet did not violate the ethic of nonmaleficence.

Another concept from virtue ethics that potentially applies is beneficence. Kyon reported early in their treatment that she was benefiting from the online counseling. However, beneficence requires an analysis of benefit versus risk or harm. The counseling provided by Harriet helped initially but not later in treatment. Another component of beneficence is the ability and knowledge to provide the help. Harriet did not have the skills she needed, nor did she seek supervision to ensure effective online counseling. The board determined that Harriet violated the concept or principle of beneficence.

A third principle that potentially applied in this case was fidelity. Harriet did not inform Kyon that this was her first online client. Harriet acknowledged she did not want Kyon to know she was just beginning her practice in online counseling.

The last principle that possibly applies is autonomy. Harriet provided Kyon with information about online counseling and encouraged her to make a free choice in seeking counseling.

Next Harriet and the licensure board discussed Buddhist concepts that potentially could be applied to this case. Harriet did not demonstrate right understanding of her client's suffering; this became evident when Kyon attempted to commit suicide. Harriet acknowledged she did not meet with Kyon in person to initially assess her symptoms before starting the online therapy. Harriet did demonstrate right thought with her compassion early in treatment, and Kyon believed she was understood. The question is whether Harriet entered into online counseling before she was fully prepared, which may be interpreted as selfish and not focused on the needs of Kyon, and which therefore violates the concept of right thought. Right livelihood is the last Buddhist concept that possibly applies. Preliminary research suggests that online counseling is effective. So Harriet is not engaging in a violation of right livelihood. If the research demonstrated that harm results from online counseling, then she may be considered to be in violation of this concept.

SUMMARY

The licensure board reiterated to Harriet that they had no jurisdiction over her, since her license was from another state. They also noted that Harriet's own state licensure board may not have jurisdiction, since the client lives in another state. But the licensure board did determine that Harriet behaved unethically based upon the hermeneutic ethical decision-making model. First, she did not complete an accurate assessment and diagnosis of the severity of Kyon's symptoms. Second, she did not assess Kyon's capacity to use computer technology. Third, Harriet failed to provide crisis procedures in working via online counseling. The board noted also that the personal characteristics of the counselor, client, and consultant/ supervisor supported the use of online counseling in this circumstance. The professional literature also supports choosing such an approach.

The licensure board made the following recommendations to Harriet based upon the review: (a) Harriet should meet with each client in person at the beginning of any online course of therapy to conduct an in-depth assessment and diagnosis, and to explain the limitations of online counseling; (b) during the initial interview and in subsequent interactions, Harriet should assess the client's capacity and understanding in using computer technology; (c) Harriet should develop clear guidelines and procedures for crisis situations.

QUESTIONS FOR DISCUSSION

1. Do you agree with the board's recommendations or would you change some or add additional recommendations?

2. Can you identify additional elements of the horizon that were not discussed?

3. How would the board's conclusions be different if they had used only virtue ethics or only Buddhist ethics?

SECTION VI

Cases

The remaining chapters, 18 through 31, are cases that provide a wide range of issues and ethical dilemmas. They are provided to give the reader an opportunity to practice applying a hermeneutic ethical decision-making model. We encourage careful consideration of the elements that have been identified in this book and of the ethical decisions to be made using this model.

Chapter 18

Natalia

A Question of Rational Suicide

Natalia is a forty-year-old Hispanic woman, referred for counseling by her primary care physician for an evaluation of depression. Natalia was assigned to Marta for counseling. When Natalia appeared for the first session, she seemed to have a constricted affect, and in a matter-of-fact manner she reported taking three extra antidepressants the previous day in order to gain the courage to kill herself. She also admitted attempting suicide by hanging but the scaffold she constructed gave way. Natalia explained how, three years ago, she was informed that she had multiple sclerosis (MS), a neurological disease that progresses slowly. Now Natalia is experiencing more severe symptoms and is wheelchair dependent. She fears that she will soon lose control over her body and emphatically states that she does not want to live under those conditions. In addition, Natalia is very upset that her medical condition is draining her family's emotional and financial resources. She feels that the MS is worsening rapidly and that she is becoming an increasing burden to her husband and two children. She emphasized that suicide is her right to ultimate control of her own destiny, framing her position as a "rational suicide." Natalia reads both popular and professional literature on the subject and follows organizations such as Compassion in Dying and the Hemlock Society. She is considering a move to Oregon where there is legislation permitting physician-assisted suicide (Oregon Death With Dignity Act, 1995). During the intake interview, Natalia explained that she wanted to see a counselor as soon as possible because she is sure that counseling to determine her competence will be required before a physician would agree to assist with her suicide. She expects that Marta will attest to her competence.

Relevant elements of the horizon based upon the case of Natalia include the ethical dilemma; the client's, counselor's, and supervisor's respective values, race, gender, and personal history; counseling agency policies; local, state, and federal laws that apply; professional knowledge; geographic region; professional ethical codes; and ethical theories.

THE ETHICAL DILEMMA

From a principle ethics perspective, the dilemma for the counselor is what to do in this situation. Should the counselor focus on treating the depression and preventing the suicide, or should the counselor allow the client to carry out the suicide without taking action? It is typical for counselors to make decisions about whether to hospitalize a suicidal client (with consultation and approval by a psychiatrist) or engage in other actions such as breaking confidentiality and informing family members of the client's intentions (Westefeld et al., 2000).

MARTA: THE COUNSELOR'S PERSONAL VALUES, RACE, GENDER, AND PERSONAL HISTORY

Marta came to New York City five years ago, shortly after finishing her counselor training at the University of Puerto Rico. She came to the United States because of business opportunities for her husband. Marta left Puerto Rico reluctantly and misses her large immediate family, consisting of her parents and five siblings, as well as many aunts, uncles, and cousins. Marta describes her family as very close and she frequently travels back to Puerto Rico for visits.

Marta tried to imagine how her own family would cope with a situation such as Natalia's. Marta's family is Catholic and would view suicide as sinful. Beyond that, she cannot imagine letting any family members end their lives to ease the burden of care. She feels all her family members would work together to take care of a terminally ill member and would be devastated by the idea of assisting in suicide.

Until now, Marta has not faced the issue of rational suicide in her counseling practice. Although Marta understands the concept of rational suicide to hasten death and relieve suffering, she is personally opposed to the idea on ethical and religious grounds. Marta is conflicted about how to address physician-assisted suicide in this case because of her own Catholic religious convictions, which she assumes Natalia shares.

Furthermore, Marta questions whether suicide can ever be considered rational, because it is always an emotional decision. She wonders to what extent Natalia's depression impairs her judgment. Marta wants to be an empathetic and compassionate counselor who cares for the welfare of her clients but also one who respects their autonomy. However, Marta also knows that in Hispanic/Latino culture, concern for family and community often outweigh individual rights. In this case, Marta is torn about what is *best* for her client, and because of the collateral effects of suicide, she is concerned about the impact of a suicide on Natalia's entire family. Marta decides to consult with her supervisor about this case.

NATALIA: THE CLIENT'S PERSONAL VALUES, RACE, GENDER, AND PERSONAL HISTORY

Natalia's parents moved from Puerto Rico to New York City when she was two years old. Her parents are now deceased and she has three older siblings who reside outside of New York state. Over the years, Natalia has occasionally traveled to visit her siblings and also to Puerto Rico to visit extended family.

Natalia is married with twin seventeen-year-old daughters. Her daughters are high-school seniors and now making plans to attend college. Since Natalia had to retire due to her illness, her husband is working two jobs to help support the family. A nurse's aide visits the home daily and her daughters also assist with Natalia's personal care. Natalia is concerned about the physical, emotional, and financial strain her MS has caused for her family, and does not want those issues to be impediments to her daughters' ability to attend college.

Natalia attended school and college in New York City, and until recently was employed as a nurse in a large metropolitan hospital. Given her nursing education and experience, Natalia is well aware of what to expect with regard to the course of her disease as well as the devastating impact it will have on her life. Since she was diagnosed with MS, Natalia has been depressed about her deteriorating condition and the burden of care she presents to her family. Natalia attends services at a Catholic church regularly and reports finding some comfort in her faith. Although Catholic religious beliefs do not view suicide as an option (see Chapter 3), Natalia rationalizes her decision because it was the answer she received through prayer as a way to care for her family's welfare and relieve their burden.

SUSAN: THE SUPERVISOR'S PERSONAL VALUES, RACE, GENDER, AND PERSONAL HISTORY

Marta's supervisor, Susan Jones, is a white American with twenty years of experience in grief counseling and end-of-life care issues. She is married with two children. Recently, her father passed away after a long battle with lung cancer. As she hears about Natalia's story from Marta, Susan recalls how her own father suffered and wanted to end his life for the same reasons of concern for the family. Since experiencing end-of-life decisions within her own family, Susan feels even greater empathy for clients suffering with terminal illnesses. Susan maintains that people have the right to choose "the least worst death" (Battin, 1994, p. 36), and she now supports efforts to legalize physician-assisted suicide.

PROFESSIONAL CODES OF ETHICS

Ethical guidelines of the American Counseling Association (2005) encourage counselor involvement in all instances in which suicide is a possible outcome. Werth (1999) also proposed ethical guidelines for mental-health professionals in such circumstances. A few potentially relevant ACA codes are*

A.1. Welfare of Those Served by Counselors

A.1.a. Primary Responsibility

The primary responsibility of counselors is to respect the dignity and to promote the welfare of clients.

A.4. Avoiding Harm and Imposing Values

A.4.b. Personal Values

Counselors are aware of their own values, attitudes, beliefs, and behaviors and avoid imposing values that are inconsistent with counseling goals. Counselors respect the diversity of clients, trainees, and research participants.

E.5. Diagnosis of Mental Disorders

E.5.a. Proper Diagnosis

Counselors take special care to provide proper diagnosis of mental disorders. Assessment techniques (including personal interview) used to determine client care (e.g. locus of treatment, or recommended follow-up) are carefully selected and appropriately used.

E.5.b. Cultural Sensitivity

Counselors recognize that culture affects the manner in which clients' problems are defined. Clients' socioeconomic and cultural experiences are considered when diagnosing mental disorders.

What are other codes that may apply?

_____

*Source: Reprinted with permission from the American Counseling Association, 2005, *ACA Code of Ethics,* Alexandria, VA.

PROFESSIONAL KNOWLEDGE

Marta's counselor training focused on preventing suicide. She knows depression is a treatable mental illness that is often overlooked in individuals with medical conditions. Marta began reviewing the professional literature that addressed suicide and rational suicide. She found that the National Center for Injury and Prevention Control had created the Center for the Study of Suicide Prevention in the 1960s, and since that time there has been considerable research on suicide. However, even with increased awareness and prevention efforts, the rate of suicide has remained constant at approximately twelve suicides for every 100,000 persons in the population (Centers for Disease Control, n.d.). Marta also learned that suicide is linked to depression (Evans & Farberow, 1988) and that researchers have found a correlation between suicide and physical illnesses; specifically, MS is associated with an increased risk of depression and suicide (Kleespies, Hughes, & Gallacher, 2000).

Marta is particularly concerned about the impact of suicide on Natalia's family and decides to review the professional literature addressing suicide and ethnicity. Portes and Rumbaut (1990) found that Hispanics have a lower rate of suicide compared to other ethnic groups and in general are not as accepting of the idea of physician-assisted suicide as are white Americans (Werth & Holdwick, 2000). Among the possible reasons that Hispanics have a lower rate of suicide are a significant dependence on family and friends, a strong belief in religion that prohibits suicide, and an acceptance of their plight in life (Westefeld et al., 2000).

Rogers, Guelette, Abbey-Hines, Carney, and Werth (2001) discussed rational suicide and counselor attitudes toward it. They described rational suicide as a consequence of the lengthening of life through medical advances, with their concomitant increase in chronic illness and protracted death. They defined rational suicide as "an attempt to control the timing and process of death" (p. 365). Werth and Cobia (1996) suggested several criteria in determining the "rational" in rational suicide. These include the following: the condition is hopeless, the dying person makes a free choice, the dying person follows a systematic decision-making process that may include discussion with a professional, and a review of how significant others will be affected.

GEOGRAPHIC REGION AND CULTURE

Because of her Hispanic surname, the administrative assistant at the counseling center simply assigned Natalia to counseling with Marta, a native of Puerto Rico. Although both Marta and Natalia were born in Puerto Rico and share a similar ethnic and religious heritage, they have had a significantly different amount of exposure to the culture of the mainland United States. Marta's formative years, both personally and professionally, were spent in Puerto Rico. Natalia lived in New York City virtually her entire life and, through her work as a nurse, was exposed to debates concerning physician-assisted suicide.

LOCAL, STATE, AND FEDERAL LAWS

Only Oregon has legislation that permits physician-assisted suicide, the Oregon Death with Dignity Act (1995), which requires two witnesses to attest that the client is competent and acting voluntarily. Marta is aware of the position of her professional organization, that is, the ACA's amicus curiae (friend of the court) brief supporting hastened-death decisions in certain circumstances when there is no hope of recovery (Brief of the Washington State Psychological Association et al., 1996).

ETHICAL THEORY: VIRTUE ETHICS

Susan, the supervisor, follows professional codes rather vigorously and encouraged Marta to use virtue ethics in her decision-making. Virtue ethics encourages the development of self- and other-regarding virtues. A virtue perspective leads the counselor to care for the best interests of the client—that is, from the client's perspective. The client's autonomy should be respected. The counselor, Marta, is aware of the ethical principle of autonomy, which affirms the client's right to make personal decisions, in this case choosing suicide. On the other hand, she is appropriately concerned about the impact of suicide on Natalia's family members, which relates to the issue of beneficence in virtue ethics. Besides the client, beneficence also implies the extension of help to others, such as the family members, involved in the situation. In addition, virtue ethics impels counselors to protect vulnerable members of society against abuse and coercion in decisions about rational suicide. Marta needs to help Natalia receive appropriate care during this time of her life.

QUESTIONS FOR DISCUSSION

1. What other ethical theories may be relevant in this case and what concepts may apply?

2. Are there any other elements to the horizon that should be considered?

3. What is the best ethical decision?

4. As a professional, how much action should Marta take to prevent Natalia's suicide?

Chapter 19

Mark

A Question of Counselor Competence

A gay man in his mid-twenties, Mark, entered counseling because of a court order as a consequence of driving while under the influence of alcohol (DUI). He is employed as an accountant with a restaurant franchise. Mark was raised in a Catholic religious tradition within his family of origin, but because of that church's position on homosexuality and gay marriage, he no longer attends services. Andrew, the counselor, is twenty-five years old. For the past six months, Andrew has been employed in a community counseling agency where his caseload primarily consists of clients with substance-abuse problems.

Initially, Mark discussed his concerns about his DUI. Mark stated that he does not usually drink to excess and that it was just his bad luck to have been arrested. Andrew has heard similar stories from other clients in the past and feels comfortable dealing with these issues. During the third counseling session, however, Mark began to talk about conflicts with his spouse, and Andrew assumed he was referring to a female partner. When Mark named his partner, Bill, Andrew realized that Mark was involved in a gay relationship. Mark reported that he had been drinking lately because of conflicts with his partner and concerns about his sexual orientation. He reported that his relationship with Bill was his first gay relationship. Now, Mark questions whether he is gay and wonders if he acted too impulsively in marrying Bill.

The counselor in this case does not have experience working with gay and lesbian clients nor does he know about homosexual issues. He left the counseling session feeling uncomfortable and unsure of what steps he should take.

Potential relevant elements of the horizon based upon the case of Mark include the ethical dilemma; the client's, counselor's, and supervisor's respective values, race, gender, and personal history; counseling agency policies; local, state, and federal laws that apply; professional knowledge; geographic region; professional ethical codes; and theories of natural law ethics.

THE ETHICAL DILEMMA

Andrew feels that he can deal with Mark's drinking problem. His initial treatment plan would be to help Mark stop drinking. However, Andrew has no experience dealing with issues presented by gay or lesbian clients, and does not know how to address issues surrounding Mark's gay relationship and sexual orientation.

The ethical question for Andrew is whether he is competent to address Mark's sexual orientation. He must decide whether to retain this client on his caseload or to request that Mark be reassigned to another counselor. Andrew is concerned about how a request to transfer a client will be viewed by his supervisor because he is a relatively new counselor at the agency and does not want to appear to be incompetent or unwilling to accept challenging cases.

ANDREW: THE COUNSELOR'S PERSONAL VALUES, RACE, GENDER, AND PERSONAL HISTORY

Andrew is an effective substance abuse and mental health counselor but has no experience counseling gay and lesbian clients. Currently, Andrew is involved in a heterosexual relationship; he has been married for two years and has a one-year-old son. He is the sole financial support for his family. Andrew was raised in a rural community. He attended a small high school and then attended a small state college where he majored in mental health counseling. Andrew decided to specialize in substance abuse treatment during his counseling graduate program where his career focus was influenced by the work of a professor whom he admired.

Through his Catholic religious affiliation, Andrew is aware of the Catholic Medical Association's (CMA, 2000) position on homosexuality, and he personally opposes same-sex marriage. The CMA's position is that there is no compelling evidence that same-sex attraction is genetic, but rather results from unfortunate childhood experiences or other psychological problems. From this point of view, therapy is directed at uncovering the root cause of the emotional trauma that gave rise to the same-sex attraction, and turns to spirituality in the healing process.

Although Andrew does not openly acknowledge his religious views among professional colleagues and supervisors, he privately agrees with the CMA diagnostic and treatment recommendations. Because natural law ethics is central to Catholic moral theology, Andrew assumes that taking a natural law point of view on homosexuality is appropriate in this case because of the client's Catholic religious upbringing.

MARK: THE CLIENT'S PERSONAL VALUES, RACE, GENDER, AND PERSONAL HISTORY

Mark was married to Bill four months ago in the state of Massachusetts. Although his family of origin is Catholic, Mark no longer practices that religion but participates in the Unitarian church that his partner attends. Mark's parents disapprove of his marriage and have let it be known to Mark that although he is welcome to attend family gatherings, his partner is not. His two siblings live out of state and maintain friendly though infrequent contacts with Mark.

The gay relationship with Bill was Mark's first sexual experience. He occasionally dated girls during high school and college. Throughout his adolescence and early adulthood, he tended to be a loner. Bill befriended Mark after they were introduced by a mutual acquaintance, and they found that they had many common interests. Within the gay community, Mark found social acceptance and companionship. Although Mark was reluctant, Bill insisted that they marry as soon as same-sex marriage became legal in Massachusetts. Mark acquiesced out of fear of losing the relationship. Since his marriage, Mark has felt increasingly isolated at work and distant from his family of origin. His relationship with Bill is now strained and they argue frequently.

Mark notes a recent shift in public opinion in the United States away from liberal political views and tolerant attitudes toward diversity to a more conservative orientation and religious fundamentalism. Religious fundamentalism and authoritarianism are associated with negative attitudes toward homosexuality (Heaven & Oxman, 1999; Hunsberger, Owusu, & Duck, 1999). Mark is concerned that he will face increasing societal discrimination as a married gay man and wonders if it is already affecting his professional relationships at work. He feels that his co-workers were somewhat more accepting of him prior to his marriage. Mark now questions his sexual identity and why he entered into a gay relationship. Because of mounting interpersonal pressures with his partner, family, and co-workers, Mark finally admitted that he has been drinking excessively.

TONY: THE SUPERVISOR'S PERSONAL VALUES, RACE, GENDER, AND PERSONAL HISTORY

The supervisor, Tony, is married with two children. He is Catholic but attends church irregularly and does not agree with some of the church's positions on contemporary issues such as birth control. There are gay members of Tony's immediate and extended families and he himself, his parents, and his relatives feel that they are quite tolerant of diversity. Tony favors civil unions for gay and lesbian couples but is opposed to same-sex marriage.

PROFESSIONAL CODES OF ETHICS

Andrew reviewed the AMHCA professional codes and found that the following possibly applied, but also knew other codes may apply:

Principle 1: Welfare of the Consumer
A. Primary Responsibility

1. The primary responsibility of the mental health counselors is to respect the dignity and integrity of the client. Client growth and development are encouraged in ways that foster the client's interest and promote welfare.

Principle 7: Competence
The maintenance of high standards of professional competence is a responsibility shared by all mental health counselors in the best interests of the public and the profession. (AMHCA, 2000)

PROFESSIONAL KNOWLEDGE

Because of Andrew's lack of experience working with the gay community, he is not familiar with the research literature and counseling recommendations for gay and lesbian clients. Andrew relies only on information he received through his connections with the Catholic religious community. He feels that this is an appropriate perspective because he and his client share a similar religious background. In fact, religious orientation is an influential context for the development of sexual identity. Individuals may suffer intense internal conflicts between their experiences of sexual attraction and their internalized sense of morality acquired through religion (Worthington, 2004).

The view of the Catholic Medical Association (CMA, 2000) concerning homosexuality as "unnatural" is at odds with the view of the American Psychiatric Association, which removed homosexuality from its list of mental disorders, the *Diagnostic and Statistical Manual of Mental Disorders* (*DSM*), in 1973. In contrast to the CMA's position, the *DSM* does not consider homosexuality pathological.

The *DSM* position notwithstanding, Pope, Tabachnick, and Keith-Spiegel (2003) indicate that efforts to eliminate pathologizing homosexuality may not yet be entirely successful. They report the results of a survey of counselors which showed that only one in five of the respondents treated homosexuality as pathological either rarely (12.7 percent) or not often (10.8 percent), whereas over half (55.7 percent) viewed as unethical the practice of treating homosexuality as pathological. Discrimination toward those who are gay or lesbian has a long history (Houser & Ham, 2004). Thirteen percent of all hate crimes today are based on sexual orientation (Strom, 2001). Even within the counseling profession, gay and lesbian clients are sometimes treated in a judgmental manner and have their behavior interpreted from a heterosexual perspective (Hall & Fradkin, 1992; Whitman, 1995).

Numerous theories have been proposed about the origins or causes of homosexuality. The APA (2004) explains that sexual orientation exists along a continuum ranging from exclusive homosexuality to exclusive heterosexuality, including various forms of bisexuality. Considerable research evidence suggests that genetic or hormonal factors play a significant role in determining a person's sexuality. Most scientists, however, agree that sexual orientation is a complex interaction of biological, cognitive, and environmental factors and that sexual orientation is shaped at an early age (APA, 2004). There are probably many reasons for a person's sexual orientation, and the reasons may be different for different people.

Because of pressure from family or religious groups, gays and lesbians sometimes seek to change their sexual orientation through so-called conversion or reparative therapies. Those therapies are controversial and potentially harmful to clients. In 1997, the APA passed a resolution opposing homophobia in treatment and reaffirming a client's right to unbiased treatment and self-determination (APA, 1997). Attempts to change the sexual orientation of gays and lesbians have had mixed outcomes (Nicolosi, Byrd, & Potts, 2000; Schaeffer, Nottebaum, Smith, Dech, & Krawczyk, 1999; Shidlo & Schroeder, 2002; Throckmorton, 2002). Hardeman (2002) also pointed out myriad methodological problems of research design and selection bias in those studies.

GEOGRAPHIC REGION AND CULTURE

Massachusetts is in the northeastern United States, known for its liberal views on same-sex marriage. The passage of the same-sex marriage law there has triggered sharp criticism from religious leaders and political debate within the state and across the country.

LOCAL, STATE, AND FEDERAL LAWS

Historically, homosexuality has been illegal in all states. Approximately forty years ago, Illinois became the first state to repeal a sodomy law (ACLU, 2003a); however, most states retained those laws until the 1970s. Repeal of many state sodomy laws coincided with the declassification of homosexuality as a mental illness (Hardeman, 2002).

Laws dealing with gay and lesbian issues are in flux. Same-sex marriage is currently legal in the state of Massachusetts where Mark lives and Andrew practices (ACLU, 2003b). This is the only state that permits same-sex marriage, though a few states allow civil unions (e.g., Vermont). Yet, there is expected to be a state referendum on the legality of same-sex marriage in Massachusetts in the next few years. Andrew notes that there have been significant positive changes in attitudes toward gays and lesbians over the past three decades. On the other hand, he recalls the strong negative reaction toward gay and lesbian issues across the United States during the 2004 elections, when eleven states voted against laws to permit same-sex marriage.

ETHICAL THEORY: NATURAL LAW ETHICS

The counselor's personal values are grounded in Catholicism and natural law ethics. Consequently, one theory used in understanding the ethical issues in this dilemma is natural law. Natural law acknowledges that humans have a tendency to seek relationships with others and to form societies, so friendship and love are good. Andrew's interpretation of natural law reflects a primarily Catholic viewpoint, however, and there are challenges to that argument because of its emphasis on biological matters. Also, from a natural law perspective, it is difficult to determine which values should take priority, i.e., procreation (biological) or love (social).

The principle of double effect does not resolve the dilemma regarding priorities. From a natural law perspective, homosexuality is considered unnatural and morally impermissible because it is does not serve the purpose of procreation;

therefore, homosexual acts cannot be used to justify a "good" result such as interpersonal bonding.

Helminiak (2004) addressed the gay community with another version of natural law. He started with the assumption of the goodness of homosexual relationships and suggested that not all people are capable of the same level of interpersonal and sexual relationships. Within that context, natural law is interpreted as a guide to do what is healthy and wholesome as determined by the best available scientific information.

What other ethical theories may apply to this case, particularly representing the client's worldview?

QUESTIONS FOR DISCUSSION

1. Should Andrew have transferred the case?

2. Should this client be given information about gay affirmative or reparative therapy?

3. How do counselors become prepared to offer educated and unbiased treatment to gay and lesbian clients?

4. What other elements are relevant in this case?

5. What is the best ethical decision?

Chapter 20

Carol

Multicultural Competence

Carol is a forty-two-year-old white female who lives in a major midwestern city. She attended public schools and she is the second oldest of five children. Carol grew up in a working-class family. She graduated from high school and was an average student. Carol's parents divorced when she was ten years old. She keeps in contact with both parents. Both parents and all siblings are alive and live within 100 miles of her. Carol was raised a Catholic but converted to the Wicca Way (witchcraft or "the craft"; also called neopaganism) at the age of thirty-five. She worked as a factory worker for over ten years (with some intermittent layoffs between jobs) and most recently has been unemployed due to her mental health problems.

Carol initially presented with the following symptoms over twenty years ago: anxiety and depression with reports of feelings of helplessness. She has had no remarkable medical problems. She has been diagnosed with major depressive disorder (as defined in *DSM*). She was first hospitalized over twenty years ago and was placed on medication for depression. She has had two subsequent hospitalizations, neither lasting for more than two weeks. The most recent hospitalization was over eight years ago. She has been stable for the past eight years. She did have one pregnancy and it resulted in an abortion; her family pushed for this outcome. Carol practices the Wicca Way and is a strong believer in her spirituality. Carol attends a day program for those with severe mental illness. She lives in an apartment with one other woman, Susan. In addition to attending the day program, she had seen a counselor at a community mental health center on a biweekly basis. Her counselor left the agency and she was assigned a new counselor, Robert.

The counselor, Robert, is a twenty-five-year-old white male who has worked as a mental health counselor since his graduation from a master's program in mental health counseling. He was born and raised in a small midwestern town. He attended a conservative Protestant church and he still attends church on a regular basis. Robert grew up in a middle-class family. He still lives in a small town and commutes to the larger city to complete his internship experience. Robert was raised in a family with a mother and father and an older brother. He is married and he has no children. He attended a public university for both his undergraduate and graduate degrees.

Robert's supervisor, Alice, has been working for the mental health center for six years and is a licensed social worker. Alice is a white, forty-seven-year-old female who is married and has three children. She lives in the suburbs of the larger midwestern city. She grew up in the area. Her family of origin was upper middle class and Alice attended a private university for both her master's and bachelor's degrees. Alice's family attended a Unitarian church. Alice started in the agency providing therapy to a wide range of clients, including those with severe mental illness. She was promoted to a supervisor position two years ago and only sees a few clients while serving as a supervisor. She was promoted because she maintained her paperwork, met regular quotas for client contact, and represented the mental health center well in interacting with other agencies.

We have identified relevant elements of the horizon based upon the case of Carol, and they include the ethical dilemma; the client's, counselor's, and supervisor's respective values, race, gender, and personal history; counseling agency policies; local, state, and federal laws that apply; professional knowledge; geographic region; professional ethical codes; and ethical theories.

THE ETHICAL DILEMMA

Robert met with Carol for the first time and she discussed her mental illness. She described her personal history, which included her thoughts about her religious beliefs—the Wicca Way or the "craft," witchcraft. She talked about her creative power and the craft. She also talked about her belief that Christianity holds an animosity toward witchcraft, and she rejects Christian attempts to restrict the freedom of other ways of religious practice, e.g., neopaganism. Carol discussed how she influenced two other members of the day program she attends to come to services.

Robert was unsure of what direction to take in addressing this issue. His personal values, which are conservative, hold that such religious practices are immoral. His initial inclination was to discuss how immoral it would be to engage in such a religion. He also was concerned about Carol influencing others to follow this type of immoral religion. However, he reserved expressing this until he had further time to think about the direction of the counseling. Thus, one ethical issue is whether Robert should focus counseling on what he perceives as an evil religious practice, witchcraft. Recall one of the major ethical dilemmas cited in Chapter 16 was multicultural competence, which includes acceptance of others' values and beliefs. Another major ethical issue is autonomy of the client.

ROBERT: THE COUNSELOR'S PERSONAL VALUES, RACE, GENDER, AND PERSONAL HISTORY

A second part of the horizon in ethical decision-making is the counselor and his or her personal values, race, gender, personal history, etc. Robert brings to the counseling sessions conservative values, religious values. He was raised in a Baptist church and he feels it is a sin for anyone to engage in religious practices such as worshiping pagan gods and practicing witchcraft. Robert grew up in a middle-class family where his mother and father were nurturing and active in his life. Odell and Stewart (1993) noted that "psychotherapy is an exercise in influence, one in which rhetoric, or conversation, is used to help the client change some problematic aspect of his or her life" (p. 128). They further cited research that revealed that clients with successful therapeutic outcomes had values closely resembling therapist values. Problems arise with the implementation of a counseling process focused on the counselor's personal values when these conflict with the values of the client. The client's values may or may not represent the larger population's view; the client may desire to seek a different but still acceptable view, acceptable meaning it is not illegal.

CAROL: THE CLIENT'S PERSONAL VALUES, RACE, GENDER, AND PERSONAL HISTORY

Carol lives with another woman, Susan, in a two-bedroom duplex in a working-class neighborhood in a large midwestern city (over 300,000 residents). Susan, who also practices the Wicca Way, is Carol's best friend and they attend services on a regular basis. Susan first introduced Carol to the Wicca Way. Carol believes in the creative power of the universe and relates to Wicca, which is an earth-centered religion. She rejects the religion of her family of origin, Catholicism, and believes that Christians seek to suppress the religious practices of her chosen religion. She is suspicious of those who practice Christianity, particularly those who are more conservative. Carol attends services and participates in the "casting of a circle" (the consecration of a sacred space) and participates in casting spells, singing, etc. Carol does talk about her religious beliefs to others at the day program and two have attended Wicca services with her and Susan.

ALICE: THE SUPERVISOR'S PERSONAL VALUES, RACE, GENDER, AND PERSONAL HISTORY

Alice, the supervisor, grew up in the suburbs of the urban area where she works. She grew up in an upper-middle-class family and she attended a Unitarian church. She is a white female with a family, a spouse and two children. She attends church on a regular basis. She considers herself liberal and open-minded with regard to religious practices and choices.

Research on supervisory relationships has examined the role of the gender of the supervisor and supervisee (Wester, Vogel, & Archer, 2004). Male supervisees have been noted to present a defensive style when working with a female supervisor (Wester et al.).

PROFESSIONAL CODES OF ETHICS

Walden, Herlihy, and Ashton (2003) stated,

> A defining characteristic of a professional organization is the formulation of a code or system of standards that prescribe acceptable professional behaviors for the members of that group. The establishment of a code of ethics signifies the maturation of a profession. (p. 106)

Counseling is a relatively young profession, but there are well-established professional codes. Hadjistavropoulos, Malloy, Sharpe, Green, and Fuchs-Lacelle (2002) also provided insight into the relevance of professional ethics and stated, "A primary purpose of a code of ethics is to assist members of an organization in making consistent choices when faced with ethical dilemmas" (p. 254). There are several professional codes that potentially apply to the ethical dilemma faced by Robert. Some of the ACA codes that may apply include*

---

*Source: Reprinted with permission from the American Counseling Association, 2005, *ACA Code of Ethics*, Alexandria, VA.

C.2. Professional Competence

C.2.a. Boundaries of Competence

Counselors practice only within the boundaries of their competence, based on their education, training, supervised experience, state and national professional credentials, and appropriate professional experience. Counselors gain knowledge, personal awareness, sensitivity, and skills pertinent to working with a diverse client population.

F.11. Multicultural/Diversity Competence in Counselor Education and Training Programs

F.11.c. Multicultural/Diversity Competence

Counselor educators actively infuse multicultural/diversity competency in their training and supervision practices. They actively train students to gain awareness, knowledge, and skills in the competencies of multicultural practice. Counselor educators include case examples, role-plays, discussion questions, and other classroom activities that promote and represent various cultural perspectives.

PROFESSIONAL KNOWLEDGE

Robert was trained in a traditional monocultural training program, where typically one course in multiculturalism is completed (Sue, Arredondo, & McDavis, 1992). Training in multiculturalism is not integrated across courses in this type of model. Is religion a culture? Falcov (1988) defined culture as "those sets of shared world views and adaptive behaviors derived from simultaneous membership in a variety of contexts: ecological settings (rural, urban, suburban), religious background, etc." (p. 336). Chi-Ying Chung and Bemak (2002) stated, "One major problem in working across cultures is the tendency for counselors to impose their cultural values on clients, which may occur in a conscious or unconscious level" (p. 159).

Sue et al. (1992) stated, "The profession of counseling oftentimes reflects the values of the larger society," which results in it being the "handmaiden of the status quo and transmitters of society's values" (p. 66). With regard to cross-cultural competence, Sue et al. stated, "a culturally skilled counselor is one who is actively in the process of becoming aware of his or her own assumptions about human behavior, values, biases, preconceived notions, personal limitations" (p. 67). Further, Sue et al. concluded that "a culturally skilled counselor is one who actively attempts to understand the worldview of his or her culturally different client without negative judgments" (p. 67). Eriksen, Marston and Korte (2002) suggested that, to maintain ethical practice, counselors should understand the beliefs and values of clients based upon religious views.

Another area of knowledge relevant in this horizon is an understanding of how to assess and counsel clients about religious beliefs (Hathaway, Scott, & Garvey, 2004). Hathaway et al. noted the importance of religiousness and adaptive mental health functioning. Religion may give the client a sense of meaning and promote hope and optimism (Hathaway et al.). Also, Hathaway et al. noted that the *Diagnostic and Statistical Manual of Mental Disorders IV TR*, or *DSM* (American Psychiatric Association, 2000), includes categories of mental health problems that focus on religious beliefs and practices, specifically found in V codes. V codes typically involve issues around relationships but also address concerns such as conversion to a new religion.

A third area that is relevant in understanding the horizon of this ethical dilemma is the history of treatment of those who have followed the religion of the Wicca Way (Barstow, 1994; Bever, 2002). For example, over 50,000 individuals were put to death for witchcraft in Europe during the Middle Ages (Barstow). Additionally, Houser and Ham (2004) suggested that religion may be considered a minority status and result in the loss of power and influence in society. More recent discrimination is found against those following the Wicca Way and includes loss of jobs and loss of custody of children (Blummer, 2000; Merriam, Courtenay, & Baumgartner, 2003).

GEOGRAPHIC REGION AND CULTURE

Geographic region can play a role in this case because both urban and rural personal experiences apply. Also, the counseling services are provided in an urban setting. Researchers have noted the unique characteristics of those living and growing up in urban and rural environments (Sears, Evans, & Perry, 1998; Silk, Sessa, Morris, Steinberg, & Avenevoli, 2004). Urban researchers have studied the development or lack of development of collective efficacy (Ford & Beveridge, 2004; Sampson, 2002). Sampson defined neighborhood collective efficacy as "an emphasis on shared beliefs in neighbors' conjoint capability for action to achieve an intended effect, and hence an active sense of engagement on the part of residents" (p. 224). Ford and Beveridge concluded that collective efficacy "emphasizes shared expectations and mutual trust among neighborhood residents and promotes an agentic sense of cohesion" (p. 27). The client, Carol, grew up in an urban environment and experienced little connection to her community or neighborhood. She felt little support from her neighborhood. Currently she lives in a working-class neighborhood again with little cohesion or sense of community or neighborhood collective efficacy.

LOCAL, STATE, AND FEDERAL LAWS

The First Amendment to the U.S. Constitution protects the right to religious freedom. Also, recent hate-law legislation has made it illegal to act violently against others due to religious beliefs (Levin, 2002). The First Amendment states,

> Congress shall make no law respecting an establishment of religion or prohibiting the free exercise thereof; or abridging the freedom of speech, or of the press; or the right of the people to peaceably assemble, and to petition the Government for a redress of grievances. (U.S. Congress, 1789)

The First Amendment does not indicate what religious beliefs or lack of beliefs are acceptable or covered, i.e., all beliefs are protected.

ETHICAL THEORY: UTILITARIAN ETHICS

There are several individuals who were potentially affected by this ethical dilemma, including Carol's roommate, those whom she knows who practice witchcraft, and possibly those at the day program. So, Robert decided to use utilitarian theory as one source in ethical decision-making. There are other theories that also may be relevant, such as Native American ethics.

The use of utilitarian ethics in practice is well accepted in counseling and psychology (Henry, 1996; Knapp, 1999). Henry identified several underlying principles of the ACA professional codes of ethics, and utilitarianism provides a foundation based upon the greatest good and the importance of assessing the consequences of an action. Knapp suggested that utilitarianism may help professionals in four ways in practice. It can "(a) identify and justify the underlying moral principles on which their ethics codes are based, (b) assist them in ethical decision-making, (c) encourage moral behavior, and (d) evaluate the culpability of their colleagues who are accused of ethics violations" (p. 383). Knapp further noted that "many standards of the APA Code of Conduct appear to be based on rule utilitarianism" (p. 390). However, Knapp stated that the use of act utilitarianism provides the professional with a foundation for ethical decision-making when professional codes are less clear about a circumstance or when codes conflict.

The basic concepts of utilitarian theory (see Chapter 4) that potentially apply to this ethical dilemma include the greatest happiness principle or GHP, utility, the consequentialist principle, rule utilitarianism, and act utilitarianism. The GHP may apply because the intent of using this theory is to determine the amount of happiness or benefit for all involved. Utility is relevant to account for how each decision may affect all involved. Ultimately, the outcome is what matters in this theory, which is the consequentialist principle. Using this principle, the ethical issue may be interpreted as how each decision ultimately affects those involved, without regard for their intentions. Applying both rule utilitarianism and act utilitarianism allows for an understanding of how each perspective may help in understanding the ethical dilemma, from either an individual or a societal perspective.

QUESTIONS FOR DISCUSSION

1. Were there any additional components of the horizon that were not listed?

2. Did Robert act ethically based upon a hermeneutic model?

3. What suggestions would you give Robert in working with Carol and dealing with the ethical dilemma?

Chapter 21

Jeff

Career Decision and Counseling Plans

Jeff, a seventeen-year-old white adolescent, began seeing his school counselor to discuss a conflict he was having over his career decisions. The issues Jeff hoped to address in counseling were directly associated with the tensions that he experienced living with parents of different religious traditions: His mother was Jewish and his father was a Christian Protestant. The most pressing issue on his mind was to decide what he wanted to do after he graduated from high school. Although this issue is not an unusual concern for a high-school senior, the decision created for him extreme tension and dominated his daily thoughts. Family tensions came to a head whenever he discussed his plans for the future with his parents together. Both his mother and his father had encouraged him to go to college, but as the time came for him to apply to colleges, their different worldviews became evident to him and his parents.

For Jeff's mother, Jeff's decision stirred up feelings she had about her own adolescence and young adulthood. These feelings about her own life decisions had lingered throughout her adult life. She had always known that her choice in marriage was not consistent with goals her parents and grandparents had had for her. They had expressed very directly to her that she had betrayed her religious and cultural heritage, and the traditions of her family, by marrying a man outside the Jewish religious faith. Since her maternal grandfather was a rabbi, her selection of a Jew as a life partner was considered essential in maintaining the family tradition of men being scholars and important members of the Jewish community. She, however, saw the men in her family as judgmental and critical; thus, her choice of a husband was a man who was a gentle, easygoing professor of literature.

Although her husband was not Jewish, her family tolerated him as a member of the family because he was at least a scholar. Also, in keeping with Jewish law, the children from the marriage would be Jewish.

During Jeff's high-school years, family tensions heightened because of Jeff's passion for writing lyrics to songs he sang while accompanying himself with a guitar. He told his parents that his future goal was to live a life like that of his idol, Bruce Springsteen. His mother opposed his dream because it was in direct conflict with the goals she had for him. She had hoped he would be a physician like her own father. His mother began to denigrate the music of Bruce Springsteen, and she also refused to pay for his guitar lessons. In contrast to his mother's response, his father slipped money to him so he could take guitar lessons. His father encouraged his interest in songwriting. In fact, when the family was together with his maternal grandparents, his father often stated that writing songs was an art form similar to writing poetry. His father even attended a Bruce Springsteen concert with him.

For Jeff, tensions in his family became unmanageable when he was told by his mother that he had to apply to colleges, preferably very prestigious colleges. Since Jeff received excellent grades and his standardized testing scores were very high, his school guidance counselor, Amy, initially encouraged him to attend college.

His father's approach was different. He often complimented Jeff about his success in school and emphasized that with his talents he could do anything he wanted. He supported Jeff's idea to take time off and focus on his music before entering college. In fact, he stated that delaying college would give Jeff time to mature. His mother frequently told Jeff that he was obligated to do as she wanted and go to a prestigious college. The situation became intolerable for Jeff. He felt helpless as he faced the choices he had before him: either to go to college or to follow his dreams.

Jeff met with Amy, the school counselor, and openly discussed his dilemma. She had not previously heard about the conflicts that Jeff was having at home. She only knew Jeff as an excellent student and someone who was well liked by his peers. She reviewed his interests and achievement test results, and these supported an artistic occupation for him, but scientific occupations were second choices. Amy did not want to see Jeff waste an opportunity to attend a prestigious college and pursue a respected career in medicine. She was skeptical of a career in music and believed it was a long shot compared to medicine for Jeff.

Amy discussed the situation with her supervisor, Sally, and questioned whose career goals would be served if Jeff were pushed into medicine. Amy returned to her office and began to question her intent to attempt to persuade him to pursue medicine.

Your task, as in earlier cases, is to discuss relevant elements from the case of Jeff that contribute to the horizon: the ethical dilemma; the values, race, gender, personal history, and any other relevant information about the counselor, the client, and the supervisor; institutional policies; applicable local, state, and federal laws; professional codes of ethics; professional knowledge; geographic region; and the ethical orientation or theories.

THE ETHICAL DILEMMA

Jeff is an adolescent with much promise and the potential to be very successful. His mother is pushing for him to pursue a career in medicine; however, his father supports the idea of Jeff attempting a career in music. Jeff expresses a strong interest in pursuing his dream of a career in music. Amy, the guidance counselor, sees Jeff as a talented and exceptional student. She agrees with Jeff's mother that he should pursue a career in medicine and apply to the prestigious colleges that she knew he could get into as an undergraduate.

Amy's supervisor, Sally, questioned whose career goal Amy was supporting. Amy began to think about her counseling efforts and the fact that she had attempted to persuade Jeff to pursue a career in medicine. She decided it was important for her to review her counseling efforts and determine the ethical nature of her efforts.

AMY: THE COUNSELOR'S PERSONAL VALUES, RACE, GENDER, AND PERSONAL HISTORY

The counselor, Amy, was a *sensei* (Mio et al., 2000), a third-generation Japanese woman in her early forties. She had been a school counselor for the past ten years in a suburban community known for its excellent schools. Because of her school experience she was familiar with the concerns that adolescents have about determining the direction of their lives after high-school graduation.

Amy was raised by parents who did not follow Japanese traditions but were aware of and interested in their Japanese heritage. However, the legacy of Amy's family included her father's experience during World War II. As a small child he had lived in California with his parents and sister in an internment (relocation) camp for Japanese. When World War II ended, Amy's grandfather wanted his family to be as *American* as possible and decided that this could only be possible if they moved to the East Coast. Amy's father was then raised in New Jersey where he continued to live with his wife and own family. Throughout her childhood and adolescence Amy felt secure, well liked, and part of her community. It was in college when she began to understand what her father's experience meant in the context of American history. In college, she had a need to find friends who were Japanese Americans, and her boyfriend was, like her, a sensei. After graduation from college, she thought she might marry her boyfriend, but she grew distant from him as she began to realize that being Japanese was not her only identity. Although she had several intimate relationships that could have concluded in marriage, she did not marry until she was forty years old. Her choice of husband was a white Jewish man who was a family therapist.

JEFF: THE CLIENT'S PERSONAL VALUES, RACE, GENDER, AND PERSONAL HISTORY

The unspoken values Jeff had learned from his family were those associated with belonging. His parents enjoyed having small parties for friends, primarily from the university where his father taught. His mother had many women friends with whom she often went on trips for weekends. She also had her women friends come to their house for evening coffee. His father liked to spend time in his study where he wrote poetry, read extensively, and prepared lectures for his courses. Jeff noticed that his father enjoyed the small parties his parents gave, but that he did not have close friends as his mother had.

Until Jeff was twelve he was not aware of religious obligations nor was he involved in any institutional religious experiences. Once a year he would go with his parents to his maternal grandparents' house for Passover. Occasionally, his father did not join his mother, sister, and him at his maternal grandparent's home for this holiday. Jeff always felt disappointed when his father did not go with them. The upper-middle-income community where Jeff and his family lived had a large number of Jews who had varying degrees of religious affiliation. Even though many of his school friends were Jewish, many of their families were not religious Jews.

On the other hand, Jeff's music friends were all white non-Jews, and not religious. He also felt at ease with friends at school. His friends meant a great deal to him, and he attached importance to loyalty and respect for each person's differences. Just to be of the same religion, go to the same school, and associate with the same group was not as important as to know that he and another person had mutual respect and loyalty.

SALLY: THE SUPERVISOR'S PERSONAL VALUES, RACE, GENDER, AND PERSONAL HISTORY

Sally was the director of guidance at Jeff's school. Her family of origin, both maternal and paternal, had come from the United Kingdom to the United States more than a century ago. For generations, her family members had been upper-middle-class, hard-working, high-school or college graduates. Members of her family were professionals and respected for their own accomplishments. Although family members were not devoted churchgoers, many attended churches in their Protestant faith. Sally had never married, but she had a small group of close friends and was an active member of several community organizations. She felt her family's values of hard work and perseverance gave her the strengths that she needed for making her a successful professional counselor and supervisor. Sally considered her respect for individual uniqueness, her patience when listening to students about their complex lives, and her ability to problem-solve as personal qualities she brought to relationships.

PROFESSIONAL CODES OF ETHICS

Amy reviewed the professional codes of the American School Counselor Association, ASCA. Some of the ASCA professional codes that potentially apply to this case include*

A.1. Responsibilities to Students
The professional school counselor:

a. Has a primary obligation to the student, who is to be treated with respect as a unique individual.

b. Is concerned with the educational, academic, career, personal and social needs and encourages the maximum development of every student.

c. Respects the student's values and beliefs and does not impose the counselor's personal values.

Other ASCA codes also apply.

PROFESSIONAL KNOWLEDGE

Amy reviewed the professional counseling literature that addressed career development, family influence on career decisions, and difficulty in career decision-making in an effort to understand this dilemma more fully (Alderfer, 2004;

Source: ASCA, 2004. Reprinted with permission.

Liezel & Meyer, 2002; Peterson & Gonzalez, 2000; Trusty & Niles, 2004; Wei-Cheng, 2004). Amy also reviewed some of the career development theories (Peterson & Gonzalez, 2000) she learned while completing her master's degree. Approaches such as Super's model of career development suggest that individuals pass through various stages and there are specific developmental tasks that are addressed (Super, 1990). Amy knew that Jeff, like most adolescents in her school, were in a crystallization phase of career development, which involves formulating a career goal.

Research into family involvement in the career choice of adolescents has shown that parental involvement generally results in more positive outcomes (Alderfer, 2004). Alderfer pointed out the importance of assessing family dynamics and reviewing the hierarchical structure in the family. She felt this was particularly important in identifying flexibility in the family system and how it adapts to changes in family members. For example, older adolescents theoretically have more input and choice. Also, Alderfer noted the importance of a family promoting differentiation of the self, e.g., allowing children/adolescents to pursue career choices. Zingaro (1983) also cited the importance of adolescents separating from their families in making their own career choices. Those who cannot separate have difficulties making free choices.

Difficulties in career decision-making have been associated with a lack of readiness, lack of information, and inconsistent information (Gati, Krasz, & Osipow, 1996; Wei-Cheng, 2004). Inconsistent information includes internal conflicts and external conflicts (Gati et al.). Amy noted that Jeff potentially fell into this category since his parents had different opinions on career options for him. How does he address these external conflicts and what should Amy do to facilitate him addressing it? Meyer (2002) suggested that counselors identify the source(s) of the difficulties in career decision-making and develop appropriate interventions.

GEOGRAPHIC REGION AND CULTURE

The institution most directly interested and invested in Jeff's decision about the future was the staff of the high school he attended. They reflected the values of the highly academic school, where ninety-two percent of the students went on to college after graduation, and the community, which promoted education through city taxes and adolescent advocacy programs. Since the Jewish population was estimated to be more than fifty percent of the community, some themes from Judaism, such as intellectual achievement and financial success (Rosen & Weltman, 1996), were recognizable in community and school priorities.

LOCAL, STATE, AND FEDERAL LAWS

While no state or federal law mandates career counseling for adolescents, the importance of going to college has been documented in state and federal government publications. For example, a federal government publication states, "One of the major benefits of acquiring a college education is having more jobs to choose from," and gives the advice, "Parents and students should talk about the kind of work that interests the students, and find out more about the kind of education that specific jobs require" (U.S. Department of Education, 2000, p. 2). These messages from state and federal publications strongly influence educators and indirectly influence the parents of adolescents.

ETHICAL THEORY: RESPECT FOR PERSONS ETHICS

Amy decided to use respect for persons as one of the theories in making an ethical decision in this case (see Chapter 5). The central theme of the ethics of respect for persons is that equal respect must be paid to the personhood of all humans. The foundation of this ethical theme comes from a refinement of Immanuel Kant's ethics theory. At the core of Kantian ethics is the claim that normal adults are capable of being fully self-governing and autonomous in making moral decisions. Foremost, we do not need to be informed by some external authority of the conditions or the demands for being moral beings, and we can effectively control ourselves through reason. As important to the Kantian argument for autonomy are the concepts of obligation and duty, which together guide us to act in a certain way. Kant also considered virtue important to ethical behavior, since virtuous behavior is a necessary moral strength of will in overcoming temptations to violate moral or social laws. Both autonomy and virtue enable human beings to take a firm position against universal injustice. Applied to this case, respect for persons interprets what is respectful and acknowledges the autonomy of Jeff.

Modern Kantians have questioned whether Kantian ethics can be of practical use. However, they have come up with proposals for universality tests and have argued that the following tests can be effective guides for ethical behavior: (1) Can we consent to everyone's adopting the moral rule presupposed by the action? (2) Can we consent to others' acting simultaneously according to the same rule(s) we use without undermining our own ability to act in accordance with it?

If the conditions of these tests cannot be met, then we must turn to the means-end principle. In a practical application, this principle implies that an act, to be morally worthy and permissible, must treat human beings as ends and not simply as means. To determine whether we are treating a person as an end and not merely as a means, two tests can be used. First, we can determine whether an action overrides the freedom or well-being of someone else or ourselves; second, we must do more than not interfere with the freedoms and well-being of others and ourselves, we must also contribute positively to the capability of others or ourselves to act as moral agents. So, in this case the question is whether the actions of Amy are universal, i.e., whether all students should be encouraged to attend college who demonstrate the ability. If a universal principle can be applied, is Jeff treated respectfully, is he treated as an end and not merely as a means, and are his freedoms unhindered? Also, do Amy's actions promote his well-being?

QUESTIONS FOR DISCUSSION

1. What are other theoretical perspectives of this case that would have relevance and meaning for you?

2. Did Amy act ethically?

Chapter 22

Vanessa

A Dual Relationship

A thirty-year-old, recently divorced woman, Vanessa, enters counseling because she is thinking about relinquishing physical custody of her two-year-old son and three-year-old daughter to her former husband. Vanessa and her ex-husband maintain a relationship only around visitation arrangements for the children. Both parents live in a large northeastern city in the United States. The children's father has not remarried, though he has a serious relationship with another woman.

Vanessa was just accepted at a prestigious law school and does not think that she can adequately care for her children while she attends graduate classes. She feels that after she completes law school and establishes herself in a career, she will be in a better position to care for the children both financially and emotionally. She hopes to be able to regain custody of the children in about five years. Vanessa's mother is opposed to this idea and told her daughter that she is an uncaring mother. Her sister and several female friends also voiced similar concerns about the plan. After a heated conversation with her mother and sister, Vanessa realized that she will face a great deal of social pressure if she "abandons her children." She wants to consider the custody matter carefully. She specifically sought a female counselor whom she felt would better understand her perspective than a male counselor.

Vanessa's case is assigned to Phyllis, a middle-aged woman who received her counseling degree three years ago. At their first meeting, Vanessa recognized the counselor as a woman whom she sometimes sees at an early morning aerobics class at a local gym, although the counselor did not recognize Vanessa during the intake interview. The counselor is unsettled by the idea that Vanessa would seriously consider "giving up" her children. She does not fully explore Vanessa's feelings of guilt about neglecting her children's care while attending law school or her conflicts about relinquishing custody to work on her career.

During the course of counseling, both women continue attending the aerobics class and exchange friendly greetings when they see each other. On one or two occasions, Vanessa asked Phyllis for information and recommendations about various community services, such as reputable day-care facilities for her children. During the aerobics class, several women suggest a weekly breakfast get-together, and both Vanessa and Phyllis join the group. During one of these breakfast meetings that Vanessa attended, Phyllis was asked about her background. Phyllis reported to the breakfast group that she was not employed outside of the home while raising her two children. She explained that she put off her career plans because young children need a stable mother figure at that critical period in their development and she did not want to regret lost time with her children. Phyllis stated that she returned to graduate school at the age of fifty when her children were no longer dependent upon her and were living on their own. Two women in the group voiced their approval of Phyllis's decision about choosing full-time motherhood over a career. Phyllis noticed that Vanessa seemed visibly upset and teary-eyed after hearing her life story.

The possible relevant elements of the horizon based upon the case of Vanessa include the ethical dilemma; the counselor and her values, race, gender, personal history, etc.; the client and her values, race, gender, personal history, etc.; the supervisor and his values, race, gender, personal history, etc.; agency policies; professional codes of ethics; applicable local, state, and federal laws; professional knowledge; geographic region; and ethical theories.

THE ETHICAL DILEMMA

Initially, Phyllis did not even consider the possibility of an unethical dual relationship because her social contact with the client was minimal. Still, the after-workout breakfast meetings between the two women occasioned an opportunity for the counselor to influence the client outside of the professional relationship. Phyllis realized that the social relationship was possibly affecting the counseling relationship. The counselor had to decide how she could stop or minimize the effects of that outside relationship.

PHYLLIS: THE COUNSELOR'S PERSONAL VALUES, RACE, GENDER, AND PERSONAL HISTORY

The counselor, Phyllis, is a middle-aged woman who chose to follow a traditional female path in her own life and sees a primary role for women as caretakers and mothers. This was the role she observed with her own mother, who raised a family of six children and was never employed outside of the home.

Phyllis is married to a high-school teacher and has two children. Even though there were financial strains, her husband insisted that she stay with the children and manage the household. Phyllis agreed with her husband, preferring to be a full-time mother rather than work outside of the home. She returned to graduate school after her children were grown. Phyllis feels that many women want to "have it all" in terms of career and family and that their children's developmental needs are neglected in the process.

VANESSA: THE CLIENT'S PERSONAL VALUES, RACE, GENDER, AND PERSONAL HISTORY

Vanessa's mother did not work outside of the home while raising her children, but returned to college when her husband passed away and Vanessa and her sister were adults. Her father, now deceased, was the sole support of the family during Vanessa's childhood. Vanessa's ex-husband is a successful computer software engineer and was easily able to support his wife and the two children. During their marriage, he insisted that Vanessa remain at home as a full-time mother.

Although Vanessa respected her mother's decision to delay a career, she saw a different path for herself in becoming an attorney. However, achieving that career goal became more complicated both financially and psychologically after her divorce. Vanessa engaged a female counselor whom she thought would intimately understand her maternal and career issues.

Vanessa is unsure that she has the strength to ignore the messages she is receiving about her maternal role and responsibilities and to continue pursuing a non-traditional course. Moreover, after hearing the counselor's life story, she is reluctant to explore in counseling the possibility of relinquishing her children out of concern that she will again be judged an uncaring mother—a message she has already received from her friends and family. Vanessa told Phyllis that the counselor's career path paralleled that of her mother.

JONATHAN: THE SUPERVISOR'S PERSONAL VALUES, RACE, GENDER, AND PERSONAL HISTORY

After hearing that comment about the similar career paths of Vanessa's mother and herself, the counselor became aware of the extent of her influence through the breakfast group. Phyllis sought the counsel of her supervisor, Jonathan, a gay man in his late thirties. Jonathan and his partner are in the process of adopting a child and are also struggling with the issue of child care in a two-career family. To satisfy the adoption agency, he and his partner must have a clear and workable day-care plan for the child. He empathized with Vanessa's child-care dilemma.

Because of his own membership in an oppressed group, Jonathan has studied feminism and is particularly interested in feminist perspectives concerning socially constructed gender roles and societal power differentials. Jonathan agreed that Phyllis may have inadvertently reinforced societal expectations regarding caretaking roles for women, and that these expectations are a likely source of Vanessa's conflicts.

PROFESSIONAL CODES OF ETHICS

Several professional ethical codes from the ACA potentially apply in this case (ACA, 2005).*

A.4. Avoiding Harm and Imposing Values
A.4.b. Personal Values
Counselors are aware of their own values, attitudes, beliefs, and behaviors and avoid imposing values that are inconsistent with counseling goals. Counselors respect the diversity of clients, trainees, and research participants.

E.5. Diagnosis of Mental Disorders
E.5.b. Cultural Sensitivity
Counselors recognize that culture affects the manner in which clients' problems are defined. Clients' socioeconomic and cultural experience is considered when diagnosing mental disorders.

PROFESSIONAL KNOWLEDGE

Phyllis reviewed the professional literature that addressed dual relationships. Nigro (2003) stated that "dual relationships exist whenever clients and therapists have a relationship outside the therapy hour" (p. 191). She further stated that "there are many types of dual relationships such as business, sexual, familial, social, and professional" (p. 191). Phyllis discovered that issues with dual relationships were the

*Source: Reprinted with permission from the American Counseling Association, 2005, *ACA Code of Ethics,* Alexandria, VA.

most frequent complaints made against counselors to state licensing boards (Neukrug, Milliken, & Walden, 2001). Some even suggested that any form of a dual relationship is unethical (Younggren & Gottlieb, 2004).

Younggren and Gottlieb (2004) warned that "engaging in multiple relationships has a high potential for harming patients, and as a general matter, should be avoided" (p. 257). They proposed a series of questions as a guide to decision-making about dual relationships in counseling:

1. Is entering into the relationship in addition to the professional one necessary, or should I try to avoid it?

2. Can the dual relationship potentially cause harm to the patient?

3. If harm seems unlikely or avoidable, would the additional relationship prove beneficial?

4. Is there a risk that the dual relationship could disrupt the therapeutic relationship?

5. Can I evaluate this matter objectively? (pp. 257–258)

Phyllis also thought it would be important to become better informed about the perspectives of feminism when working with female clients. In dealing with a client whose issues relate to gender role concerns, the counselor must understand, and must help the client to understand, the social, cultural, and political context and pressures that may be the source of the turmoil, or that are at least contributing to the problem. Cummings (2000) proposed that counselors learn specific feminist responses that would (a) empower clients, (b) decrease the power differential between the counselor and client, (c) use a gender role perspective, and (d) place client issues in a sociocultural context. At the core of feminist counseling is the acknowledgment of the client's sociocultural context, which places personal issues in a broader political framework. The goal is to normalize feelings about being a woman in a particular culture. Radov, Masnick, and Hauser (1977) isolated five components that differentiate feminist approaches to counseling from traditional counseling: (1) assuming that all roles are open to women, (2) using a sociological perspective, (3) developing a new feminist ego ideal, (4) emphasizing balance in work and relationships, and (5) assessing the value of relationships with other women as opposed to relationships with men. Feminist supervisory practices parallel the feminist counseling process. It is described as a collaborative relationship between supervisor and counselor characterized by mutual respect, attention to social and cultural factors, advocacy, analysis of boundaries and power, and sensitivity to diversity (Szymanski, 2003).

GEOGRAPHIC REGION AND CULTURE

Vanessa lives in a large metropolitan area in the Northeast where there is greater tolerance for alternative lifestyles, single mothers, and career women than in other parts of the country. It is likely that she could find support groups for women dealing with the same parenting and career issues.

LOCAL, STATE, AND FEDERAL LAWS

There are no laws that specifically address dual relationships in the counseling relationship. There have been civil and criminal lawsuits filed against counselors for engaging in dual relationships, such as sexual intimacy with a client.

ETHICAL THEORY: FEMINIST ETHICS

With its emphasis on relationships, a feminine care perspective may provide the counselor and client a viewpoint from which to understand dual relationships in counseling. But the feminine care perspective may also serve to reinforce care-taking roles for women and idealize mother-child relationships as virtuous. Therefore, in the case of Vanessa, taking a *feminist,* rather than *feminine,* perspective is important because the issues are gender-related and deal with societal expectations for mothers and career women. Feminist approaches seek to overcome societal barriers and increase options for women, not to dictate a particular outcome.

A dual relationship can confuse the client with regard to the counselor's expressions of caring within a professional relationship versus those expressed within a social relationship, e.g., an exercise group. Baier's (1986) notion of trust is also pertinent to ethical issues concerning dual relationships. The problem with dual relationships is that they typically involve asymmetric power relationships. In counseling, the counselor holds a very influential position and must be vigilant not to abuse the power that the client has entrusted to him or her. The potential for the differential in power influencing the counseling as well as the social relationship is significant.

What other ethical theory(ies) may apply to this case?

QUESTIONS FOR DISCUSSION

1. Can Phyllis continue to work with Vanessa given the circumstances of their dual relationship?

2. Did the client indicate in any way that she was experiencing gender-role conflict?

3. How should gender issues be addressed?

4. How could the counselor have made the client more aware of the socio-cultural context of her issue?

5. What is the best ethical decision?

Chapter 23

David

Supervisor-Supervisee Conflict

David is a mental health counselor in Oregon. He is of American Indian descent and he has worked as a mental health counselor for the past two years. His primary caseload is with clients who have severe mental illness and who are American Indians. David has fairly frequent conflicts with his supervisor over what the supervisor considers to be sharing too much information, or sharing information that the client theoretically cannot handle. For example, David has given feedback to clients that they were not being responsible in changing their lives despite having severe mental illness. David's supervisor has indicated that he feels such feedback is not helpful because this population cannot always control their behaviors.

David recently was assigned a new client, Sarah, who is a twenty-eight-year-old Native American woman diagnosed with schizophrenia. She has been inconsistent in attending a day program for those with severe mental illness and has come into counseling sessions with bruises on her arms. Sarah lives with her family—parents and several siblings. David suspects someone in the family is physically abusing her. He wants to comply with a state law that protects abuse of those with disabilities, including those with mental illness. David asked the client how she received the bruises on her arms and Sarah answered that she fell.

David informed his supervisor, Dennis, about the situation with his client and his concern about abuse. The supervisor stated that he would be reluctant to report any abuse without further information. Dennis believes doing so will jeopardize David's relationship with the client and the family. Dennis suggests that David not file a report of potential abuse but to gather more information.

The potentially relevant elements of the horizon include the ethical dilemma; the counselor and his values, race, gender, personal history, etc.; the client and her values, race, gender, personal history, etc.; the supervisor and his values, race, gender, personal history, etc.; agency policies; local, state, and federal laws that apply; professional codes of ethics; professional knowledge; geographic region; and ethical theories.

THE ETHICAL DILEMMA

One dilemma for David is whether to break the confidentiality of the counseling sessions and report suspected abuse of his client. A second ethical dilemma is whether he should ignore his supervisor's recommendation and make the report. The information from the client is not absolutely clear, and David can only suspect abuse. Disclosure to an outside source may impact the family and the client, who may decide to withdraw from counseling services. Typically, physical abuse of those with disabilities does not involve the counselor monitoring the abuse as carefully as is required with potential abuse of children. David believes in honest disclosure to his clients, and if he reported suspected abuse, he would share with his client that he had done so.

David has had frequent disagreements with his supervisor over honest disclosure to clients. His supervisor, Dennis, believes that sharing information that the client can handle is the criterion for disclosure. David likes working with this agency and he enjoys the clients with whom he works. He is concerned that his supervisor may use such conflicts to fire him from his position. Additionally, David believes he should be respectful of his supervisor and follow his recommendations.

DAVID: THE COUNSELOR'S PERSONAL VALUES, RACE, GENDER, AND PERSONAL HISTORY

David is twenty-five years old and lives in a medium-size city. He grew up on a reservation in eastern Oregon and his parents educated him about the traditions and customs of his ancestors. He spent his first eighteen years on the reservation and thus feels proud of his heritage.

Currently, David is single and lives in an apartment with a roommate. He continues to practice the traditions and customs of his heritage. He shows honor and respect to his parents and he returns to the reservation frequently to visit his family and provide service to the community. David attended a public university for his bachelor's and master's degrees. His master's degree is in mental health counseling. During his training, he completed an internship working with those who had a severe mental illness. Consequently, he decided to pursue employment working with this population. Additionally, he felt it necessary to work with Native Americans because of his own heritage and understanding of the population. He also felt a responsibility to his community to work with this population.

SARAH: THE CLIENT'S PERSONAL VALUES, RACE, GENDER, AND PERSONAL HISTORY

Sarah received the diagnosis of schizophrenia when she was twenty-two. She had been working as a clerical staff person in a dentist's office. She lives with her family, which includes her mother, father, and two younger siblings. Her family had moved off a reservation in eastern Oregon before she was born. The family still observes Native American traditions and customs, and they return to the reservation frequently to see relatives and participate in community activities.

Sarah was a below-average student in school, and upon graduation she started a clerical job. She moved from job to job and did not stay long in any position. She reports having difficulty getting along with co-workers. After her initial hospitalization with psychosis, she attempted to return to work but felt co-workers were talking about her so she quit her job again. The family was unhappy with Sarah's decision to leave her job because she was expected to contribute financially to the family.

DENNIS: THE SUPERVISOR'S PERSONAL VALUES, RACE, GENDER, AND PERSONAL HISTORY

Dennis is a forty-eight-year-old white male who is married without children. He grew up in a small family of four and has an older sister. Dennis lived a rather comfortable and protected childhood. He and his spouse were married after they graduated from college over twenty years ago. Dennis grew up in the midwestern part of the United States. He did not have much contact with Native Americans until he took a position in the agency where he now works. He started practicing as a counselor over fifteen years ago, and became a supervisor ten years ago.

He has become more aware of Native American culture the longer he lives in Oregon. Over the years, he has had several clients who were Native American and felt he got along well with them. The agency where he works is a mental health center that provides services to a wide range of clients and backgrounds. The primary ethnic and racial groups served include Native Americans, Asian Americans, and whites.

PROFESSIONAL CODES OF ETHICS

A number of ACA (2005) professional codes of ethics may apply to the ethical dilemma:*

A.1. Welfare of Those Served by Counselors
A.1.a. Primary Responsibility
The primary responsibility of counselors is to respect the dignity and to promote the welfare of clients.

C.2. Professional Competence
C.2.a. Boundaries of Competence
Counselors practice only within the boundaries of their competence, based on their education, training, supervised experience, state and national professional credentials, and appropriate professional experience. Counselors gain knowledge, personal awareness, sensitivity, and skills pertinent to working with a diverse client population.

D.1. Relationships With Colleagues, Employers, and Employees
D.1.b. Forming Relationships
Counselors work to develop and strengthen interdisciplinary relations with colleagues from other disciplines to best serve clients.
D.1.e. Establishing Professional and Ethical Obligations
Counselors who are members of interdisciplinary teams clarify professional and ethical obligations of the team as a whole and of its individual members. When a team decision raises ethical concerns, counselors first attempt to resolve the concern within the team. If they cannot reach resolution among team members, counselors pursue other avenues to address their concerns consistent with client well-being.

PROFESSIONAL KNOWLEDGE

David determined that several areas of professional knowledge were possibly relevant and should be considered in understanding his ethical dilemma: supervisor-supervisee relationship, supervisor competence, and physical abuse of those with disabilities.

Source: Reprinted with permission from the American Counseling Association, 2005, *ACA Code of Ethics,* Alexandria, VA.

First, David discovered that there have been attempts to understand supervisor-supervisee relationships based upon the working alliance (Borden, 1983), a concept also used to understand the client-counselor relationship (White & Queener, 2003). Berlin (1983) proposed that the working alliance consisted of three components: bonds, goals, and tasks. *Bonds* refers to emotional bonds and feelings of attachment. This component does not appear to be directly relevant to David's ethical dilemma. *Goals* concerns the supervisor and supervisee agreeing on goals, both those of clients and those of supervision. David and Dennis do not appear to share the same goals for the client. David wants to promote more client responsibility and ensure the safety of the client. Dennis appears to want to maintain confidentiality and protect client rights. *Tasks* refers to the activities of the supervision or the activities of working with clients, e.g., the interventions to reach the goals. David and Dennis also appear to disagree on tasks. David wants to contact an outside agency to assist in the protection of the client from abuse. Dennis wants to use agency or counselor resources to monitor any suspected abuse.

Next, David reviewed the professional literature addressing supervisor competence. Muratori (2001) suggested that the inability of the supervisor to perform certain supervisory functions and roles is indicative of supervisor impairment. She stated that these supervisory functions include functions addressed by the Association for Counselor Education and Supervision (Bernard & Goodyear, 1998):

(a) monitoring client welfare; (b) encouraging compliance with relevant legal, ethical, and professional standards for clinical practice; (c) monitoring clinical performance and professional development of supervisees; and (d) evaluating and certifying current performance and potential of supervisees for academic, screening, placement, employment, and credentialing purposes. (p. 306)

Function (b)—encouraging compliance with relevant legal, ethical, and professional standards—is potentially relevant and may be an example of the supervisor, Dennis, not performing adequately.

The third knowledge area that may apply is abuse of those with disabilities. There is a dearth of research about abuse of those with disabilities (Calderbank, 2000). Several authors suggested that abuse of those with disabilities is founded upon a power and control relationship (Hendey & Pascall, 1998). Furthermore, Hendey and Pascall suggested that issues of control and power are linked to personal caregiving for those with disabilities. They also found that women with disabilities are more vulnerable to abuse than men. An individual providing personal care for an adult with a disability usually does so in private, and therefore the community may not become aware of abuse as readily as it does with children who attend school.

GEOGRAPHIC REGION AND CULTURE

The mental health agency where David works is located in western Oregon, close to a large American Indian reservation. David was raised on a reservation in eastern Oregon. His client, Sarah, and her family lived on a reservation in eastern Oregon prior to her birth and still return to participate in tribal community activities. Several writers have noted the uniqueness of the American Indian reservation (Pandey, Zhan, & Collier-Tenison, 2004; Yurkovich, Clairmont, & Grandbois, 2002). Yurkovich et al. concluded that the mental health system is not well prepared to address the needs of American Indian groups.

David knows the American Indian culture intimately from growing up on a reservation. However, Pandey et al. (2004) observed that "American Indian communities differ in size, extent of geographic remoteness, economic opportunities, levels of welfare dependency, and structure of social services" (p. 94). In addition, Yurkovich et al. (2002) advised recognizing the importance of using caution in assuming an understanding of others based upon similarity, which may result in a cultural blind spot: believing that if a person is similar to you in appearance and behavior that there are few other differences.

LOCAL, STATE, AND FEDERAL LAWS

Oregon has a state law for the protection of people with disabilities who are abused, the Elderly Persons and Persons with Disabilities Abuse Protection Act—EPPDAPA (2003). As with child abuse, there are mandated reporters, professionals who are mandated to report abuse by law. A state worker will investigate a claim of abuse and can ask the court for a protection order on behalf of a victim. The EPPDAPA defines abuse as "conduct, within the last six months, that has caused physical injury. It can be physical injury inflicted on purpose or as a result of neglect, abandonment, or desertion of the victim when the abuser was supposed to be taking care of the victim in some way. Abuse also means the use of intimidating or harassing language threatening serious physical or emotional harm."

ETHICAL THEORY: NATIVE AMERICAN ETHICS

David and his client share similar backgrounds and values in Native American ethics, so this is one theory that potentially applies. Several concepts from Native American ethics potentially apply to this dilemma. These include respect for elders and respect for others, truthfulness, serving others, and taking responsibility for one's actions. The first dilemma, whether to break confidentiality and report suspected abuse, may involve being truthful. David values being truthful, and if he does not disclose the suspected abuse to the appropriate agency, then he may not be acting truthfully. Also, if he does decide to break confidentiality and report the suspected abuse, he feels he should also disclose such an action to the client, which would be a truthful act.

David also values taking responsibility for his actions. This means making a difficult decision such as breaking confidentiality and reporting suspected abuse. Breaking confidentiality may result in the client not continuing counseling, and David must decide whether he wants to take this risk.

David also agrees with Native American ethics and the concept of serving others. Will he be serving others if he breaks confidentiality and reports the suspected abuse? Will he be serving his agency by breaking confidentiality, which may result in the Native American community not using this service in the future?

Showing respect for elders and others is another concept that possibly applies. David's supervisor, Dennis, disagrees with him about reporting suspected abuse in the case of Sarah. Should David ignore his value of respect for others by reporting suspected abuse, despite his belief that he should respect his elders, i.e., his supervisor?

QUESTIONS FOR DISCUSSION

1. Are there any circumstances that warrant ignoring a supervisor's recommendations?

2. What is the impact of having a counselor and client from the same racial background on ethical decision-making?

3. Do you think the supervisor behaved ethically based upon a hermeneutic model?

Chapter 24

Shi-Jiuan

*Conflict Between Laws
and Client Worldviews*

Shi-Jiuan is a thirty-three-year-old female who emigrated from Hong Kong to the United States three years ago. She is Chinese. She is married and her spouse, also Chinese, holds a graduate degree in electrical engineering and works in a large corporation in New York City. The couple has two children: a twelve-year-old daughter and a younger son who is nine. Shi-Jiuan was diagnosed with depression and been coming to counseling for the past two months. She initially reported fatigue, memory loss, irritability, and sleep disturbances. Zoloft was prescribed for her and she has been on this medication for two months. She states the medication has helped and she feels less fatigue and irritability.

Another complaint, along with her depression, was that she missed her homeland, Hong Kong, and that she was having difficulty with her children in maintaining cultural values—i.e., Confucian values, such as respect for one's elders—and retaining many of their Chinese views and traditions. Shi-Jiuan was the oldest of three children and she grew up in a traditional Chinese family. She and her husband, who grew up in a similar environment, were socialized into traditional Confucian values and beliefs, including respect for elders, loyalty to family, and respect for social order. The family valued education and attempted to instill the importance of education in their children.

Shi-Jiuan has seen the same counselor for the past two months on a biweekly basis to monitor her medication and provide counseling. The counselor, Joan, is a white, middle-aged, forty-two-year-old mother of one. Counselor and client have developed a good relationship despite the initial hesitance Shi-Jiuan expressed about seeing a counselor. She felt it was a sign of weakness to see a counselor and to discuss personal feelings outside the family. She stated she felt ashamed that she had to receive such help, but acknowledged counseling was helpful to her. Shi-Jiuan described her marital relationship as that of a woman in a traditional Chinese family, with the male dominant and her primary role as caretaker of the children.

After two months of counseling, Shi-Jiuan presented a new issue in the counseling session. She was discussing her frustrations about some of the behaviors of her children, particularly the older, her daughter. Her daughter has shown some disrespect and talked back to her. Shi-Jiuan stated that she had slapped her daughter on the face when the daughter talked back. Joan, the counselor, listened to Shi-Jiuan's account of the face-slapping incidents and asked her about the response of her daughter to this type of discipline. Shi-Jiuan stated that the daughter became more compliant after the slapping. Shi-Jiuan recalled how she saw her brother slapped for being disrespectful when she was growing up and how she learned to become more respectful of elders. Joan notes that she is a mandated reporter of child abuse and decides she must review the situation carefully to make an important decision at this juncture in counseling.

The relevant elements of the horizon based upon the case of Shi-Jiuan include the ethical dilemma; the counselor and her values, race, gender, personal history, etc.; the client and her values, race, gender, personal history, etc.; the supervisor and his values, race, gender, personal history, etc.; agency policies; local, state, and federal laws that apply; professional codes of ethics; professional knowledge; geographic region; and ethical theories.

THE ETHICAL DILEMMA

Joan must decide what course of action to take: Should she continue working with Shi-Jiuan and attempt to address her parenting actions, or should she submit a report of child abuse to the New York Office of Children & Family Services? As a counselor, Joan is a mandated reporter according to New York state law (New York Office of Children & Family Services, 2002). Joan has worked with many Asian clients and families previously and knows that an authoritarian parenting style is typical and that corporal punishment is used on a frequent basis. Joan believes she has developed a good but still tentative relationship with Shi-Jiuan. The counselor is concerned that if she reports the abuse, even though it is anonymous, Shi-Jiuan will deduce who filed the report because she probably has not talked about slapping her daughter to anyone else, and she may withdraw from treatment. If the client withdraws from treatment, she may stop taking her medication; in addition,

Joan would lose an opportunity to work with her around her parenting skills. Alternatively, how severe is the physical abuse and what damage has it done to the twelve-year-old adolescent? Last, Joan is a mandated reporter, and failure to report child abuse is a Class A misdemeanor and subject to criminal penalties. Joan knows her supervisor, Greg, has very strong feelings about reporting child abuse because he worked for the Office of Children & Family Services prior to coming to the counseling agency.

JOAN: THE COUNSELOR'S PERSONAL VALUES, RACE, GENDER, AND PERSONAL HISTORY

Joan grew up in a middle-class family where discipline was person-centered and resulted in no physical punishment. She was the oldest of three children and she did not see any of her siblings receive any corporal punishment. Joan used verbal praise, feedback, removal of problem stimuli, and time-outs to educate her son, now eighteen, as to expected prosocial behaviors, and never used physical punishment. Her spouse shared her view of child rearing. She received her graduate training from a public university and took a course on behavioral theories that addressed parent training and behavioral principles.

SHI-JIUAN: THE CLIENT'S PERSONAL VALUES, RACE, GENDER, AND PERSONAL HISTORY

Shi-Jiuan is the younger of two children; she had an older brother growing up. Her mother and father worked hard and provided a comfortable living environment for her and her brother. Her parents expected their children to follow Confucian practices such as showing respect and obedience. Shi-Jiuan remembers seeing her brother being slapped for talking back to his mother. She always listened to her parents and she was never slapped, but she knew it would happen if she was disrespectful. She married when she was nineteen, while her spouse was attending college. After graduating from engineering school, her spouse began working in Hong Kong. Shortly after, she became pregnant and she had their first child, a daughter. Shi-Jiuan and her husband were disappointed that the child was not a boy, but she provided good care for the child. Her husband became involved in his work, and, as a traditional Chinese mother, she cared for the child. Three years later they had a son.

Then three years ago her husband's company acquired a major project in New York, so he took a position there and the family moved there. Shi-Jiuan has never been employed outside the home; instead, she has cared for the children. At first, her children did not want to come to New York, but since the move they have done relatively well in school. Shi-Jiuan gets out of the house through shopping and parties with her husband's company. She is ambivalent about living in the United States and hopes to return to Hong Kong in the future. She misses the traditions and cultural opportunities in Hong Kong.

GREG: THE SUPERVISOR'S PERSONAL VALUES, RACE, GENDER, AND PERSONAL HISTORY

Greg, Joan's supervisor, is a forty-two-year-old African American. He worked for five years for the New York Office of Children & Family Services before coming to the mental health facility six years ago. He is married without children. He was educated during his master's program as a counselor and shares the professional codes of ethics that Joan follows. His parents at times disciplined him using corporal punishment when he was growing up.

PROFESSIONAL CODES OF ETHICS

A review of the ACA professional codes finds that several professional codes potentially apply to this situation:*

A.1. Welfare of Those Served by Counselors
A.1.a. Primary Responsibility
The primary responsibility of counselors is to respect the dignity and to promote the welfare of clients.

A.2. Informed Consent in the Counseling Relationship
A.2.a. Informed Consent
Clients have the freedom to choose whether to enter into or remain in a counseling relationship and need adequate information about the counseling process and the counselor. Counselors have an obligation to review in writing and verbally with clients the rights and responsibilities of both the counselor and the client. Informed consent is an ongoing part of the counseling process, and

---

Source: Reprinted with permission from the American Counseling Association, 2005, *ACA Code of Ethics,* Alexandria, VA.

counselors appropriately document discussions of informed consent throughout the counseling relationship.

B.1. Respecting Client Rights

B.1.d. Explanation of Limitations

At initiation and throughout the counseling process, counselors inform clients of the limitations of confidentiality and seek to identify foreseeable situations in which confidentiality must be breached.

B.2. Exceptions

B.2.a. Danger and Legal Requirements

The general requirement that counselors keep information confidential does not apply when disclosure is required to protect clients or identified others from serious and foreseeable harm or when legal requirements demand that confidential information must be revealed. Counselors consult with other professionals when in doubt as to the validity of an exception. Additional considerations apply when addressing end-of-life issues.

C.2. Professional Competence

C.2.a. Boundaries of Competence

Counselors practice only within the boundaries of their competence, based on their education, training, supervised experience, state and national professional credentials, and appropriate professional experience. Counselors gain knowledge, personal awareness, sensitivity, and skills pertinent to working with a diverse client population.

The goal of all counseling is to promote the welfare of the client (A.1.a). It is important for the counselor to be aware of how her own values about corporal punishment differ from her client's beliefs and how her own views may impact her counseling decisions (A.2.a). In the case presented here, the counselor must consider informing the client of the limitations of confidentiality specifically relating to disclosure to a protection agency, such as the New York Office of Children & Family Services. Second, if the counselor decides to file a report of suspected child abuse, she must inform the client of this decision, even though the New York Office of Children & Family Services has an option for submitting a report anonymously (A.2.a and B.2.a). Clients come into counseling with the expectation that the information shared will be kept in the strictest confidence. Such confidentiality allows a client to self-disclose without fear of retribution or judgment by the other hearing the situation (B.1.d). According to this code, the counselor needs to consider breaking confidentiality based upon an evaluation of the potential for danger to the child(ren) and the extent to which the law applies: Does the evidence suggest child abuse in this case (B.2.a)?

PROFESSIONAL KNOWLEDGE

A review of the professional research literature reveals that there is considerable research into the efficacy and effects of corporal punishment (Andero & Steward, 2002; Baumrind, Larzelere, & Cowan, 2002; Deater-Deckard, Lansford, & Dodge, 2003; Gershoff, 2002; Schenck, Lyman, & Bodin, 2000). Andero and Steward stated that the use of corporal punishment is one of the "most controversial parental practices" (p. 90). Straus and Donnelly (1993) defined corporal punishment as "spanking and/or slapping as the use of physical force with the intention of causing a child to experience pain but not injury, for purpose of correction or control of the child's behavior" (p. 420).

Straus (1991) noted that an estimate of the use of corporal punishment in the United States is approximately ninety percent among parents of younger children, ages three to four, and the use of corporal punishment in older children and adolescents is around thirty percent. Researchers found that the use of corporal punishment has varied outcomes (Andero & Steward, 2002; Baumrind et al., 2002; Giles-Sims, Straus, & Sugarman, 1995; Simons, Johnson, & Conger, 1994). Simons et al. investigated whether corporal punishment predicted specified negative adolescent outcomes. They found no detrimental impact on adolescent aggressiveness, delinquency, or psychological well-being. However, Straus and Yodanis (1996) found that adults who had experienced corporal punishment in adolescence had an increased likelihood of approving of spousal violence.

A review of Chinese parenting practices shows that such parents have been found to be more authoritarian than American parents (Leung, Lau, & Lam, 1998), suggesting that the use of corporal punishment is a fairly common cultural parental practice among Chinese families. Rao, McHale, and Pearson (2003) pointed out that "it is considered a mother's duty to bring up her children well" (p. 478). Chao (1994) further proposed that the authoritarian approach in Chinese populations does not affect academic achievement as it does in American children (Dornbusch, Ritter, Leiderman, Roberts, & Fraleigh, 1987). Ho (1986) concluded that "Chinese parents place great emphasis on obedience, proper conduct, moral training, and the acceptance of social obligations" (p. 61). Fontes (2002) noted that common corporal punishment tactics in Asian families included slapping the face and pulling the hair.

GEOGRAPHIC REGION AND CULTURE

Different regions have different interpretations of laws affecting the reporting of child abuse, particularly physical abuse. For example, Mississippi defines physical abuse as "any type of contact that results in bodily harm such as bruising, abrasions, breaking bones, internal injuries, burning, missing teeth, and skeletal injuries" (Mississippi Code, 1972). Flynn (1993) discovered that those living in the southern United States had more positive attitudes toward corporal punishment than other regions of the country, and that those living in the Northeast had the least favorable attitude toward corporal punishment. Giles-Sims et al. (1995) surmised that those living in rural areas are more likely to approve of corporal punishment, a finding that is potentially related to lower levels of education among this group. Cheng Lai, Zhang, and Wang (2000) found that Chinese parents from Hong Kong and those from Beijing differed in disciplinary styles despite sharing common values, i.e., Confucianism. They found that mothers of children in Hong Kong dominated their children more than those from Beijing.

LOCAL, STATE, AND FEDERAL LAWS

State laws that potentially apply to this case involve New York state laws and regulations governing mandated reporters of child abuse. Those who are identified as mandated reporters of child abuse include mental health professionals, substance-abuse counselors, psychologists, and alcoholism counselors. The guidelines state, "Mandated reporters are required to report suspected child abuse or maltreatment or cause a report to be made when, in their professional roles, they are presented with reasonable cause to suspect child abuse or maltreatment" (New York Office of Children & Family Services, 2002, p. 3). Further, abuse "encompasses the most serious harms committed against children. An abused child is one whose parent or other person legally responsible for his or her care inflicts serious physical injury or commits a sex offense against the child" (p. 4). Additional important information found in state law concerns penalties for failure to report child abuse. The mandated reporters' guide states,

Anyone who is mandated to report suspected child abuse or maltreatment, and fails to do so, could be charged with a Class A misdemeanor and subject to criminal penalties. Furthermore, mandated reporters can be sued in civil court for monetary damages for any harm caused by the mandated reporter's failure to make a report. (p. 10)

ETHICAL THEORY: CONFUCIAN ETHICS

Since Shi-Jiuan is Chinese and holds Confucian values, Joan decides to use Confucian ethics as one of the theories to consider in her ethical decision-making (see Chapter 8). The concepts and ethics that potentially apply to this ethical issue include Li, Ren, reciprocity, sincerity, and the ability to know right from wrong. Li concerns following standards of acceptable social behavior. The acceptable behavior in the ethical dilemma is, for the counselor, following the law, i.e., the mandated reporter law in New York. Ren also potentially applies and concerns the ideal relationship between human beings. In this case it may be interpreted to include benevolence toward the client and the client's children. Two ways to manifest Ren are through reciprocity (shu) and sincerity (zhong). Reciprocity is expressed through the silver rule, i.e., do not do unto others what you would not want others to do unto you. Thus, the counselor must decide whether she would want someone to submit a child abuse report against her under the circumstances.

The concept of sincerity is relevant because the counselor may need to decide, if she reports child abuse, whether to inform the client or to make the report anonymously. The ability to know right from wrong is relevant in this ethical dilemma because interpretation of the state laws is important. What constitutes child abuse is an integral part of the ethical decision.

QUESTIONS FOR DISCUSSION

1. Based upon the fusion of horizons, what is the best ethical decision in this case?

2. Should Joan attempt to change her client's child-rearing practices to use less corporal punishment?

3. What role and importance should client culture have in ethical decision-making? For example, if a state, federal, or local law conflicts with the practices of a particular culture, should the counselor defer to the cultural values and ethics?

Chapter 25

Melissa

Minors' Rights and Confidentiality

Melissa is a seventeen-year-old Taiwanese female who is a junior in high school. She lives with her mother and father in a medium-size city in the northwestern United States. Also, she has an older brother who is a college student and lives away from home. She is a good student and is active in student government and sports in her high school. She is planning to attend college and she expresses aspirations of becoming a veterinarian.

Melissa visited her school counselor and asked to talk about concerns she had for several peers who were having difficulty with some other girls. Donna, a twenty-eight-year-old white female, is the school counselor, and she noted that Melissa was pleasant and sensitive. Donna has spoken to Melissa on other occasions about her career aspirations, so the counselor feels she has a positive relationship with this student. At a second meeting, Melissa spoke about her friends and how they were getting along with another group. Then she asked Donna about how an adolescent can go about getting an abortion. This was quite a change in the conversation and Donna asked Melissa who was looking for an abortion. At first, Melissa stated it was a friend, but after a few minutes she confirmed it was herself and she began to cry. Melissa stated she was two months pregnant and did not want to tell her parents. She decided it would be best to get an abortion.

Donna thought it would be a good idea to meet with Melissa and spend time discussing this decision. She explained that an adolescent can receive an abortion without the consent of her parents in the state in which they live, but Donna wanted to discuss with Melissa whether she should include her parents in the decision. Donna wondered whether she should contact Melissa's parents and share this information with them. This was an important decision, and Donna thought that she herself would want to know this about her daughter if she were the parent of such a child. Also, Donna was Catholic and did not believe in abortion. Donna knew that the primary decision she had to make was whether to contact the parents, because her school had a policy of informing parents when issues arose with their children.

The elements of the horizon in this case potentially include the ethical dilemma; the counselor and her values, race, gender, personal history, etc.; the client and her values, race, gender, personal history, etc.; the supervisor and his values, race, gender, personal history, etc.; institutional policies; local, state, and federal laws that apply; professional codes of ethics; professional knowledge; geographic region; and ethical theories.

THE ETHICAL DILEMMA

After the meeting where Melissa shared her secret about being pregnant, Donna set up another meeting a few days later. Donna had an opportunity to review the hermeneutic model of ethical decision-making and come prepared to address the issue. Donna defined the ethical dilemma in terms of maintaining confidentiality with an adolescent. Furthermore, she noted that parental rights were an issue here. What do parents have a right to know about their child? Do parents have a right to know that their child is pregnant and is seeking an abortion? Taiwanese culture is collectivistic and family oriented. Expectations are that children represent the family honorably.

Also, a critical value in the school in which Donna works is open communication and sharing information with parents. However, the school has not had a situation where the adolescent chose to seek an abortion without parental consent, so this is a new dilemma for the counselor and the school.

A secondary ethical issue is the personal values of the counselor that conflict with the primary choice of the client, i.e., seeking an abortion. Donna is Catholic and she strongly believes abortion is morally wrong. Can Donna provide counseling that is objective and free of her personal values?

DONNA: THE COUNSELOR'S PERSONAL VALUES, RACE, GENDER, AND PERSONAL HISTORY

Donna is single and lives with her roommate in an apartment in a small town in Oregon. The school where she is employed as a counselor is in the community in which she lives. She grew up in a small town not too far from where she now resides. Her parents were supportive and caring of her and her brother, who is two years younger. She received her undergraduate degree in psychology at a small private Catholic college and her master's degree in school counseling from a state university. She took a course in ethics and uses the hermeneutic model of ethical decision-making in her practice.

She has been employed as a school counselor for the past four years. She likes the school and the students. Her colleagues are pleasant and share feedback openly. The administration is supportive of the school counseling program and recognizes the importance of good counseling services.

Donna was raised as a Catholic and attended both a Catholic high school and a Catholic undergraduate institution. She holds strong beliefs in her faith and she describes herself as living her religion. She does not believe in abortion and is pro-life.

MELISSA: THE CLIENT'S PERSONAL VALUES, RACE, GENDER, AND PERSONAL HISTORY

Melissa is a B-plus student and she is active in student government. She also participates in various sports in her high school. She attends church regularly and is planning to attend college. Melissa began dating when she was fifteen and over the past year has been dating a senior at her high school. He is planning on furthering his education and was recently accepted into a prestigious private college.

Melissa reportedly gets along well with her parents. Her mother, in particular, has encouraged her to excel in school and pursue a college degree. She knows her parents would not agree to an abortion. She also knows they would be very upset if they knew that she had gotten pregnant. Melissa believes that her pregnancy would not only disappoint her parents but also prevent her from attending college.

DAVID: THE SUPERVISOR'S PERSONAL VALUES, RACE, GENDER, AND PERSONAL HISTORY

David, Donna's supervisor, is the director of guidance at the school. He is a forty-eight-year-old white male. He has been employed in the school for over twenty years, and he has fostered relationships between parents and the school that he feels are effective. He supports his counselors in sharing information with parents if the students in question are at risk of serious harm. He is pro-choice and believes that women should be able to decide for themselves whether to have an abortion. He grew up in the 1970s when the Supreme Court decision to legalize abortion was hotly debated.

PROFESSIONAL CODES OF ETHICS

Donna completed a review of the ASCA professional codes and she found that several professional codes potentially applied to this situation. These included some of the following codes:*

A.1. Responsibilities to Students
The professional school counselor:

a. Has a primary obligation to the student, who is to be treated with respect as a unique individual.

b. Is concerned with the educational, academic, career, personal and social needs and encourages the maximum development of every student.

c. Respects the student's values and beliefs and does not impose the counselor's personal values.

A.2. Confidentiality
The professional school counselor:

a. Keeps information confidential unless disclosure is required to prevent clear and imminent danger to the student or others or when legal requirements demand that confidential information be revealed. Counselors will consult with appropriate professionals when in doubt as to the validity of an exception.

PROFESSIONAL KNOWLEDGE

Donna reviewed the professional literature addressing an adolescent's right to confidentiality in obtaining an abortion. She also reviewed research on the impact on an adolescent of obtaining an abortion versus that of carrying a pregnancy to term. She found that approximately 350,000 girls under the age of eighteen become pregnant each year, and thirty-one percent of those have abortions (ACLU, 2001). Additionally, sixty-one percent of pregnant adolescents who choose abortion decide to discuss the decision with their parents, while thirty-nine percent decide not to discuss the issue with their parents, instead pursuing an abortion without parental consent (ACLU).

Source: ASCA, 2004. Reprinted with permission.

There has been considerable research and writing on the issue of adolescents having the right to choose to obtain an abortion without informing their parents (Gardner, Scherer, & Tester, 1989; Griffin-Carlson & Schwanenflugel, 1998; Gruber & Anderson, 1990; Melton, 1990; Worthington et al., 1989). For example, Worthington et al. (1989) discussed adolescents' ability to make competent decisions about choosing an abortion. They suggested that, in general, based upon psychological research, adolescents show less ability in making competent decisions than do adults. However, there appears to be an association with age; younger adolescents do not make as good decisions as older adolescents, i.e., those younger than fifteen make worse decisions than those sixteen and over (Liebowitz, Eisen, & Chow, 1984). Other researchers have found no difference in adolescent versus adult decision-making as to whether to obtain an abortion (Blum & Resnick, 1982). However, Gardner et al. (1989) suggested that not enough is known about adolescent decision-making to conclude whether adolescents are competent or not to make a decision such as whether to pursue an abortion.

The American Academy of Pediatrics (AAP, 1996) noted that minors have a right to obtain an abortion without parental consent despite state laws that require parental consent. The U.S. Supreme Court has concluded that states must provide for judicial bypass if state laws require parental consent to obtain an abortion. Judicial bypass allows adolescents to petition courts to request an abortion without parental consent. The decision is made based upon an assessment of the adolescent's capacity to make an informed decision.

Donna also reviewed the professional literature on adolescent pregnancy and abortion. Wang, Wang, and Hsu (2003) noted that the pregnancy rate among adolescents in Taiwan is lower than in the United States, but it is still considered an issue. The United States has the highest adolescent pregnancy rate among developed countries (Griffin-Carlson & Schwanenflugel, 1998). Melissa grew up in the United States and is likely influenced by both cultures.

Stone (1990) concluded that pro-choice advocates believe that choosing an abortion is the least costly and safest choice in an unwanted pregnancy. Adler, Ozer, and Tschann (2003) further stated that "abortion itself carries relatively few medical risks, especially compared with the risks of childbearing" (p. 212). Additionally, researchers have found few negative psychological problems associated with adolescents choosing abortion (Zabin, Hirsch, & Emerson, 1989). Other researchers have found a significant impact on adolescents who become parents (Milan et al., 2004). Jaffee (2002) summarized many of the negative outcomes for teenage mothers and stated, "Compared with women who delay childbearing, they have lower incomes, less education, and more children. Women who first give birth as teens experience increased welfare dependency, higher unemployment, higher rates of depression, more marital instability" (p. 38). Research seems to support a negative association between adolescents becoming mothers and future successful adult functioning.

GEOGRAPHIC REGION AND CULTURE

Twenty states have parental consent laws for minors seeking an abortion, while sixteen require parental notification, that is, an adolescent can choose to have an abortion, but parents must be informed (Americans United for Life, 2003). Melissa lives in a northwestern state, Oregon, which does not have state parental involvement laws for minors seeking an abortion. If she lived in another state that had such a law, her options would be more restricted, and she may have had to obtain a court bypass to receive an abortion without informing her parents. Melissa lives in a medium-size city, and because of this, even if the state did have a parental involvement law, her confidentiality would more than likely be maintained. However, if she lived in a smaller town and attempted to petition for a court bypass, she might have lost her privacy, since many of those working in the court would know her and her family.

LOCAL, STATE, AND FEDERAL LAWS

Parent involvement laws typically restrict adolescent access to abortion and require permission from one or both parents. However, the U.S. Supreme Court requires that there must be a process for not involving the parents in cases where states have parental involvement laws, and this is accomplished through judicial bypass of parental involvement (Adler et al., 2003). So, if an adolescent decides not to include her parents in deciding to seek an abortion, she must petition the court to bypass parental involvement. The court must decide whether the adolescent is competent to make the decision. The court's decision is not whether the adolescent should have the abortion, but whether she is competent to make the decision by herself without parental involvement. Finally, the U.S. Court of Appeals affirmed that adolescents have a right to obtain an abortion without parental consent, even in states that require it, if no means of bypassing this requirement (e.g., a court bypass) is available (*Blackard v. Memphis,* 2001).

ETHICAL THEORY: TAOIST ETHICS

Melissa is Taiwanese, and so Donna decided to review and use Taoism as one ethical theory she wanted to apply to the situation (see Chapter 9). She found that three major concepts potentially applied to this ethical dilemma: Tao, yin and yang, and wu wei. Donna knew that Tao is defined as a way or a path that is true and desirable to follow. The Way or Tao must be experienced to understand it. So Donna believed that the action or way to pursue would become clear through her interaction with Melissa. This would involve carefully listening to Melissa and respecting her perspective. Additionally, Donna would need to place the decision in the context of the school and the school environment and rules.

Donna recalled from her ethics course that yin and yang refer to the interaction of two opposites. These opposites include the yin, which is the receptive and weaker aspect of the union and may be considered negative and destructive; and the yang, which has been referred to as strong, positive, and constructive. In this dilemma, Melissa may be considered as the yin and the weaker partner of the union when coming together (because she is an adolescent) and Donna may be considered as the yang, the stronger partner of the union. Donna noted that the ideal relationship is a balance between the yin and the yang, not too much strength or dominance and not too little. To act ethically based upon Taoism, Donna will want to be aware of the balance in the relationship; for example, how assertive or dominant should she become in encouraging or acting in informing the parents?

Wu wei is another concept that may apply. Donna recalled it referred to non-action and involved following nature and being natural, spontaneous, and harmonious with nature. The dilemma for Donna is discovering what is natural or spontaneous in this situation. Nonaction may be interpreted in this situation as not letting the adolescent decide naturally whether to contact the parents. Additionally, the question becomes: How much information or influence does Donna exert on Melissa if she follows wu wei?

What other ethical theories may be relevant to this case?

QUESTIONS FOR DISCUSSION

1. Were there any important components of the horizons presented that were not addressed and should have been?

2. Should Donna inform the parents if Melissa decides against including them in the decision to obtain an abortion?

3. What is the best ethical decision based upon a hermeneutic model?

4. Would the decision be different if Melissa lived in a state where obtaining parental consent is required?

Chapter 26

Raj

*Counselor Competence and
Minor Informed Consent*

Raj, a severely depressed seventeen-year-old adolescent male from India, checks in at a college counseling center and is immediately assigned to see a white female counselor, Vicki. Raj has been in the United States for a short time and is experiencing new academic and personal adjustment challenges. He shares an apartment with one other student and has frequent contact with a sponsoring Indian family living in the vicinity.

Raj, a first-year engineering student at a prestigious technical university, was referred for counseling by one of his professors. Raj is not sleeping well, has lost weight, and seems unmotivated in class. To account for his considerable weight loss, Raj explains that he does not find the traditional American diet appetizing. He denies suicidal ideation. Raj knows that there are expectations for high academic achievement from his family and professors, and he is very concerned that if his parents are informed of his difficulties, they will be disappointed in him or blame him for his problems.

After the first meeting, the counselor, Vicki, felt that, in addition to counseling, Raj would benefit from medication and should be referred for psychiatric care. She discussed the case with a psychiatric consultant, who agreed to evaluate Raj for medication. Following her consultation with the psychiatrist, Vicki suggested to Raj the need for an evaluation for medication, and she reassured Raj that he had sufficient medical insurance through his college medical plan to cover psychiatric treatment. But Raj refused, stating that he would rely on his Hindu religious beliefs.

Vicki shared her counseling efforts and strategies with her supervisor, Dr. Smith, during a supervision session. He listened to her description of the case and decided to use a hermeneutic ethical decision-making approach to help Vicki understand the case and determine the course of counseling.

The relevant elements of the horizon based upon the case of Raj include the ethical dilemma; the client's, counselor's, and supervisor's respective values, race, gender, and personal history; counseling agency policies; local, state, and federal laws that apply; professional knowledge; geographic region; professional ethical codes; and relevant ethical theories.

THE ETHICAL DILEMMA

Rather than using medication, Raj prefers to seek spiritual guidance through a Hindu temple to achieve inner peace. Vicki's initial reaction was that this was superstitious behavior, and she began encouraging Raj to consider being evaluated for medication during subsequent counseling sessions. Raj agreed to continue in counseling but not to pursue medication. Moreover, he did not want his parents notified by the counselor because he is concerned that a call will alarm his parents about his mental health. Raj further explains that he felt guilty about having the opportunity to study in the United States while his parents and siblings remain in India. In seeking counseling, he already sees himself as disappointing his family. Vicki is concerned that if she informs his parents about Raj seeking mental health counseling, he will drop out. She questions whether it would be best not to contact Raj's parents as he requested. Vicki believes she is knowledgeable about the use of psychiatric medication and she does not believe in the effectiveness of spirituality in treating depression.

Dr. Smith questions whether Vicki should seek informed consent from Raj's parents. Raj is considered a minor in the United States, and states require parental consent for medical and psychological treatment. Second, Dr. Smith questions Vicki's competence in aggressively pursuing the use of medication and in understanding the use of alternative treatments such as the use of spirituality.

VICKI: THE COUNSELOR'S PERSONAL VALUES, RACE, GENDER, AND PERSONAL HISTORY

Vicki attended a traditional mental health counseling graduate program in the midwestern United States. Although she interned in clinics that served diverse populations, she had no experience with recent immigrants. Now Vicki occasionally has international students in her caseload at the college counseling center where she has worked for the past five years. She presumes that Raj is experiencing culture shock and misses his family; however, she is very concerned about his reports of eating and sleeping disturbances.

Vicki recalled her own difficult adjustment when she first left home to attend college. The first semester, she was in danger of failing all of her courses as she tried to cope with overwhelming depression. At that time, Vicki visited the college counseling center to obtain antidepressant medication and engage in counseling, which helped her immensely. She perceives her own past college experience as comparable to Raj's, and she feels that the same treatment is a reasonable plan for him.

Vicki's recommendations come from a Western medical model and she is skeptical of the spiritual healing proposed by Raj. She is also concerned that Raj may use spirituality as a way to bypass or avoid dealing with unresolved emotional or personal issues (Cashwell, Myers, & Shurts, 2004).

RAJ: THE CLIENT'S PERSONAL VALUES, RACE, GENDER, AND PERSONAL HISTORY

Raj is the eldest of six children and he knows his parents are having difficulty supporting their large family. Raj has always excelled in school, particularly in math and science, and was granted a full scholarship to study engineering in the United States. He now has a more affluent lifestyle than his family in India, with the promise of even greater financial success when he obtains his degree. Indian firstborn sons are often sent abroad for education, and Indian immigrants to the United States are often regarded as exceptional (Sharma, 2000). This may place additional stress on Raj to be successful academically. Beyond acculturative stress (stress related to entering a new and unfamiliar culture), Raj has expressed during his counseling sessions feelings of guilt over leaving behind family members in India.

The fact that Raj came to see a counselor is a big step for him. In Raj's native India, psychology is devalued because there is a cultural belief that psychological problems are the result of one's own making (Sharma, 2000). His family is Hindu and would recommend a spiritual counselor or guru to improve mental health. Raj shared with Vicki a personal ethical perspective for the liberation of the soul that is stressed in the Bhagavad Gita (van Buitenen, 1985):

Let a man lift himself up by his own self; let him not depress himself; for he himself is his friend and he himself is his enemy. . . . The self is the friend of the self for him who has conquered himself by the self, but to the unconquered self, this self stands in the position of an enemy like the (external) foe. (6.5–6)

This quotation from the classical religious text of India suggests that individuals should look inward and not to others for help with problems. This outlook has been influential in Raj's life and may explain his reluctance to seek professional help or to inform his family about his personal adjustment problems.

Raj has a sponsoring family who met him at the airport upon arrival in the United States. This sponsoring family is originally from Madras, a city in southern India close to Raj's parents' community. They are U.S.–educated physicians who have welcomed Raj to their home and who serve as U.S. "culture brokers" to ease his adjustment to the new environment. The sponsoring family is invested in Raj's personal welfare and academic development and has offered to help him in whatever way they can.

DR. SMITH: THE SUPERVISOR'S PERSONAL VALUES, RACE, GENDER, AND PERSONAL HISTORY

Dr. Smith is the director the College Counseling Center. His work is primarily administrative and he is responsible for the financial management of the center. Recently, the center was sued by a student for incompetent treatment, and the malpractice lawsuit was settled out of court.

At present, Dr. Smith does not see clients. Because of the recent lawsuit against one of his staff members, he has started to closely supervise the work of the counseling staff. The counselors are often frustrated with him because his supervision sessions always emphasize legal liability and how to protect the center in case of another lawsuit. Many counselors see him as overly legalistic, putting the welfare of the counseling center above that of the clients.

PROFESSIONAL CODES OF ETHICS

Dr. Smith discussed with Vicki several professional codes of ethics from the ASCA that potentially apply to this case.*

A.1. Responsibilities to Students
The professional school counselor:

a. Has a primary obligation to the student, who is to be treated with respect as a unique individual.

Source: ASCA, 2004. Reprinted with permission.

b. Is concerned with the educational, academic, career, personal and social needs and encourages the maximum development of every student.

c. Respects the student's values and beliefs and does not impose the counselor's personal values.

d. Is knowledgeable of laws, regulations and policies relating to students and strives to protect and inform students regarding their rights.

A.2. Confidentiality

The professional school counselor:

a. Informs students of the purposes, goals, techniques and rules of procedure under which they may receive counseling at or before the time when the counseling relationship is entered. Disclosure notice includes the limits of confidentiality such as the possible necessity for consulting with other professionals, privileged communication, and legal or authoritative restraints. The meaning and limits of confidentiality are defined in developmentally appropriate terms to students.

b. Keeps information confidential unless disclosure is required to prevent clear and imminent danger to the student or others or when legal requirements demand that confidential information be revealed. Counselors will consult with appropriate professionals when in doubt as to the validity of an exception.

c. Recognizes his/her primary obligation for confidentiality is to the student but balances that obligation with an understanding of the legal and inherent rights of parents/guardians to be the guiding voice in their children's lives.

PROFESSIONAL KNOWLEDGE

Dr. Smith requested that Vicki investigate three important areas relevant to the dilemmas in the professional literature: counselor competence, spirituality and counseling, and confidentiality and informed consent with minors. Vicki first reviewed relevant literature on counselor competence, both on multicultural competence and on expertise in areas beyond one's training. She found that Constantine (2002) defined multicultural competence as "the awareness, knowledge, and skills that mental health professionals display in the context of working with culturally diverse individuals" (p. 255). Researchers have found a significant relationship between client satisfaction and differences in race and ethnicity between counselor and client (Constantine).

Sue, Arredondo, and McDavis (1992) identified three dimensions of multicultural competence: counselor awareness and biases of multicultural groups, an understanding of the worldviews of multicultural groups, and the ability to develop appropriate intervention strategies. Dr. Smith asked Vicki to review her competence in these three dimensions, including her ability to understand and choose appropriate interventions. In the dilemma in this case, does Vicki understand how spirituality can be used in counseling and is she able to use it?

Vicki next reviewed the professional literature on spirituality and counseling. She discovered that the link between spirituality and counseling is an increasingly frequent topic in the professional literature (Chappelle, 2000; Hathaway, Scott, & Garvey, 2004; Wig, 1999). Hathaway et al. concluded that "the spiritual and religious domain is significantly associated with many facets of adaptive functioning" (p. 98). She also noted that researchers have found that there are lower levels of religiousness among counselors than in the general population, suggesting that counselors may not be aware of the importance of spirituality in clients' lives. Vicki further discovered through her literature review that Hinduism is not exactly equivalent to religion in other perspectives like Christianity. It is a combination of spirituality and philosophy. Additionally, Hinduism is focused on pursuing truth through experience and self-exploration. Wig noted that many mental health professionals in other countries use spirituality in the treatment of mental health problems. Eriksen, Marston, and Korte (2002) concluded that "counselors can certainly do harm if they fail to grasp the significance of the client's organizing system" (p. 49), i.e., if they fail to understand the client's spirituality or religion. There is some evidence of the curative and restorative mental health benefits provided by spiritual healers and healing temples in India (Raguram, Venkateswaran, Ramakrishna, & Weiss, 2002) as well as a growing interest in the connections between spirituality and mental health in the United States (APA, 2003b). It has been argued that the use of spirituality and religion can be an effective intervention because it provides a clear moral frame, helps to construct meaning, conveys a sense of purpose, and offers optimism and emotional support (Dull & Skokan, 1995; George, Larson, Koenig, & McCullough, 2000; Maton & Wells, 1995).

The issue of confidentiality is another ethical dilemma, and researchers have found that this is one of the more frequently cited issues in therapy (Pope & Vetter, 1992). Goesling, Potts, and Handelsman (2000) noted the importance of maintaining confidentiality in promoting a trusting therapeutic relationship. Confidentiality is defined as regulating disclosure of information based upon professional rules and ethics. Watkins (1989) defined *relative confidentiality* as maintaining confidentiality and privacy of information disclosed in a therapy session, but with breach of confidentiality under certain conditions. An example of a condition allowing for breach of confidentiality is a clinical judgment of danger to a client or another, where disclosure would decrease the likelihood of injury or risk, e.g., the intended victim is warned. Another condition under which confidentiality can be breached is through a client releasing the information through informed consent.

Kuther (2003) pointed out the complexity of obtaining informed consent and releasing confidentiality with minors. Most states in the United States require parental consent to release information. The philosophy is that minors cannot make informed decisions and thus are not considered competent. Kuther noted a few exceptions in which minors *are* given the right to make informed consent; they include an emancipated minor, special situations where minors are pursuing certain types of treatment such as an abortion, and mature minors. Kuther defined emancipated minors as "those who live independently of their parents" (p. 345). States define emancipated minors differently and use criteria such as marriage, parenthood, financial independence, etc. Vicki noted that Raj may meet the criterion for being an emancipated minor, specifically the category of financial independence, since he receives scholarships for his education and living expenses.

GEOGRAPHIC REGION AND CULTURE

For sixteen years of his life, Raj lived in a rural area in southern India; he is now attending college in a large city in the United States. The community surrounding the university is composed of many different racial and ethnic groups representing a range of countries, including many immigrants. Raj's sponsoring family is Hindu and provides a supportive respite for Raj as he negotiates a new culture. This is a common practice among Indian families; it is used to bridge the geographic distances and cultural differences that Indians feel in the United States. Raj's parents have talked with the sponsoring family by phone and are comfortable with the arrangement.

LOCAL, STATE, AND FEDERAL LAWS

Because Raj may be considered a minor in the state in which he resides, the consent of a parent or guardian is necessary for treatment unless he is considered an emancipated minor. One criterion for being an emancipated minor is financial independence and Raj receives considerable scholarship funding that may qualify him. In most states, the legal age is eighteen years, which is the universal voting age under the Twenty-Sixth Amendment to the U.S. Constitution, ratified in 1971. Legal age is the age at which an individual is legally permitted to enter into contracts without adult consent.

ETHICAL THEORY: HINDU ETHICS

Since the client is Hindu, Dr. Smith and Vicki thought this ethical theory should be considered in making an ethical decision. There are several Hindu concepts that Dr. Smith and Vicki thought may apply to the dilemmas in this case, which included deciding whether to break confidentiality and determining whether the counselor was competent. The concepts that possibly apply are dharma, ahimsa, and karma (see Chapter 10). *Dharma* concerns virtue and duty or fulfillment of roles. Specifically, dharma involves virtues such as truthfulness. Vicki needs to decide what she will do in regard to breaking confidentiality. Should she break confidentiality and obtain informed consent from the parents? If she does so, will she be truthful and inform Raj of her intended actions? Dharma also concerns fulfilling one's role. In this case it refers to Vicki performing her role as a counselor and doing it competently.

Ahimsa refers to noninjury or not causing harm. Vicki may consider whether her actions may cause harm to Raj. If she continues to promote the use of medication and Raj agrees to an evaluation, will this harm him? A second question is whether Vicki's lack of knowledge of alternative treatments, such as the use of spirituality, will harm Raj. Her use in counseling of only traditional counseling methods, and not combining these with alternative treatment, may potentially harm Raj.

The third concept that potentially applies is *karma,* which refers to creating established patterns. For example, if Vicki persuades Raj to try medication, will this result in him pursuing the use of medication with future mental health problems, and is this bad for him? Also, if Vicki discourages the use of spirituality by Raj, does this have a negative effect on future situations where he might use spirituality to cope with problems?

QUESTIONS FOR DISCUSSION

1. How should the confidentiality issue be handled?

2. How can a minor's confidentiality be safeguarded, while at the same time respecting the parents' right to know?

3. Are there ways to enlist the sponsor family to support Raj without breaking his confidences?

4. Can the medical and spiritual healing models be reconciled?

5. What is the best ethical decision based upon a hermeneutic model?

Chapter 27

Smith Family

Assisted Suicide

Alan Smith's parents had met at a military installation in Japan after World War II. His father, John Smith, was an American naval officer from a small affluent community outside Boston; his Japanese mother, Kyoko, was fluent in English and the secretary for one of the high-ranking naval officers. John and Kyoko had met at the military base, and several months after they met they married and moved to the United States. Fortunately, John was able to be stationed in the Boston area close to his own parents. The couple adjusted to their community, and Kyoko's charm and fluency in English, as well as her knowledge of Western culture, made it possible for her to be easily accepted by John's family, friends, and colleagues. Within the next six years they had three children: two boys, Alan and Ted, and a girl, Jessica. From the onset of their life in the United States, Kyoko maintained many of her Japanese traditions, and for her the most important was her continued and faithful following of Buddhism. Alan, the oldest son, had been close to his mother and he integrated his mother's beliefs in Buddhism into his life. He had also integrated his mother's beliefs in Buddhism and Japanese tradition into his own ways of adapting to United States culture. Ted and Jessica, while devoted to their mother, were more aligned with their father's ways of behavior and more similar to him in their appearance.

The next forty years for the couple and their children were filled with both happiness and some disappointments, but were without crisis. Then, when Kyoko was close to becoming sixty-four years old, she was diagnosed with a virulent and terminal cancer. John was devastated and could not accept the possibility of his wife's death. Alan, Ted, and Jessica were also distraught. Alan found that he was the most sympathetic to his mother's suffering, while Ted and Jessica were focused on their father's emotional state in response to his wife's illness. What complicated the family's crisis was that Kyoko was experiencing intense pain. All of the family members found her pervasive suffering unbearable to watch. When John was with Kyoko, he would sob uncontrollably and would frequently leave her bedside to vomit. He also had continuous throbbing headaches whether he was with her or not. Ted was impatient with his father's behavior and felt that a "navy man" should hold up better than his father was. He also seemed indifferent to his mother's suffering, and was often unavailable when other family members tried to contact and inform him of his mother's prognosis. Jessica conveyed understanding of her father's response to her mother's critical illness. She often visited him, cooked for him, and was available to comfort him. Alan was the one family member who could accept his mother's suffering. He spent as much time as he could with her. From talking with her while he was at her bedside, he learned that his mother wanted to end her life. She felt that she could bear her own suffering, but she did not want her husband, John, to experience such intense pain from watching her suffer.

Kyoko asked Alan if he would adjust her morphine drip, given to her to relieve her pain, so that the amount she received would kill her. Alan understood and was sympathetic to his mother's request, but he felt that he could not follow her wishes without the consent of his father and siblings. He told his father, his brother, and his sister what his mother had asked him to do. John was adamant about keeping his wife alive and not accepting her wish for death. His opinion was that she was delusional with pain, but as she responded to treatment her attitude would change. Ted was noncommittal and finally said that whatever his mother wanted would be all right with him. Jessica made it known that she would support her father's decision because his well-being was important to the entire family. Alan was alone in firmly supporting his mother's wish. He conveyed his mother's position that her wish and subsequent death were consistent with her Buddhist beliefs and Japanese tradition. Soon the family's discrepant positions made communication among the family members intolerable. The hospital social worker suggested that the family seek counseling to improve their communication and their ability to cope with Kyoko's illness. They took the advice of the hospital social worker and began counseling with Theresa.

This case demonstrates the complexity of decision-making when a counselor is faced with many different perspectives, in this case the dissimilar perspectives of family members. Identified elements of the horizon are the ethical dilemma; the values, race, gender, personal history, and any other relevant information about the counselor, the client, and the supervisor; institutional policies; applicable local, state, and federal laws; professional codes of ethics; professional knowledge; geographic region; and relevant ethical theory, in this case Buddhism.

THE ETHICAL DILEMMA

When Alan told his father, brother, and sister of his mother's request to die, the dilemma for the family members seemed irreconcilable. The choices they had were both indefensible: Either they were going to condone and assist in the death of Kyoko, or they were going to continue to experience her suffering, and their own, by approving and continuing with the medical care she was currently receiving. At the first session, they presented their choices to Theresa, their counselor. In listening to the family's situation, she experienced both personal and professional dilemmas, which began with the question of whether she could condone self-imposed death. Her personal dilemma was whether she would facilitate a behavior—assisted suicide—that was contrary to her earliest instruction about the value of life, or would accept assisted suicide as a behavior to enhance human autonomy and the free choice of this family. The mother had requested that her eldest son increase her medication with the intent of ending her life and pain. Such a method of assisted suicide is not legal. What would Theresa do, knowing this was an option the family was considering?

THERESA: THE COUNSELOR'S PERSONAL VALUES, RACE, GENDER, AND PERSONAL HISTORY

Theresa's parents were both from South America and had come to the United States as graduate students. Her parents decided to settle permanently in the United States after completing their education, and soon began to have a family. Theresa was the youngest of her parent's four daughters. She was raised as Catholic; however, Theresa's Catholic faith as a child and adolescent was not fully formed, and her beliefs were based on rules she learned in her religious education classes. She entered college, a Catholic university, and completed both her bachelor's degree and master's degree. Her master's degree was in counseling.

Kyoko's wish to die was in direct conflict with Theresa's beliefs. Theresa's mother passed away several years ago after a long illness. The Smith family did not handle Kyoko's illness in the same way that Theresa's family handled her mother's illness. Theresa's father was completely aware and supportive of her mother's strong Catholic belief, which was to fight for her life as long as she could.

THE SMITH FAMILY: THE CLIENTS' PERSONAL VALUES, RACE, GENDER, AND PERSONAL HISTORY

Theresa realized as she gathered information about the Smith family members that the complexity of their situation stemmed from the fact that every member of the family had a different perspective about the meaning and approach of death. John, who was raised in New England and who was from a well-established Protestant New England family, was not completely attuned to the significance of Buddhism in Kyoko's life. Even though John had met Kyoko in Japan, he experienced her as an American rather than as Japanese. Jessica, the couple's only daughter, was a caring and empathic person. Alan, the eldest son, had adopted his mother's beliefs in Buddhism. For Kyoko and Alan, Buddhism was practiced from a culturally Japanese perspective. Of most importance to Japanese Buddhists is that the manner of dying at the moment of death is very important. This belief comes from Buddha's teachings that declared the crucial variable governing karma and rebirths was the nature of the consciousness at the moment of death. Thus, Buddhists consider that the most important behavior at the moment of death is to hold proper and wholesome thoughts, if possible with the encouragement of those with you at the time of death (Becker, 1990, as cited in Shanahan & Wang, 1996). For Kyoko, death was not the end of anything, but a personal right to determine when she should move on from this existence to the next. Her consideration was not whether her body lived or died, but whether her mind could remain at peace and in harmony with itself (Becker). Alan, in hopes that his mother would attain nirvana, supported Kyoko's beliefs. He saw himself as someone who could help his mother to achieve calm and peace with her own death.

THOMAS: THE SUPERVISOR'S PERSONAL VALUES, RACE, GENDER, AND PERSONAL HISTORY

Because the Smith family was in constant contact with members of the medical profession, Theresa sought the supervision of a psychiatrist whose specialty was in working with terminally ill patients. Thomas, a psychiatrist, was also very knowledgeable about oncology and terminal illnesses and brought to the supervision his medical expertise. Thomas was a man close to sixty years old. He had experienced the death of both his parents as well as one of his siblings. When his brother died in his mid-thirties of cancer, and this was followed by his father's death from a heart attack, and then his mother's death from cancer several years later, he realized that no one escapes death. Because of his experiences with hospice care when his mother and brother were dying, he was aware of the importance of dying with dignity. In his work with terminally ill patients, he made a point of conveying to them their right as competent patients to refuse consent to any medical treatment (Hospice, n.d.). He encouraged them to use the services of hospice, whose basic principle is "to affirm that the intention of good palliative care for dying patients is to relieve their physical, emotional, social and spiritual suffering in the context of respect for their individuality and without intent to shorten life" (Hospice, n.d.).

PROFESSIONAL CODES OF ETHICS

Theresa found that the AAMFT Code of Ethical Principles for Marriage and Family Therapy (American Association of Marriage and Family Therapy, 2001) provided guidelines for her treatment of the Smith family. Committed to her work with families, Theresa understood the importance of her ethical responsibility to her clients: "Marriage and family therapists provide professional assistance to persons without discrimination on the basis of race, age, ethnicity, socioeconomic status, disability, gender, health status, religion, national origin, or sexual orientation" (AAMFT Code: 1.1). Since the Smith family presented a conflict of values for her, she knew that she needed to seek appropriate professional assistance for conflicts that could impair her work performance or clinical judgment (AAMFT Code: 3.3). There are other codes that possibly apply.

PROFESSIONAL KNOWLEDGE

Theresa was aware that she needed to be more knowledgeable about two issues in particular. First, she realized that she needed to be more culturally competent. Her challenge would be to have enough knowledge about the Buddhist's perspective of assisted suicide so she could discern her own values, taken from natural law, from Buddhism and its moral framework. Second, Theresa wanted to know more about the accepted policies about cancer care.

Theresa discovered that modern interpretations of the Buddhist position were not in agreement. These disparate positions she found in Keown's (1995) comprehensive discussion about Buddhism and bioethics. Keown critiqued three points of view, which he considered to be a reasonable sample of the range of views found in the literature about assisted suicide and Buddhism. Kapleau suggested that Buddhism would reject the practice of euthanasia:

> Buddhism holds that because death is not the end, suffering does not cease
> thereupon, but continues until the karma that created the suffering has played

itself out; thus it is pointless to kill oneself—or aid another to do so—in order to escape. (Kapleau, 1989, as quoted in Keown, 1995, p. 135)

Kapleau concluded that assisted suicide is wrong from his conclusion that it is futile to attempt to evade one's karma.

Lesco (1986, as quoted in Keown, 1995), writing from a Tibetan Buddhist perspective, suggested, "The objections to assisted suicide would be on two grounds, that of karma and the mode of death" (p. 55). In regard to karma, as Lesco explained, "In Buddhism, a terminal illness is not considered a chance event. . . . A terminal illness represents the repayment of a karmic debt" (p. 55). Keown's interpretation of Lesco's explanation was that, since an illness is due to the maturation of karma, it is undesirable to try to prevent it from taking its course (p. 177). If the illness were prevented from taking its course in this life, it would only have to be faced again at another point. However, this interpretation of karmic debt does not exclude the relief of pain:

This non-interference with karma, however, does not exclude the compassionate intervention of relief of physical pain with analgesics . . . or to soothe mental distress with sympathetic listening and counsel. For the terminally ill, Buddhism advocates hospice care, not euthanasia. (Lesco, 1986, as quoted in Keown, 1995, p. 55)

Lesco's second argument does not directly address the argument against euthanasia but focuses on how the terminally ill patient should be treated and cared for:

Buddhists would strongly disagree with this ideal of the comatose death. The act of dying and the dying process are felt to be a vital link between this and subsequent existences. The state of consciousness and the level of mindfulness are of crucial importance. (Lesco, 1986, as quoted in Keown, 1995, p. 55)

Keown (1995) concluded that Lesco's arguments were in harmony with Buddhist values because neither of his main points led to the conclusion that assisted suicide is immoral; rather, the Buddhist concern with death is treated in the context of life. For Keown there were two implications: One was that life should not be preserved as an end in itself at the cost of losing perspective on its overall meaning and purpose. The other was that we should approach death in a clear and mindful state rather than in a drugged and comatose condition.

Whereas Kapleau and Lesco considered Buddhism to be opposed to the practice of euthanasia, for van Loon (1978, as cited in Keown, 1995), the important concept for argument is the criterion of "volition death," which determines whether a life any longer has human value. A summation of van Loon's position follows:

> Whether a patient is conscious or unconscious, and expressly requests assisted suicide or not, . . . the general rule should be applied that where a disease . . . induces in a patient either volitionless, unconscious vegetative existence or an overwhelming awareness of distress, pain and suffering to the exclusion of almost any other sensation or conscious activity, then such a patient should be eased into as "natural" a death as possible. (van Loon, 1978, as quoted in Keown, 1995, p. 184)

Keown found van Loon's position problematic. One argument for Keown was that Buddhism does not distinguish mental and bodily lives. "To lose the capacity for volition is to lose an ability, not to lose one's life" (Keown, 1995, p. 184). Keown also concluded that van Loon's definition of death can only apply to human beings. Since animals lack the capacity to reflect and intuit, there would be two definitions of death. However, Buddhism requires a definition of death that applies to all karmic life. Keown concluded that van Loon's arguments in favor of assisted suicide were not consistent with traditional Buddhist views of life, death, and karmic lives.

Theresa also searched for information about care of cancer patients in their last phase of life, and found the recommendations approved in 1998 by the American Society of Clinical Oncology (ASCO) to be helpful. Although ASCO acknowledged that there is a great need for research on the problems of care at the end of life, there have been two areas that have received attention: pain management and advanced care directives (ASCO, 1998). Of interest to Theresa in her reading of ASCO literature was their identification of the importance of spirituality in the process of dying and also the importance of the existential meaning of life. Another area addressed by ASCO was the importance of recognizing the impact of a patient's death on family members. ASCO's research has shown that a patient's death and dying process can have serious adverse effects on family members, which can lead to increased rates of illness and even death. Currently, there is almost no information about the predictors for adverse outcomes of family members, nor is there information about which caregivers and family members of terminally ill patients are most susceptible to illness and death (ASCO). The most difficult conclusion was that researchers and clinicians do not know which interventions and at what times would be most effective in reducing adverse outcomes for family members of the terminally ill patient.

GEOGRAPHIC REGION AND CULTURE

Although federal legislation would affect any decision and action Theresa would take in her work with the Smith family, she reviewed the history of legislation regarding the practice of assisted suicide in Massachusetts, the state where she was a practicing counselor. No legislation regarding assisted suicide had been introduced to the state senate or house, and no cases regarding assisted suicide had been brought to the Massachusetts courts. However, Massachusetts, with its abolition of the death penalty in 1984, held true to the belief that a civilized people will not tolerate the state putting a human being to death (*Commonwealth v. Colon-Cruz,* 1984). Theresa surmised that if there is a parallel between the death penalty and euthanasia, the attitude of citizens in the Commonwealth of Massachusetts would probably not support assisted suicide or any right-to-die legislation.

LOCAL, STATE, AND FEDERAL LAWS

The Nightingale Alliance (2004) has a comprehensive discussion on its Web site of the legal and ethical issues of assisted suicide as they have evolved in the history of the United States. Citizens in the United States did not begin to support assisted suicide until the 1970s. Until this time, primarily because of policies promoted and carried out by Nazi Germany that brought death to 275,000 men, women, and children with mental illness, mental retardation, epilepsy, multiple sclerosis, and other afflictions, assisted suicide was a dormant issue.

In the 1970s, the states of Wisconsin and Montana introduced bills to their respective state legislatures for the "right to die." Neither of these bills received legislative action; it was thought that society was not ready for such extreme measures. In the late 1980s, groups advocating euthanasia, such as the Hemlock Society, openly advocated assisted suicide and attempted to place a referendum question on the ballot to allow active assisted suicide in the state of California. The effort failed because not enough signatures were obtained.

During the 1990s, actions promoting assisted suicide were more successful. A pivotal action occurred in the state of Oregon, where a measure amending Oregon's living-will law to allow an individual to request from a physician drugs to commit suicide passed by a margin of fifty-one percent to forty-nine percent.

The state of Oregon became the first governmental body in the United States to legalize physician-assisted suicide. The measure was battled in courts, but in 1997 it was finally able to go into effect.

In order to implement this measure, the then-director of Oregon's Medicaid program expressed the expectation that Medicaid funds would likely be used to fund assisted suicide. In response to this proposed policy, the U.S. Congress passed the Assisted Suicide Funding Restriction Act in 1997 to prevent such a scenario, and to focus instead on promoting projects to care for the elderly and the terminally ill. In 1998, the Oregon Health Division issued its first official report that sixteen Oregonians had died of overdoses from a legal federally regulated drug. However, in 1997 the Drug Enforcement Administration (DEA) had begun to claim that assisted suicide could not be considered a legitimate medical purpose, and thus it would be impermissible for Oregon physicians to use federal registrations to prescribe lethal overdoses of federally regulated drugs. To respond to the DEA restrictions, then Attorney General Janet Reno in 1998 allowed the use of federally regulated drugs to assist suicide, but only in states that had legalized the practice, and only in accordance with the state's assisted suicide law.

To clarify the issue of assisted suicide, the Pain Relief Promotion Act was introduced the U.S. Congress in 1999 to protect aggressive pain management while prohibiting the use of controlled substances for the purpose of carrying out assisted suicide and euthanasia. It passed in the U.S. House of Representative and the Senate Judiciary Committee, but there was not a vote in the Senate. This controversy continues, with the most recent ruling occurring in 2002 when a federal judge in Oregon struck down a directive by U.S. Attorney General John Ashcroft that it was not legal to use drugs controlled by federal law to assist suicide or carry out euthanasia. The federal government has appealed this decision. To date there is no ruling on this matter (Nightingale Alliance, 2004).

An important issue in this case is that Kyoko requested that a family member assist her in her suicide; the family member's action could be interpreted as murder. For example, in Oregon there is a systematic process and not just a decision between two or more individuals. Such an act by a family member may be considered a homicide in most states.

ETHICAL THEORY: BUDDHIST ETHICS

Because of Kyoko's strong belief in Buddhism, Theresa decided to use Buddhism as the ethical theory to apply in this case (see Chapter 11). The major concepts that potentially apply include suffering, impermanence, and no-self. The family is experiencing considerable suffering and Buddhism interprets this to be a fact of life. In an effort to live with and understand suffering and impermanence, one reviews and attempts to understand the Four Noble Truths: (1) the truth of humanity, with misery and suffering a part of humanity; (2) the truth from recognizing what gives rise to suffering and from knowing that suffering originates within us from the craving for pleasure; (3) the truth that this craving can be eliminated; and (4) the truth that elimination is the result of a methodical way or path to be followed. All four truths possibly apply. The family is suffering by seeing the pain Kyoko is experiencing and the possibility of a future loss of Kyoko through death. Theresa understands that the family is suffering because of craving for the mother to be well. Elimination of craving may be achieved by understanding impermanence and accepting it as part of life. Finding the middle way and balance may result in elimination of craving.

From the Buddhist perspective, the right individual intention combined with appropriate karmic effects can develop into good mental attitudes. Theresa believed this possibly applied to Kyoko's wish to die with a good mental attitude. Other concepts that Theresa thought applied were the liberating process toward purification and some of the concepts of the Noble Eightfold Path. The concepts that potentially applied included right understanding, right thought, and right action. Right understanding may be applied so that Theresa can fully understand the suffering that Kyoko and her family are experiencing and the source of the suffering, i.e., expecting permanency and immortality in physical life. Right thought may apply so that Theresa makes an ethical decision that is unselfish and compassionate. Right action addresses certain precepts such as avoiding taking life, even suicide. This may be a key consideration in coming to an ethical decision in this case.

QUESTIONS FOR DISCUSSION

1. Are there any other aspects of this case that would conflict with your own values?

2. What Buddhist teaching and concept might be consistent with your own values?

3. What specific Buddhist teaching or concept would you rely upon in working with the Smith family?

4. What is the best ethical decision based upon a hermeneutic model?

Chapter 28

Christine

Appropriate Termination

Christine, who is non-Jewish, is engaged to marry a young Jewish man, Jeremy, whom she met in college. Her future in-laws, Orthodox Jews, are opposed to the marriage and have voiced their disapproval of the "outmarriage." Christine, an English Protestant, does not intend to convert to Judaism. She is offended by Jeremy's parents' rejection simply because of her religious preference and ethnicity. Christine promised her future in-laws that she will follow Jewish holiday traditions in raising her children. Jeremy, who does not practice his religion and leans toward the more liberal reform or reconstructionist positions of Judaism, feels that his family will adjust eventually and that they should just keep moving ahead with their marriage plans. Christine, troubled by her future in-laws' rejection, wonders about its effect on her forthcoming marriage and is reconsidering her plan to marry Jeremy. A friend recommended that she seek counseling to assist her in resolving this issue.

Christine sought counseling through a private practice. She requested to see a Jewish counselor because she felt that he or she will have a thorough understanding of the outmarriage (interfaith or mixed marriage) issue and would be able to advise her about dealing with her future in-laws.

Steve was assigned her case; prior to the session, the insurance clerk for the private counseling center informed Steve that his client, Christine, had coverage for ten counseling sessions. As Steve listened to Christine recount her problems and vent her anger toward her potential future in-laws, he realized that he has a strong reaction to her. Although he did not state it, Steve agreed with Jeremy's parents in disapproving marriages between non-Jews and Jews. Steve tried to contain his strong emotional reaction to Christine's anger toward Jeremy's parents and Jews in general because of the restrictions about intermarriage. As Christine told her story, he thought she would have a difficult time accepting Judaism. He found himself siding with Jeremy's parents and believed that his goal was to convince her to end the engagement.

Steve shared his goal with his supervisor, Marvin, who cautioned him against imposing his own values on the client. When Marvin asked how sessions with Christine were going, Steve simply stated that the client was still defensive.

Steve met with Christine weekly and attempted to explore her understanding of Jewish beliefs and traditions. He continually challenged her lack of understanding of Jeremy's religion and background. Christine ignored these challenges and presented arguments in favor of marriage because she and Jeremy love each other and get along well. Steve became convinced that Christine should not marry Jeremy and he was increasingly frustrated that she appeared to show no insight into the reason why. At the tenth session, Steve decided to be more blunt and told Christine that, in his opinion, she should not marry Jeremy. He explained that after ten counseling sessions, she still did not seem to understand what it means to engage in a religious intermarriage. Christine told Steve that she thought he was wrong about her understanding of intermarriage, but she did not realize that he was opposed to her marriage to Jeremy. Christine wanted to continue counseling but could not pay the fees. Steve did not believe she would benefit from any further counseling, so she was informed that he could not see her since her insurance coverage had been used up. He informed her that she might try a community mental health center where she would be charged based upon her ability to pay. Christine was not pleased when she left the session. She felt the counselor had not really helped her with her problem but had depleted her insurance coverage.

Christine was angry that she received little or no help from Steve and felt he was prejudiced in his views of religious intermarriage. She also was upset that counseling ended without giving her specific information on where to go for further treatment. She contacted the state licensure board and filed a complaint. Her complaint accused Steve of prejudice and not providing an appropriate referral to another agency for counseling.

Potential elements of the horizon include the ethical dilemma; the counselor's values, race, gender, personal history, etc.; the client's values, race, gender, personal history, etc.; the supervisor's values, race, gender, personal history, etc.; counseling agency policies; local, state, and federal laws that apply; professional knowledge; geographic region; professional codes; and ethical theories.

THE ETHICAL DILEMMA

The state licensure board received Christine's complaint and assigned an investigator to determine its legitimacy. The investigator determined that the complaint met requirements on the grounds of failure to adhere to acceptable standards of practice.

The board investigator interviewed Christine, Steve, and his supervisor, Marvin. The investigator found that Steve reacted strongly to Christine's anger toward her future in-laws. Steve stated to the investigator that Christine displayed little understanding of Judaism and pursuing marriage would be wrong in his personal opinion. Steve acknowledged he attempted to influence Christine to end her engagement. He also acknowledged that he was relieved that her insurance coverage was expended and he would not have to meet with her again. Steve finally acknowledged that he did not make a referral to another counseling agency because he did not believe she could benefit from counseling. Based upon the investigator's findings, the licensure board decided there was enough evidence for a complaint of failure to adhere to acceptable standards of practice. Steve potentially demonstrated bias and insensitivity to client diversity and did not provide appropriate referral to another counselor. The licensure board decided to hold an informal conference with Steve to have him further explain his actions in this case. A subcommittee of board members was formed to review the case. This subcommittee would decide on whether sanctions were appropriate or whether Steve should go before the full committee for a formal review.

STEVE: THE COUNSELOR'S PERSONAL VALUES, RACE, GENDER, AND PERSONAL HISTORY

Steve is a twenty-four-year-old Jewish male and both of his parents are Jewish. He has two siblings, a brother and sister. He grew up as an observant, Orthodox Jew and understands the in-laws' concern about outmarriage involving the potential loss of Jewish identity of the children (Fishman, 2004). Steve knows that Christine's future in-laws' concern goes beyond accepting Judaism and celebrating holidays, to questions about accepting the concept of Jewishness as an ethnicity or national destiny. His sister married a non-Jew and after three years of marriage obtained a divorce because of numerous conflicts, some related to following Jewish traditions.

Steve, a graduate of a mental health counseling program that offered numerous opportunities to work in diverse and minority communities, has not had experience dealing with the diversity conflicts and questions within his own Jewish cultural group. He received his master's degree four years ago and he became a licensed counselor two years ago.

CHRISTINE: THE CLIENT'S PERSONAL VALUES, RACE, GENDER, AND PERSONAL HISTORY

Christine is a twenty-five-year-old white female who was raised in a Methodist religious tradition. Her large family is tolerant of diversity and there are three interfaith marriages among Christine's five siblings, primarily between Protestants and Catholics. The family members are primarily members of the working class. Christine was the first in her family to attend college. Her parents are pleased that she met Jeremy, who appears to care for their daughter. Christine has known Jeremy for almost three years and they have been engaged for six months. Christine's family welcomes Jeremy and does not have concerns about his Jewish background. Christine met Jeremy's parents over two years ago and at first they were pleasant with her until it became apparent that she and their son were becoming more serious about their relationship. Since their engagement, Jeremy's parents are distant and unsupportive of their future marriage.

Christine does not understand Jewish law or the concern of Jeremy's parents that their grandchildren would not be considered Jewish. She feels personally offended and rejected by her future in-laws, and she is also uncomfortable with Jeremy's siblings and ostracized by his extended family. She feels that Jeremy's family will seek to undermine her marital relationship by continuing to find fault with her and rejecting her children.

MARVIN: THE SUPERVISOR'S PERSONAL VALUES, RACE, GENDER, AND PERSONAL HISTORY

Marvin, the supervisor, is a forty-year-old Jewish male. He received his master's degree in social work and he has worked in the field for over fifteen years. He has been a supervisor for the past five years. Marvin maintains a Reform Jewish position with more liberal views on outmarriage than the Orthodox position. There are several interfaith marriages among his immediate family members and they have easily incorporated diverse customs in their lives while still adhering to Jewish religious traditions.

Marvin agrees with Steve that his values may interfere with his ability to work with Christine. He suggests to Steve that they devote a certain portion of their supervision session to address his work with Christine.

PROFESSIONAL CODES OF ETHICS

The licensure board decided to use the ACA codes of ethics in their review of this case. They noted that several professional ethical codes possibly apply to this dilemma and they include*

A.1. Welfare of Those Served by Counselors
A.1.a. Primary Responsibility
The primary responsibility of counselors is to respect the dignity and to promote the welfare of clients.

A.4. Avoiding Harm and Imposing Values
A.4.b. Personal Values
Counselors are aware of their own values, attitudes, beliefs, and behaviors and avoid imposing values that are inconsistent with counseling goals. Counselors respect the diversity of clients, trainees, and research participants.

A.11. Termination and Referral
A.11.a. Abandonment Prohibited
Counselors do not abandon or neglect clients in counseling. Counselors assist in making appropriate arrangements for the continuation of treatment, when necessary, during interruptions such as vacations, illness, and following termination.

A.11.c. Appropriate Termination
Counselors terminate a counseling relationship when it becomes reasonably apparent that a client no longer needs assistance, is not likely to benefit, or is being harmed by continued counseling. Counselors may terminate counseling when in jeopardy of harm by a client, or another person with whom the client has a relationship, or when clients do not pay fees as agreed upon. Counselors provide pretermination counseling and recommend other service providers when necessary.

PROFESSIONAL KNOWLEDGE

The licensure board committee determined that there are several areas from the professional literature that are possibly relevant with this case: the impact of

---

Source: Reprinted with permission from the American Counseling Association, 2005, *ACA Code of Ethics,* Alexandria, VA.

religious intermarriage, prejudice based upon religion, and counseling termination. The review found that there is a higher rate of divorce for religious intermarriages than for marriages between individuals of the same religion (Ho & Johnson, 1990; Sussman & Alexander, 1999). Researchers also have found that *religious homogamy* is related to marital satisfaction (Chintz & Brown, 2001; Heaton & Pratt, 1990). Chintz and Brown define religious homogamy as "similar attitudes and beliefs about specific religious practices" (p. 723). They propose that problems arise not when there is a marriage between specific religions, e.g., Judaism or Catholicism, but when there is disagreement on practices of faith. So, one interpretation for this case is that the assumption Steve had about a negative outcome for Christine's marriage to Jeremy is not necessarily accurate. If, as Christine indicated, she is open to discovering agreement on the observance and practices of Judaism in her marital relationship and in her family, then there may not be the problems Steve has assumed.

There has been consistent research linking religion and prejudice (Duck & Hunsberger, 2000; Hunsberger, 1995). An explanation for prejudice based upon religious affiliation is founded on social identity theory (Tajfel & Turner, 1986), which suggests that when one identifies with a particular group, one reports a more positive attitude toward members of the group. Jackson and Hunsberger (1999) stated, "Affiliation and identification with a religious group could lead one to prefer the religious ingroup over the outgroup" (p. 511). Furthermore, because Jews have always been a small subset of the larger society in which they live, outmarriage threatens group identity (Miller & Lovinger, 2000; Rabinowitz, 2000).

Steve reported concern that intermarriage between a Jew and non-Jew creates significant problems for the couple and likely will result in divorce. Also, he had a strong visceral reaction to Christine marrying a Jew that went beyond simple cognitive understanding. He acknowledged that he does not support intermarriage. The question here is whether Steve is being realistic with his conclusions or prejudiced against those not from his religious group.

Termination of the relationship between counselor and client is another area of the professional literature that is relevant to this case (Hunsley, 1999; Hunsley, Aubry, Verstervelt, & Vito, 1999; Pearson, 1998; Wachtel, 2002). The termination of therapy or counseling has been described as a loss, and consequently models of mourning and grieving have been used (Kubler-Ross, 1969) to assess the effects of termination. Termination also has been described as a critical phase or stage of counseling (Kramer, 1990).

Termination appears to be a complex and significant part of the counseling process and not necessarily well understood. Researchers have identified several types of client reactions to termination, such as sadness, feelings of abandonment and rejection, and anger (Gillman, 1991; Kramer, 1990). Additionally, researchers have found that counselors and clients do not agree on the reasons for termination (Hunsley et al.,1999). Pearson (1998) proposed strategies for effectively and sensitively terminating counseling. For example, a review of the client's progress can be helpful. Suggested questions to help with such a review include (1) How disruptive is the timing of termination to the client's current work in counseling? and (2) What would be Steve's answer to this question in his counseling and rather abrupt termination with Christine?

GEOGRAPHIC REGION AND CULTURE

Christine and Jeremy live in a large city in Virginia. The counseling center is located in this community. Jeremy's family resides in the midwestern United States in a predominantly Jewish neighborhood in the suburbs of a large city. They maintain close ties with family members in Israel. Christine's family resides in an eastern state with a liberal reputation. Her great-grandparents emigrated from England.

LOCAL, STATE, AND FEDERAL LAWS

In the United States, there is a long history of intolerance toward *interracial* marriage. An aptly named case, *Loving v. Commonwealth of Virginia*, was invalidated by the U.S. Supreme Court only fairly recently, in 1967. When the Supreme Court ruled antimiscegenation laws unconstitutional, Virginia and fifteen other states had to erase those statutes from their books (Kennedy, 2002). However, there have been no legal prohibitions to *interfaith* marriages. The issue of outmarriage is a concern that stems from Jewish law. Jewish law considers only someone born of a Jewish mother, or a convert, Jewish, although Reform and Reconstructionist Jews do include those born of Jewish fathers and gentile mothers if the children are raised to follow the Jewish religion.

ETHICAL THEORY: JEWISH ETHICS

Christine, the client, is planning to marry a Jewish man. The client came to counseling focusing on the issue of a non-Jew marrying a Jew. There a several concepts from Judaism that possibly apply to this case (see Chapter 12), and they include social action, honesty and truthfulness, beneficence, nonmaleficence, and the ethic of responsibility. Recall that social action is defined as a commitment to repair the world. Steve was engaged in providing counseling to help Christine. His attempts at help concerned advising against an intermarriage. His efforts may be consistent with Judaic ethics in this situation.

Honesty and truthfulness are other concepts in Judaic ethics. Steve initially attempted to subtly challenge Christine's belief that she could accommodate Jewish practices and traditions. At the last counseling session, he gave Christine his honest reaction and feedback about her impending marriage to Jeremy. He informed her that he was concerned about her decision to marry Jeremy and that such marriages frequently end in divorce based upon his experience. The question here is whether this is *the* truth or is just Steve's interpretation of the truth.

The next concepts that possibly apply are beneficence and nonmaleficence. The first concept is defined in terms of helping and the second is the related idea of "do no harm." Steve believed he was doing good by honestly telling Christine that he thought her marriage to Jeremy would be problematic. However, Steve's actions may have caused harm, because Christine is unhappy and angry about his predictions and about his lack of follow-through with an appropriate referral to another counselor after her insurance coverage was expended.

The last concept that applies is the ethic of responsibility. An important question for the licensure board committee is whether Steve provided an adequate referral for Christine to continue services and whether his termination of counseling with her was appropriate.

QUESTIONS FOR DISCUSSION

1. Should the counselor inform the client of his values?

2. What was Steve's responsibility in ensuring continuation of counseling services given that her insurance was expended and he did not believe she could benefit from further counseling?

3. Was there enough evidence to support a charge of bias or prejudice by Steve?

4. Should the supervisor also have been reviewed by the licensure board?

5. What is the best ethical decision based upon a hermeneutic model?

Chapter 29

Ahmed

A Mandated Client

Ahmed is a twenty-four-year-old male of Middle Eastern descent who has entered counseling as a mandated client. He was charged with assault and battery against his spouse and he was found guilty. As part of his sentence he must attend individual and group counseling focusing on anger management.

Ahmed has a history of aggressive acts. He would often get into physical fights with his brothers when they were adolescents. During his college years, he had an arrest for assaulting another student when they had an unpleasant verbal exchange. Most recently, he acknowledges that he becomes angry at his spouse about different issues, but primarily about money and family finances. The incident that resulted in his physically attacking his spouse involved her spending money on items he felt were unnecessary. His wife told him that she worked and had a right to buy whatever she wanted. Ahmed felt his wife was being disrespectful of him because he thought they could not afford the items she purchased. He admitted hitting her several times. His wife then called the police, and he was arrested. Ahmed was found guilty of assault and battery, and mandated to obtain counseling for anger management or go to jail. With counseling, his two-year sentence was reduced to probation. After the incident he and his spouse did decide to remain together to try to work through this situation.

Ahmed attends an anger management group in a local mental health agency. The group meets for two hours weekly, and this will last for sixteen weeks. The group focuses on psychoeducational and insight-oriented approaches. Typically, psychoeducational information is provided in the first couple of sessions, and the remaining sessions are process oriented and self-reflective. Session participants are informed when the sessions begin that the agency policy is that any potential threats of violence will require the counselors to contact the spouse and give him or her a warning. Clients sign a release of information acknowledging that they were informed and give permission to disclose if necessary.

Ahmed attended the first three sessions but did not participate in any significant way. During the fourth session, the group focused on the triggers that set up the anger and aggression for group members. Ahmed described a recent trigger for him, that is, his spouse spending money on things he felt she did not need. Then, during the second part of a session, Ahmed stated he would still physically assault his spouse if she overspent. He said that his spouse would argue with him about her expenditures. He felt it was his obligation to correct his spouse's behavior. The group was led by two counselors, Jeremy and Sally. Jeremy and Sally were pleased that Ahmed participated in the fourth session, but they were concerned about his continued belief in aggressive acts toward his spouse. They do not want to hinder the continued participation of Ahmed in future groups, but they felt they needed to consider breaching confidentiality and inform the spouse of the threat.

Relevant elements of the horizon include the ethical dilemma; the counselors and their values, race, gender, personal history, etc.; the client and his values, race, gender, personal history, etc.; the supervisor and her values, race, gender, personal history, etc.; agency policies; local, state, and federal laws that apply; professional codes of ethics; professional knowledge; geographic region; and ethical theories.

THE ETHICAL DILEMMA

Jeremy and Sally must decide whether to break confidentiality and contact Ahmed's spouse about the potential threat of violence. The fact that he signed a release of information prior to beginning the group sessions gave them legal authority to do so, but they also think that such a breach of confidentiality may hinder his participation and honesty in future anger group sessions. Their possible courses of action are to (1) contact the spouse and share the information that he expressed violent thought toward her or (2) not share the threat of violence with the spouse and work with Ahmed in the group sessions to address his anger. Several issues need to be considered in the decision. What if they do not inform the spouse and she is physically abused? What responsibility do they have in tacitly allowing this aggressive behavior? Another issue is that Ahmed may become more aggressive if his spouse confronts him with information she receives from the counselors. Alternatively, Ahmed may be more open to treatment in the group if he feels accepted and can express himself without negative consequences. This may result in more openness to treatment and ultimately better management of his anger. Jeremy and Sally decide to use the hermeneutic approach to making this decision; this will include a consultation with the agency director and their supervisor, Cheryl.

JEREMY AND SALLY: THE COUNSELORS' PERSONAL VALUES, RACE, GENDER, AND PERSONAL HISTORY

Jeremy is an African American male in his early thirties who is married without children. He is a practicing Muslim and so is his spouse. He lives in a suburban community of middle-income families. He grew up in a middle-class family where both parents were teachers. While growing up he attended a Christian church; then he converted to Islam in his early twenties. He is the oldest of three boys. His parents provided a good model for a marital relationship; they rarely argued and he never observed any aggressive acts on the parts of his parents toward each other or toward his siblings or himself.

Jeremy attended a small, private, liberal-arts college and earned a degree in psychology. He furthered his education with a master's degree in mental health counseling at another small, private college. He has been a practicing counselor for over five years. He is licensed by the state as a counselor and is a member of the ACA, so he follows the ACA code of ethics.

Sally is a forty-year-old divorced white female. She lives with her two children, ages fifteen and seventeen, in the urban community where the counseling center is located. She and her older brother grew up in a working-class family. The family was not particularly religious, but on occasion she did attend a Protestant church. Her mother and father argued frequently and she observed their conflicts. At times, her father did become physically abusive toward her mother, but they did not divorce. She attended college and obtained her bachelor's degree in social psychology. She met her husband in college and they married after graduation.

Sally divorced as a consequence of an abusive relationship with her husband. She lived with physical abuse for the first eight years of their marriage. She then sought help to get out of the abusive relationship and lived in a shelter for a period of time with her children. After the divorce, she decided to return to school while working to support her two children. She attended a local urban university for her master's degree in community counseling. She completed an internship in the same counseling center where she works now. She became involved in the anger management groups working with males who engaged in violence against their partners. Sally has become an advocate for women in abusive relationships and is passionate about her work. She graduated with her master's degree two years ago and began working in the counseling center full-time. She sees clients individually and runs several groups focusing on anger management and abused women.

AHMED: THE CLIENT'S PERSONAL VALUES, RACE, GENDER, AND PERSONAL HISTORY

Ahmed was born and grew up in the United States. His parents entered the United States in the 1970s and they received master's degrees in engineering and in education, respectively. He is the oldest of his siblings; he has two younger brothers. He attended college but did not complete a degree. Ahmed currently works in construction as a laborer. He has been married for three years and has no children.

Ahmed recalls that his parents were emotionally distant. He observed his father physically abusing his mother on a relatively frequent basis. His father would not hit his mother in the face or head, but hit her on the arm, back, or stomach. Ahmed was teased in school for his Middle Eastern complexion and he would fight back. He was expelled from school on two occasions as a consequence for fighting. Also, he would get into fistfights with his two brothers on occasion. Even though Ahmed was the oldest, his middle brother was larger than he and picked on him at times. Ahmed was an average student in school and graduated with an undistinguished academic record. He attended a public university for one year before dropping out and getting a job in construction. He liked construction work because the pay was good.

He only began dating women in his late teens and he found it hard to find another Muslim even though he lived in a relatively large Muslim community. After attending college he met his current spouse and after a short courtship they decided to marry. He was physically aggressive toward his spouse early in their relationship, and after dating for only a few months he twisted her arm when she was teasing him about his dark complexion.

After their marriage, the couple lived in an apartment and seemed to have enough money to meet their monthly expenses. Currently, Ahmed lives in an apartment with his spouse in a large urban area in the Midwest. He is a practicing Muslim and is planning a pilgrimage to Mecca in the next few years. He attends a mosque in his community. His spouse also is Muslim and is of Middle Eastern descent. She works as a clerical staff member in an insurance agency. Because Ahmed views his role as a man as the head of the household, he believes it is his responsibility to limit what he considers his spouse's excessive spending. Ahmed manages the household funds and feels pressure to manage the money well.

CHERYL: THE SUPERVISOR'S PERSONAL VALUES, RACE, GENDER, AND PERSONAL HISTORY

Cheryl is the agency director and the supervisor for Jeremy and Sally. She is a forty-six-year-old white female who has been married for five years. This is her second marriage. Her first marriage ended in divorce from a man who was physically and psychologically abusive. She was married to her first husband for five years and she had two children with him. Cheryl raised the children alone and remarried when they were adults. She received her master's degree in social work ten years ago and began working in an agency providing services to abused women. After four years in this agency, she became the director of the current community agency, which provides counseling services primarily to abused women and their abusive partners.

AGENCY POLICIES AND VALUES

The agency is committed to reducing physical and psychological abuse of spousal partners, and particularly abuse of women. Its staff has developed policies that are designed to protect abused partners, e.g., informed consent that gives permission to disclose potential violence to a spouse and break confidentiality.

PROFESSIONAL CODES OF ETHICS

A number of professional codes potentially apply to this case. Jeremy and Sally decided to use the codes from the Association for Specialists in Group Work, ASGW (1998). Relevant codes include

A.6. Professional Disclosure Statement
Group Workers have a professional disclosure statement which includes information on confidentiality and exceptions to confidentiality.

A.7. Group and Member Preparation
a. Group Workers facilitate informed consent. Group workers provide in oral and written form to prospective members . . . : the professional disclosure statement; group purpose and goals; group participation expectations including voluntary and involuntary membership; . . . procedures for mandated groups.

b. Group Workers define confidentiality and its limits. . . . (ASGW, 1998)

PROFESSIONAL KNOWLEDGE

Estimates of the number of individuals who are victims of violence by partners or former partners range from approximately one million to four million a year, with eighty-five percent of these victims being women (Hassouneh-Phillips, 2001; Rennison & Welchans, 2002). Many theorists and researchers studying violence and spousal abuse suggested that a social learning theory model best represents an approach to understanding the problem (Bevan & Higgins, 2002; Rosenbaum & Leisring, 2003). Social learning theory is based upon a view that behaviors are learned through exposure and modeling. So, observing a parent abusing another parent may result in intergenerational transmission of violence (Bevan & Higgins; Margolin, Gordis, Medina, & Oliver, 2003).

Ahmed reportedly observed his father physically abusing his mother when he was a child. Bevan and Higgins (2002) stated that social learning theory suggests that children identify with their parents, particularly the parent of the same sex as the child. When a child observes aggression by a parent, and the child later identifies with the aggressor, the aggression may be repeated. Thus, Ahmed had a model for aggressive acts from his father, and this aggression appears to have been passed on to Ahmed in his relationship with his spouse. Researchers also have found a strong connection between adult spousal abuse and witnessing spousal violence during childhood (Cappell & Heiner, 1990). Bevan and Higgins also found a strong association between observing family violence during childhood and physical spousal abuse. Rosenbaum and Leisring (2003) noted that domestic violence is "about power and control" and Ahmed sought control over his spouse's spending habits.

Both group leaders, Jeremy and Sally, were concerned whether Ahmed would continue active participation in treatment if they broke confidentiality. A concept that focuses on the process of counseling that may be relevant here is the therapeutic alliance (Bordin, 1979). One of the three important components of the therapeutic alliance according to Bordin is mutual liking, attachment, and trust between the client and therapist. Researchers have found that the therapeutic alliance is an important variable in treatment outcome (Brown & O'Leary, 2000). If the group leaders broke confidentiality, what impact would this have on the therapeutic alliance? Would Ahmed trust the group leaders and continue sharing his thoughts and feelings?

Also, researchers have found that self-esteem among Muslim men and women is associated with support for physical abuse of partners (Ali & Toner, 2001). More specifically, Ali and Toner found that Muslim men with low self-esteem were more likely to support physical abuse of spouses. Also, Muslim men expressed more supportive attitudes toward physically abusing partners than did Muslim women.

The recidivism rate of abusive partners has been found to be around forty percent within a five-year period (Shepard, 1992). There have been several different attempts to develop a method for assessing that danger that an offender will return to physically abusing his or her spouse (Kropp, Hart, Webster, & Eaves, 1999; Stuart & Campbell, 1989). However, results are mixed in predicting significant harm to a spouse as a consequence of recidivism (Hilton, Harris, & Rice, 2001). So, based upon the literature, it is difficult to predict significant harm to Ahmed's spouse if he relapses into violent acts.

GEOGRAPHIC REGION AND CULTURE

Geographic region can play a role in this case because of some characteristics of urban settings. Ahmed lives in an urban area and the counseling center is located in an urban area. Researchers noted the different characteristics of those living and growing up in urban and rural environments (Sears, Evans, & Perry, 1998; Silk, Sessa, Morris, Steinberg, & Avenevoli, 2004). Urban researchers studied the development or lack of development of collective efficacy (Ford & Beveridge, 2004; Sampson, 2002). Sampson defined neighborhood collective efficacy as "an emphasis on shared beliefs in neighbors' conjoint capability for action to achieve an intended effect, and hence an active sense of engagement on the part of residents" (p. 224). Ford and Beveridge concluded that collective efficacy "emphasizes shared expectations and mutual trust among neighborhood residents and promotes an agentic sense of cohesion" (p. 27). The client, Ahmed, lives in an urban area and may not feel close to his neighbors; however, his belonging to the Muslim community may make up for any lack of connection to his physical community. The concept of *ummah* (Kelly, 1984) refers to a particular community that is instituted by Islamic teaching and practice. Islam encourages the development of bonds by the moral and social codes espoused. Islam also has been described as "a community of believers which transcend tribal difference" (Kelly, 1984, p. 164).

LOCAL, STATE, AND FEDERAL LAWS

Waller (1995), in describing federal and state laws governing confidentiality, stated that they are "a crazy quilt of federal and state constitutional, statutory, regulatory and case law" (p. 44). The surgeon general's report on mental health observed that there are no national standards governing confidentiality (Satcher, 1999). The report also noted the significant differences in state laws on confidentiality. However, there appear to be some similarities that may apply to the case of

Ahmed. It has been suggested that each state has identified exceptions to confidentiality (Satcher). One obvious exception is if the client gives informed consent to release information. This appears to be the case with Ahmed, but it may be more complex than simply a record of release. The circumstances of how the release was obtained are relevant. Beauchamp and Childress (1989) suggested that informed consent involves free choice. Ahmed was mandated into counseling, and if he did not comply he could be surrendered to the court and sent to jail for his remaining sentence. Therefore, an important consideration is how the consent was obtained. Did Ahmed have a free choice in choosing to sign the release? If he did not have free choice, then his signature on the consent form may be considered invalid.

Another exception to maintaining confidentiality is based upon a court decision, *Tarasoff v. Regents* (1976). The Tarasoff case involved a client, Prosenjit Poddar, who was being seen in the student services office at the University of California, Berkeley. He expressed a threat toward a woman, Tatiana Tarasoff, in a counseling session with a psychologist, Dr. Moore. The intended victim, Tatiana Tarasoff, was out of the country at the time of the threat; she was in Brazil. However, Dr. Moore concluded that Mr. Poddar was a serious threat and needed psychiatric hospitalization, and he contacted the campus police to detain Mr. Poddar for an evaluation. Dr. Moore also informed his supervisor of the threat and the actions he took. The campus police initially did detain Mr. Poddar and determined that he was not a danger, so they released him. Upon returning from Brazil, Ms. Tarasoff was killed by Mr. Poddar.

The parents of Tatiana Tarasoff filed a lawsuit against Dr. Moore, the campus police, and the university. Ultimately, the California Supreme Court ruled in favor of the parents against the university. The court determined that Dr. Moore was responsible for accurately determining the level of dangerousness of his client and taking appropriate action, including warning the intended target or victim, and the family in this case since Ms. Tarasoff was away. Thus, "duty to warn" the intended victim of a threat requires that counselors contact an intended victim. There are two conditions of duty to warn: First, there must be a specified target, not a general threat against humanity; and second, the individual making the threat must be able to carry out the threat. For example, an incarcerated individual serving a twenty-year sentence who threatens to harm a relative when he or she gets out of prison may not be considered a threat; however, if the person makes the threat closer to the time of release, then duty to warn is in effect.

The question in the case of Ahmed is the level of potential harm and a clinical judgment of whether he intends to act on his threat. This is always the issue with duty to warn—the responsibility of the counselor to determine the seriousness of the threat and to assess the dangerousness of the individual making the threat.

ETHICAL THEORY: ISLAMIC ETHICS

Jeremy and Sally decided to use Islamic ethics in their ethical decision-making since it is the worldview of the client (see Chapter 13). Islamic ethics defines five major classes of acts: forbidden acts, undesirable acts, neutral acts, desirable acts, and required acts. More specifically, good or required acts potentially help others or they remove harm. For example, rescuing a drowning person if you can swim well is a good and required act. Also, there are four components of good: justice, benefit, truthfulness, and willing good (Hourani, 1971). Justice refers to performing socially good acts to bring about help or, alternatively, to bring about injury if the recipient is deserving of it. Benefit accordingly refers to acts that bring pleasure (Hourani). Truthfulness is considered good if such acts bring about pleasure and avoid pain (Hourani). Conversely, if truthfulness hurts someone who is undeserving of pain, then it is considered undesirable. The solution is not to tell a mistruth, but to remain silent or avoid speaking such a mistruth (Hourani). The will for good is based upon an evaluation of the intent of the actor and it refers to motivation or intent. Having an intention of bringing about benefit is considered good; however, not all good intentions remain good if pain and suffering occurs with an intended good act. One can have a good intent, e.g., wanting to help a client get better, but if the counselor does not have the skills to be helpful and tries to help anyway, the counselor's action may become an undesirable act. The outcome may be harmful and therefore the act would be undesirable.

QUESTIONS FOR DISCUSSION

1. What do you imagine you would say to Ahmed's spouse in explaining the potential threat of violence made toward her?

2. What suggestions would you give Sally and Jeremy in working with Ahmed and dealing with him in future group counseling sessions?

3. What other ethical theories would you apply?

4. What would be your ethical decision in this case using a hermeneutic model?

Chapter 30

Liz

A Student Intern

For the past three months, Liz has been counseling Luis, a twenty-one-year-old young adult with mild mental retardation. Liz is a first-semester counseling intern. Counseling was initiated to ensure that Luis made appropriate personal adjustments as he transitioned from school to a work environment. Luis is competitively employed (i.e., a paid employee) in a supported work program in a grocery store in the community. He has good social skills, relates well to his co-workers, and can perform basic activities of daily living. Because he does not have the skills to manage complex activities, his family has limited guardianship to assist him with financial matters, but he is considered legally competent to make other personal decisions. All family members provide Luis with supervision and direction at home. Luis is included in all family activities and his primary social contacts are within his extended family.

Liz reported that Luis showed flat affect in their counseling sessions and she concluded that Luis is mild to moderately depressed. She explained his depression as socially induced, that is, a result of not being encouraged to develop an individual identity separate from his family or to pursue outside friendships and personal interests. Liz concludes that Luis needs to become more independent now that he has reached adulthood and that his siblings should not be "burdened" with his future care. She recommended that Luis move into a group home with other adults with mental retardation.

When Liz presented this idea to Luis, he did not ask any questions or voice a strong opinion about such a move. His father mentioned that he had always taken care of his family and had intended to support Luis during adulthood. Luis's mother agreed with her husband's plan and mentioned her trust that the Virgin of Guadalupe will provide for her son's special needs in the future. Nevertheless, Liz persisted by explaining her recommendation to both Luis and his parents as something that is expected of all children when they become adults. At first, the parents were greatly saddened by the thought of having Luis move. They thought that they had made mistakes in his upbringing. Even though they never considered a group home option for Luis, they acquiesced to the recommendation that they thought was made in Luis's best interest because of their past failures. Liz reported to her supervisor, Maria, that the family readily agreed with her suggestion that Luis move to a group home setting.

The move caused significant emotional distress for the entire family, including Luis. Having Luis removed from the home disrupted their family's functioning. Luis began exhibiting difficulties adjusting to household routines in the group home, and the staff described daily behavior management problems, mainly resistance and irritability.

The parents arranged to meet with Liz and told her that they wanted Luis to return home. Liz talked to the parents and reassured them that Luis's reaction was normal and that he would eventually adjust to the situation. The parents saw the counselor as the expert and agreed to continue with the placement despite feeling that Luis probably would not adjust.

Luis continued to have adjustment problems in the group home. He called his family frequently and cried that he wanted to come home. The parents decided to contact the agency where Liz was interning. The secretary referred the parents to Liz's supervisor after they explained their concerns. Maria was unaware of Luis's difficulties in adjusting to the group home. After speaking with his parents, she told them she would speak with Liz, and Liz would be contacting the family.

Maria spoke with Liz during supervision, and Liz stated that she felt the family was overreacting and that Luis would adjust to the situation. Maria asked Liz why she had not discussed the case more during supervision. Liz explained that she felt things were going well with the case so she did not bother to bring it up. Maria expressed her concern that Liz was not using supervision well and did not appear open to feedback. Liz became angry and stated that she worked hard and her clients liked her.

Maria asked Liz to set up a meeting with Luis's parents. She reluctantly agreed. Luis's parents came to the meeting with Liz and her supervisor, Maria. Liz discussed Luis's adjustment and continued to try to persuade the family that placement in the group home was good for him. Maria listened during the session and decided after the meeting that Luis should be transferred to another counselor. She also decided to contact Liz's university supervisor to discuss whether Liz could continue with the internship at the agency. Maria contacted Dr. Martin, the university supervisor, and he came to the site to meet with Liz and Maria. Maria expressed her concerns about Liz's reluctance to engage in supervision, her lack of cultural sensitivity, and her clinical judgment. Liz stated she thought things were going well and felt the supervisor did not like her. Maria concluded the meeting by stating she could not have Liz continue as an intern at this site.

Dr. Martin informed Liz that she would need to go before a counseling department ethics committee composed of three faculty members. He stated this was standard procedure when a student intern is discharged from an internship site.

The primary elements of the horizon based upon the case of Liz include the ethical dilemma; the counselor and her values, race, gender, personal history, etc.; the client and his values, race, gender, personal history, etc.; the supervisor and her values, race, gender, personal history, etc.; agency policies; applicable local, state, and federal laws; professional knowledge; geographic region; ethical theories; and professional codes of ethics.

THE ETHICAL DILEMMA

Liz was in the first semester of her internship and she was feeling confident about her work. However, despite almost three months of exposure to Hispanic/Latino individuals and issues, Liz did not seem to have acquired the cultural competencies that are critical to understanding the context of Luis's life and to intervening in a supportive way with his family. The field supervisor was particularly concerned that Liz would be graduating next semester and that she would obtain a license to practice. Maria was also concerned about Liz's lack of openness to supervision and her lack of willingness to learn. Maria informed the university supervisor about these concerns and decided that she had to transfer Liz's client, Luis, to a more seasoned counselor who would be sensitive to cultural issues. Finally, Maria determined that she could not allow Liz to continue her internship at the agency because she believed that Liz would be harmful to clients. Liz had not demonstrated good clinical judgment, nor did she show a willingness to learn from feedback and supervision.

Dr. Martin, the university supervisor, determined that Liz should go before the counseling department's ethics committee. The counseling department has a written statement in the student handbook that any student discharged from an internship site must be reviewed. Dr. Martin informed the other two faculty members, Drs. Jones and Harrison, that Liz had been discharged from her internship and they would need to meet. The department ethics committee decided to use a hermeneutic ethical decision-making model in their deliberations. They had to decide whether the actions of Liz were ethical and whether she should continue in the program.

LIZ: THE COUNSELOR'S PERSONAL VALUES, RACE, GENDER, AND PERSONAL HISTORY

Liz, the youngest of three children, was raised in a small, rural, midwestern town in the United States. While attending a high school, she developed a good relationship with the guidance counselor who helped her resolve some adolescent adjustment issues concerning identity and independence. Because of her admiration for the school counselor and the positive impact counseling made in her own life, Liz decided to major in psychology and pursue a career in counseling.

Liz enrolled in a traditional graduate counselor education program with a homogeneous, white, middle-class student population. Liz's thinking is influenced by traditional Western developmental psychology, which is based on Anglo American values and reflects the dominant ethic of individualism in the United States. She performed well in the didactic portion of her training, earning an A average in academic courses prior to beginning field experiences. To fulfill the final requirement for her master's degree, Liz was assigned to a year-long counseling internship in a community agency that serves a predominantly Hispanic/ Latino population in a large urban area.

LUIS: THE CLIENT'S PERSONAL VALUES, RACE, GENDER, AND PERSONAL HISTORY

Luis is a young adult with a history of cognitive impairments. He soon will be twenty-two years old, and he lives at home with his parents, who are in their early sixties. His parents moved from Mexico to the United States about twenty-five years ago. Spanish is the primary language of the home, but the family has sufficient English language skills to easily negotiate everyday matters in the community. Luis's two younger sisters attend college and live at home. His older sister, her husband, and their infant son also reside in the parents' home. Many extended family members live in the vicinity and the family often travels to Mexico to visit other family and friends. Luis's parents have not made financial and living arrangements for him in the future but expect that his sisters will cooperate in his care. The family holds strong Catholic religious beliefs. They view themselves as specially chosen by God to care for Luis and report that their caretaking has spiritual significance for them. Luis's mother is convinced that her devotion to the Virgin of Guadalupe saved Luis's life following his extremely premature birth. The family feels that Luis has given meaning and purpose to their lives.

MARIA: THE SUPERVISOR'S PERSONAL VALUES, RACE, GENDER, AND PERSONAL HISTORY

Maria is of Mexican descent, though she has resided in the United States her entire life. Her family circumstances are similar to those of Luis's family. One of her brothers had Down syndrome and died in his mid-twenties. Maria is aware of how her brother's life impacted her entire family and her own childhood, as she was called upon to assist with his daily care.

Maria was surprised by Liz's apparent lack of cultural competence and insensitivity to the dynamics of this case after three months in the agency. In particular, the etiology of Luis's depression was not thoroughly addressed, his understanding of the implications of the move to a group home was not considered, and the potential impact of the group home recommendation on family functioning was not assessed. Maria assumed Liz understood the cultural limitations and biases of Western psychological theories of adult development and had acquired intercultural sensitivity through her fieldwork in the community agency. Yet Liz's handling of the case was incompetent and insensitive. Before she became aware of the issues in this case, the supervisor had not formally evaluated Liz's cross-cultural counseling competencies.

PROFESSIONAL CODES OF ETHICS

Professional codes of the ACA that potentially apply in this case include*

A.1. Welfare of Those Served by Counselors
A.1.d. Support Network Involvement
Counselors recognize that support networks hold various meanings in the lives of clients and consider enlisting the support, understanding, and involvement of others (e.g., religious/spiritual/community leaders, family members, friends) as positive resources when appropriate with client consent.

Source: Reprinted with permission from the American Counseling Association, 2005, *ACA Code of Ethics,* Alexandria, VA.

F.1. Counselor Supervision and Client Welfare

F.1.a. Client Welfare

A primary obligation of counseling supervisors is to monitor the services provided by other counselors or counselors-in-training. Counseling supervisors monitor client welfare and supervise clinical performance and professional development. To fulfill these obligations, supervisors meet regularly with supervisees to review case notes, check samples of clinical work, or make live observations. Supervisees have a responsibility to understand and follow the *ACA Code of Ethics.*

F.6. Responsibilities of Counselor Educators

F.6.a. Counselor Educators

Counselor educators who are responsible for developing, implementing, and supervising educational programs are skilled as teachers and practitioners. They are knowledgeable regarding the ethical, legal, and regulatory aspects of the profession, are skilled in applying that knowledge, and make students and supervisors aware of their responsibilities. Counselor educators conduct counselor education and training programs in an ethical manner and serve as role models for professional behavior.

F.6.g. Field Placement

Counselor educators develop clear policies within their training programs regarding field placement and other clinical experiences. Counselor educators provide clearly stated roles and responsibilities for the student or supervisee, the site supervisor, and the program supervisor. They confirm that site supervisors are qualified to provide supervision and inform site supervisors of their professional and ethical responsibilities in this role.

F.9. Evaluation and Remediation of Students

F.9.b. Limitations

Counselor educators, throughout ongoing evaluations and appraisal, are aware of and address the inabilities of some students to achieve counseling competencies that might impede performance. Counselor educators

1. assist students in securing remedial assistance when needed,

2. seek professional consultation and document their decision to dismiss or refer students for assistance, and

3. ensure that students have recourse in a timely manner to address decisions to require them to seek assistance or to dismiss them and provide students with due process according to institutional policies and procedures.

PROFESSIONAL KNOWLEDGE

The university counseling program ethics committee decided to review the professional literature in several areas before meeting with Liz. The areas included supervisor-supervisee relationships and styles of supervision, counseling student diversity competency, and supervisee/student competency.

There has been considerable writing and research on the supervisor-supervisee relationship (Granello, 2000; Ladany, Marotta, & Muse-Burke, 2001; Ladany, Walker, & Melincoff, 2001). The most frequent supervisor-supervisee model used is a developmental model (Granello). The model is based upon the view that students pass through developmental stages, from novice to expert, as they progress toward professionalism. Watkins (1994) identified three assumptions of a developmental supervisor-supervisee model: (1) that trainees pass through a series of identifiable, definable, sequential, hierarchical stages; (2) that different trainee needs exist across the different stages of development; and (3) that supervisors should vary their supervision to match the needs of their trainees (p. 417). The goal in a developmental supervisory model is to discover the developmental stage of the student intern and provide supervisory techniques and experiences that are congruent with the students' stage of professionalization. The issue here is whether the supervisor, Maria, provided the appropriate level of supervision for the developmental stage of Liz.

Developing multicultural competence is more complex than taking a single course (Arthur & Achenbach, 2002). Arthur and Achenbach suggested that the best method of developing multicultural competence is through experiential learning. They further proposed that students can be encouraged to reflect on experiential learning to enhance their understanding of multicultural issues and promote cultural competence. Finally, Arthur and Achenbach stated, "Experiential exercises need to be tailored to the learning needs of students" (p. 5).

Competency in diversity requires self-knowledge of personal biases, attitudes, and assumptions about the world as well as knowledge about the various dimensions of diversity (Daniel, Roysircar, Abeles, & Boyd, 2004). Coleman, Wampold, and Casali (1995) suggested that clients desire counselors who share their values and can understand them. The essential component of multicultural counseling is to demonstrate to clients that their whole world, not just their psychological problem, is understood and appreciated. Therefore, multicultural counseling is the only perspective in which effective counseling can occur (Coleman, 1998).

Hensley, Smith, and Thompson (2003) concluded that "the evaluation of student competence is a fundamental part of counselor preparation" (p. 219). It is the ethical responsibility of training programs to conduct regular evaluation of student progress (Frame & Stevens-Smith, 1995). The standards of the Council for Accreditation of Counseling and Related Educational Programs (CACREP) require systematic evaluation of student progress and development of counseling competencies (CACREP, 2001).

Competencies and characteristics have been identified for evaluating and dismissing problem students in counseling programs (Hensley et al., 2003). These include willingness to accept feedback, personal responsibility, maturity, flexibility, and awareness of impact on others. The counseling program ethics committee can review Liz in these areas.

GEOGRAPHIC REGION AND CULTURE

Luis and his generation are the first in his family to be born outside of Mexico. The nuclear and extended families of both of his parents now live in the same community in the United States and interact frequently. The family returns to Mexico periodically and maintains connections with family and friends there.

LOCAL, STATE, AND FEDERAL LAWS

At the age of twenty-two, Luis will no longer be eligible for special education services at his school under the Individuals with Disabilities Education Act (1999) and will need to be transitioned to adult services. Luis's parents are conservators for their son, having legal guardianship only in financial matters. Luis is considered competent to make other personal decisions.

ETHICAL THEORY: HISPANIC/LATINO ETHICS

One ethical theory that potentially applies is Hispanic/Latino ethics (see Chapter 14). The client, Luis, holds Hispanic/Latino views as does the supervisor, Maria. There are three Hispanic/Latino ethical concepts that may be applicable in this case: machismo, marianismo, and solidarity. Solidarity and family cohesion are core values in Hispanic/Latino culture. This is evident within the client's family, as they have drawn together to support Luis's development and care. The family initially resisted any attempt to violate solidarity and move Luis out of their home to a group home. Subsequently, they experienced regret about the decision to move Luis because it violated the concept of solidarity. The actions of Liz probably interfered with solidarity rather than promoting it for this family.

Liz's training as a counselor can be understood to some degree in terms of solidarity. The counseling program faculty can decide either to discharge Liz from the program or to work with her to resolve her difficulties. Attempting to work with her to resolve her difficulties may be interpreted as an example of solidarity on the part of the counseling faculty and department.

In the true sense of machismo, Luis's father took responsibility for his entire family by providing for the educational, social, and physical needs of his wife and each of his children. Liz appears to have entered into the family's decision-making process and violated the concept of machismo. Her pressuring the family to make the change and move Luis out of the family home resulted in the family losing control and no longer being responsible for Luis.

The counseling program ethics committee is acting within the concepts of machismo by taking responsibility for Liz's training as a counselor. They must decide what is best for Liz and what is best for the counseling program, i.e., what impact will a student with limitations in her counseling skills have on the reputation of the counseling program? Negative perceptions of the counseling program by community agencies can affect hiring of graduates.

The last Hispanic ethical concept is the influence of marianismo, which is evident in the family's strong religious beliefs and personal sacrifices in caring for the family members, in particular, attending to the special needs of Luis. They expressed considerable discomfort when this core value was violated because they could no longer provide direct care for Luis.

The counseling faculty may choose to implement the concept of marianismo and be nurturing to Liz. This may involve designing a remedial program to improve her counseling skills. Special attention could be paid to obtain another counseling internship with a very nurturing supervisor.

QUESTIONS FOR DISCUSSION

1. Should the student be endorsed for a degree?

2. Are the field and university supervisors culpable for failure to ensure multicultural learning?

3. Can cultural sensitivity be taught? How?

4. What is the ethical course of action?

Chapter 31

Berice

Culturally Sensitive Assessment

Berice is a thirty-five-year-old married Jamaican male who sustained a closed-head injury approximately six months ago. He fell off a ladder while painting a friend's house. He was employed by a painting company at the time of the injury, but the injury did not occur on the job. He was knocked unconscious and was discovered by his friend, who called an ambulance. He was taken to the hospital where he was admitted. He regained consciousness after a few hours. He was diagnosed with a moderate head injury, based upon the Glasgow Coma Scale. Residual effects of the head injury included difficulty in concentration, mild memory loss, sudden mood swings from happy to sad, and anger either unprovoked or inconsistent with the circumstances for the situation.

Berice entered the United States approximately two years ago. His brother, who is a U.S. citizen, owned the painting company, and this brother had sponsored him.

After the injury, Berice was able to return to work, but he was unsteady on a ladder and the company did not want to risk further injury. His family noted how the residual side effects impacted his relationships with others. Berice would forget what he was talking about, and he was emotionally unpredictable. A relative of Berice informed him that he may be eligible for services at the state vocational offices. He decided to visit an office and apply for services.

Jim, a twenty-five-year-old white male vocational rehabilitation counselor, was assigned Berice's case. Jim had worked at the state vocational rehabilitation office for several years and he had had a few clients with head injuries. Jim found Berice to be pleasant and motivated to become employed again. Berice expressed an interest in employment as an alarm-system installer. He wanted to receive training for this type of occupation and requested that the state vocational rehabilitation program fund the training. Jim did not know whether this was a viable goal given Berice's head injury and the residual effects. Berice gave permission for Jim to speak to his physician, family, and former employer as part of the initial informational-gathering process.

A review of job tasks showed that the occupation of alarm-system installer involved

- Consulting with clients to assess risks and to determine security requirements

- Drilling holes for wiring in wall studs, joists, ceilings, and floors

- Feeding cables through access holes

- Inspecting instillation sites

- Studying work orders, building plans, and instillation manuals (Occupational Information Network [ONET], 2004)

Jim questioned whether Berice had the ability and skills to perform such job tasks. He decided to obtain further formal assessment information and determined that a neuropsychological assessment would be helpful. His office typically used a psychologist, Dr. Kinney, who was knowledgeable in neuropsychological assessment, but who did not use any assessments that accounted for cultural differences. Counselors in the office knew this was a limitation of Dr. Kinney. Jim decided to use Dr. Kinney despite these limitations because Jim had a large caseload and did not have the time to locate another neuropsychologist that might provide a more culturally sensitive assessment.

Berice completed the assessment with Dr. Kinney and then met with Jim to discuss the results. Jim explained to Berice that the results indicated that Berice had limitations that prevented him from pursuing employment as an alarm-system installer. Berice was upset with the results and stated that he did not believe Dr. Kinney understood him. Jim decided to discuss the case of Berice with his supervisor, Shirley, to decide if he acted ethically and whether he should take additional steps to obtain another assessment.

The possible elements of the horizon relevant to the case of Berice include the ethical dilemma; the counselor's values, race, gender, personal history, etc.; the client's values, race, gender, personal history, etc.; the supervisor's values, race, gender, personal history, etc.; counseling agency policies; applicable local, state, and federal laws; professional knowledge; geographic region; professional codes of ethics; and ethical theories.

THE ETHICAL DILEMMA

Jim and Shirley discussed whether Berice's referral to Dr. Kinney was ethical and appropriate, or whether another assessment is warranted. Several questions were identified by Jim and Shirley as important to determine whether the assessment process was ethical. First, did the referral by Jim constitute an appropriate referral based upon Dr. Kinney's known skills and the knowledge Dr. Kinney had demonstrated in past assessments? Jim and Shirley are aware of Dr. Kinney's limitations in the use of culturally sensitive assessments. For most of their referrals to Dr. Kinney this is not an issue; they provide services to relatively homogeneous ethnic and racial groups. A second related question is whether the results are valid "enough" to make reasonable decisions and determine whether Berice is able to pursue the type of occupation he wants, i.e., as an alarm-system installer. The answer to the second question will determine whether they decide to order a second assessment, which will cost the organization more money.

JIM: THE COUNSELOR'S PERSONAL VALUES, RACE, GENDER, AND PERSONAL HISTORY

Jim has worked for the state vocational rehabilitation agency since his graduation from a master's program two years ago. He is married and his spouse is also white. He grew up in a homogeneous ethnic and racial community that is a suburb of a large urban area that was predominantly a white community. His family did not travel far outside the community, and so he had minimal exposure to other ethnic and racial groups.

He completed an internship during his master's program in a state vocational rehabilitation agency serving the same area where he grew up. His exposure to primarily homogeneous racial and ethnic groups continued with this internship. He took courses in cross-cultural counseling and he did not feel he was prejudiced against minority groups. He had not grown up hearing any negative stereotypes expressed toward individual minority groups in his family or the schools he attended.

After completing his internship, he was hired to work in an urban state vocational rehabilitation office where he had his first significant exposures to minorities and different racial and ethnic groups. After a few years working as a vocational rehabilitation counselor, he believed he understood the issues facing those from minority groups. Approximately ten percent of his caseload was minorities, and of these he had a few who were Jamaican.

BERICE: THE CLIENT'S PERSONAL VALUES, RACE, GENDER, AND PERSONAL HISTORY

Berice is married with two children, a boy and girl, ages eight and ten. He grew up in rural Jamaica near Mandeville. He was the youngest of three boys. He was employed in odd jobs including taxi-driving prior to coming to the United States. He also worked in maintenance positions and maintained apartment complexes. He speaks English and Patois, which is a combination of English, Portuguese, Spanish, and African words. Jamaica was one of the first areas in the Western Hemisphere to receive slaves, and the island residents have been oppressed for centuries, both physically through slavery and later more economically.

Berice has been married for twelve years and his spouse is from the same rural community where he grew up. The two children attend public schools. His spouse, Olivia, works as a secretary at a local university. Berice sees his brother and his family on a regular basis so there is a connection to extended family.

SHIRLEY: THE SUPERVISOR'S PERSONAL VALUES, RACE, GENDER, AND PERSONAL HISTORY

Shirley is a fifty-year-old African American woman who is married and who has worked at the state vocational rehabilitation agency for over twenty years. She has one child and she grew up in the urban area where she works. Over her years of experience she has worked with numerous minorities, including many Jamaicans. Prior to coming to the current office, Shirley worked for five years in a state vocational rehabilitation office in which over half of the clients were minorities. She grew up in a middle-class family and was the oldest of three children. She has been a supervisor for the past eight years and supervises ten other counselors in her office.

She completed her master's degree in rehabilitation counseling over twenty-five years ago and she had courses in testing, but no courses in multicultural counseling or ethics. However, she has attended several workshops and conferences addressing multicultural counseling and ethics. She believes she is knowledgeable about current issues in these areas. She encourages her counselors to attend various workshops that address competence in multiculturalism and ethics.

PROFESSIONAL CODES OF ETHICS

Several professional codes potentially apply in this situation. These include the following ACA codes:*

A.1. Welfare of Those Served by Counselors
A.1.e. Employment Needs
Counselors work with their clients considering employment in jobs that are consistent with the overall abilities, vocational limitations, physical restrictions, general temperament, interest and aptitude patterns, social skills, education general qualifications and other relevant characteristics and needs of clients. When appropriate counselors appropriately trained in career development will assist in the placement of clients in positions that are consistent with the interest, culture, and welfare of clients, employers, and/or the public.

A.4. Avoiding Harm and Imposing Values
A.4.b. Personal Values
Counselors are aware of their own values, attitudes, beliefs, and behaviors and avoid imposing values that are inconsistent with counseling goals. Counselors respect the diversity of clients, trainees, and research participants.

D.2. Consultation
D.2.a. Consultant Competency
Counselors take reasonable steps to ensure that they have the appropriate resources and competencies when providing consultation services. Counselors provide appropriate referral resources when requested or needed.

E. Evaluation, Assessment, and Interpretation
E.1. General
E.1.b. Client Welfare
Counselors do not misuse assessment results and interpretations, and they take reasonable steps to prevent others from misusing the information these

---

Source: Reprinted with permission from the American Counseling Association, 2005, *ACA Code of Ethics,* Alexandria, VA.

techniques provide. They respect the client's rights to know the results, the interpretations made, and the basis for counselors' conclusions and recommendations.

PROFESSIONAL KNOWLEDGE

Jim and Shirley reviewed the professional literature that concerned assessment and
multiculturalism. They also reviewed the appropriate selection of a consultant
and referral. Dana, Aguilar-Kitibutr, Diaz-Vivar, and Vetter (2002) noted that
counseling and therapy have addressed cultural competence fairly extensively;
however, there has been little consensus concerning standards for assessment and
cultural competence. Dana (2002) stated,

> Assessment training continues to be accomplished primarily in a traditional
> manner with several courses covering standardized tests of intelligence, psy-
> chopathology, and personality. The assumption is generally made that standard
> tests are appropriate for all persons regardless of their cultural, ethnic, and
> racial identities. (p. 196)

Dana concluded the following about multicultural assessment:

> To provide reasonable access to unbiased, equitable psychological assessment
> services for multicultural populations in the United States, training for cultural
> competence should be coextensive with basic assessment training rather than
> provided by subsequent multicultural assessment courses now available in some
> programs. (p. 196)

Jim and Shirley found that researchers have concluded that doctoral programs
note the importance of training in multicultural competence (Rogers, 1992).
However, it has been found that few doctoral programs devote as much classroom
time as they suggest is important to multicultural competency (Rogers). Jim and
Shirley found that there appears to be little research into specific multicultural
competencies in assessment practices. Dr. Kinney was trained over twenty years
earlier, so his exposure to multicultural assessment is consistent with what the
practices and training models provided at the time.

Jim and Shirley also reviewed the professional literature on use and selection of
psychological consultants (Conoley & Conoley, 1992; Tombari & Bergan, 1978).
Conoley and Conoley investigated the effect of the consultee's framing of the
problem on the consultant's understanding, conclusions, and recommendations.

The way Jim framed the questions he asked Dr. Kinney to address may have influenced Dr. Kinney's assessment and conclusions. Others have noted the generalized approach to psychological assessment, which ignores the unique needs of individual clients and more so the unique characteristics of minority individuals (Brenner, 2003). It is suggested that a way to prevent the use of a generalized approach to assessment is through focused referral questions (Brenner, 2003; Wiener, 1985). Referrals of African Americans by white professionals have demonstrated a bias in expectations (Moore, 2002), which may reflect how assessment referrals and questions are framed.

GEOGRAPHIC REGION AND CULTURE

The state vocational rehabilitation office is located in an urban area that is fairly homogeneous and composed primarily of whites, with less than fifteen percent of the population made up of African Americans, Latinos, Jamaicans, and Asians. Berice grew up in Jamaica, a tropical mountainous country. He lived in a relatively rural community. The unemployment rate was high so he took the opportunity to immigrate to the United States and work for his brother. At the time his accident occurred, he had been in the United States only a few years and he was still adjusting to the density of the population and environment.

LOCAL, STATE, AND FEDERAL LAWS

There are no local, state, or federal laws that apply to this particular situation involving assessment and cultural competence. However, if the client were of school age and had a developmental disability, federal laws may have applied.

ETHICAL THEORY: PAN-AFRICAN ETHICS

Berice is Jamaican and the supervisor is African American. Consequently, one theory to review for this case is Pan-African ethics (see Chapter 15). Several Pan-African concepts possibly apply. The first concept that potentially applies and is the foundation of Pan-African ethics is acting in a way that does not harm others in the community. Referring Berice to a psychologist who was not competent in multicultural assessment may have harmed him. The assessment results may either over- or underestimate Berice's abilities and potential for a particular occupation. A related concept is trust and involves being entrusted with another's care. Berice trusted Jim to provide quality care. He believed that Jim was making decisions that would benefit him and result in a desired and appropriate occupation.

Shirley asked Jim to think about whether he had fulfilled his duty as a state vocational rehabilitation counselor in making the referral to Dr. Kinney. Also, Jim and Shirley discussed whether they were fulfilling their roles if they approved a second assessment. They had a responsibility to make judicious decisions in approving expenditures for client rehabilitation. State vocational rehabilitation services are paid for through federal and state tax dollars.

QUESTIONS FOR DISCUSSION

1. What other ethical theories are relevant?

2. Do you think the supervisor bears responsibility for the ethical problem? Explain.

3. What would you recommend to Jim and Shirley?

4. What is the ethical course of action based upon a hermeneutic model?

Appendix A

Web Sites for Professional Codes of Ethics

American Association for Marriage and Family Therapy
http://www.aamft.org/resources/LRMPlan/ethics/ethicscode2001.asp

American Counseling Association
http://www.counseling.org/Resources/CodeOfEthics/TP/Home/CT2.aspx?

American Mental Health Counselors Association
http://amhca.org/code/

American Psychological Association
http://www.apa.org/ethics/code2002.html

American School Counselor Association
http://www.schoolcounselor.org/content.asp?contentid=173

Association for Specialists in Group Work
http://www.asgw.org/best.htm

Commission on Rehabilitation Counselor Certification
http://www.crccertification.com/pdf/code_ethics_2001.pdf

National Board for Certified Counselors
http://www.nbcc.org/extras/pdfs/ethics/NBCC-CodeofEthics.pdf

Appendix B

Web Sites for State and Federal Laws Affecting Counseling Practice

FEDERAL LAWS

Family Education Rights & Privacy Act (FERPA)
http://www.ed.gov/policy/gen/guid/fpco/ferpa/index.html

Health Insurance Portability and Accountability Act (HIPAA)
http://www.hhs.gov/ocr/hipaa/

Individuals with Disabilities Education Act (IDEA)
http://www.cec.sped.org/law_res/doc/law/index.php

INFORMATION ABOUT FEDERAL PROTECTIONS

Child Protection—Native Americans
http://straylight.law.cornell.edu/uscode/html/uscode25/usc_sup_01_25_10_21.html

Genetic Information—Privacy
http://www.genome.gov/10002336

Substance Abuse Treatment—Privacy
http://www.access.gpo.gov/nara/cfr/waisidx_00/42cfr2_00.html

Veterans Employment and Training Service—Laws and Regulations
http://www.dol.gov/vets/regs/main.htm

SUMMARIES OF STATE LAWS (ALL STATES)

Child Abuse
http://nccanch.acf.hhs.gov/general/legal/statutes/resources.pdf

Child Abuse—Mandatory Reporters
http://nccanch.acf.hhs.gov/general/legal/statutes/manda.pdf

Confidentiality (Surgeon General's Report)
http://www.mentalhealth.samhsa.gov/features/surgeongeneralreport/chapter7/
  sec3.asp

Domestic Violence
http://www.ilj.org/dv/98legis.html

Involuntary Commitment (Assisted Treatment)
http://www.psychlaws.org/LegalResources/statechart.htm

Mental Health Coverage
http://www.ncsl.org/programs/health/Mentalben.htm

Minors' Access to Contraceptive Services
http://www.guttmacher.org/statecenter/spibs/spib_MACS.pdf

STATES' LAWS

Alabama Laws

Child Abuse and Mandatory Reporting
See summaries of state laws above

Confidentiality and Rights
http://www.legislature.state.al.us/CodeofAlabama/1975/coatoc.htm

Domestic Violence
http://www.legislature.state.al.us/CodeofAlabama/1975/coatoc.htm

Elder and Disabled Abuse
http://www.legislature.state.al.us/CodeofAlabama/1975/coatoc.htm

Involuntary Commitment

http://www.psychlaws.org/LegalResources/ATCriteria.htm#alabama

Licensure

http://www.archives.state.al.us/officials/rdas/examcounseling.pdf

Mental Health

http://www.legislature.state.al.us/CodeofAlabama/1975/coatoc.htm

Alaska Laws

Child Abuse and Mandatory Reporting

See summaries of state laws on page 258

Involuntary Commitment

http://www.psychlaws.org/LegalResources/ATCriteria.htm#alaska

Licensure

http://www.dced.state.ak.us/occ/pub/pco4403.pdf

Arizona Laws

Child Abuse and Mandatory Reporting

See summaries of state laws on page 258

Involuntary Commitment

http://www.psychlaws.org/LegalResources/ATCriteria.htm#arizona

Licensure

http://www.azca.org/government.html

Arkansas Laws

Child Abuse and Mandatory Reporting

See summaries of state laws on page 258

Domestic Violence

http://www.womenslaw.org/AR/AR_statutes.htm

Involuntary Commitment

http://www.psychlaws.org/LegalResources/ATCriteria.htm#arkansas

Licensure
http://www.ark.org/abec/

California Laws

Child Abuse and Mandatory Reporting
See summaries of state laws on page 258

Domestic Violence
http://www.caadv.org/docs/2005leg.pdf

Involuntary Commitment
http://www.psychlaws.org/stateactivity/California.htm

Licensure
No counseling licensure law

Colorado Laws

Child Abuse and Mandatory Reporting
See summaries of state laws on page 258

Domestic Violence
http://www.womenslaw.org/CO/CO_statutes.htm#13-14

Involuntary Commitment
http://www.psychlaws.org/LegalResources/ATCriteria.htm#colorado

Licensure
http://www.counseling.org/Content/NavigationMenu/JOINRENEW/STATE
    LICENSURECERTIFICATIONDETAILEDCHART/Colorado.htm

Connecticut Laws

Child Abuse and Mandatory Reporting
See summaries of state laws on page 258

Domestic Violence
http://www.womenslaw.org/CT/ct_statutes.htm

HIV Privacy

http://www.glad.org/rights/connecticut_hiv.shtml#confidentiality

Involuntary Commitment

http://www.psychlaws.org/LegalResources/ATCriteria.htm#connecticut

Licensure

http://www.counseling.org/Content/NavigationMenu/JOINRENEW/STATE
LICENSURECERTIFICATIONDETAILEDCHART/Connecticut.htm

Delaware Laws

Child Abuse and Mandatory Reporting
See summaries of state laws on page 258

Domestic Violence

http://courts.delaware.gov/How%20To/Protection%20From%20Abuse/

Involuntary Commitment
http://www.psychlaws.org/LegalResources/ATCriteria.htm#delaware

Licensure
http://www.counseling.org/Content/NavigationMenu/JOINRENEW/STATE
LICENSURECERTIFICATIONDETAILEDCHART/Delaware.htm

Florida Laws

Child Abuse and Mandatory Reporting
See summaries of state laws on page 258

Domestic Violence
http://www.dcf.state.fl.us/domesticviolence/

Involuntary Commitment
http://www.psychlaws.org/LegalResources/ATCriteria.htm#florida

Licensure
http://www.doh.state.fl.us/mqa/491/soc_home.html

Georgia Laws

Child Abuse and Mandatory Reporting

See summaries of state laws on page 258

Domestic Violence

http://www.womenslaw.org/GA/GA_statutes.htm#1

Involuntary Commitment

http://www.psychlaws.org/LegalResources/ATCriteria.htm#georgia

Licensure

http://www.counseling.org/Content/NavigationMenu/JOINRENEW/STATE
LICENSURECERTIFICATIONDETAILEDCHART/Georgia.htm

Hawaii Laws

Child Abuse and Mandatory Reporting

See summaries of state laws on page 258

Domestic Violence

http://www.hscadv.org/laws.asp#709-906

Involuntary Commitment

http://www.psychlaws.org/LegalResources/ATCriteria.htm#hawaii

Licensure

http://www.counseling.org/Content/NavigationMenu/JOINRENEW/STATE
LICENSURECERTIFICATIONDETAILEDCHART/Hawaii.htm

Idaho Laws

Child Abuse and Mandatory Reporting

See summaries of state laws on page 258

Domestic Violence

http://www3.state.id.us/cgi-bin/newidst?sctid=180090018.K

Involuntary Commitment

http://www.psychlaws.org/LegalResources/ATCriteria.htm#idaho

Licensure

http://www.counseling.org/Content/NavigationMenu/JOINRENEW/STATE
LICENSURECERTIFICATIONDETAILEDCHART/Idaho.htm

Illinois Laws

Child Abuse and Mandatory Reporting
See summaries of state laws on page 258

Domestic Violence
http://www.ilcadv.org/legal/Booklet.pdf

Involuntary Commitment
http://www.psychlaws.org/LegalResources/ATCriteria.htm#illinois

Licensure
http://www.idfpr.com/dpr/WHO/prfcns.asp

Indiana Laws

Child Abuse and Mandatory Reporting
See summaries of state laws on page 258

Domestic Violence
http://www.womenslaw.org/IN/IN_statutes.htm

Involuntary Commitment
http://www.psychlaws.org/LegalResources/ATCriteria.htm#indiana

Licensure
http://www.counseling.org/Content/NavigationMenu/JOINRENEW/STATE
LICENSURECERTIFICATIONDETAILEDCHART/Indiana.htm

Iowa Laws

Child Abuse and Mandatory Reporting
http://www.dhs.state.ia.us/dhs2005/dhs_homepage/children_family/abuse_reporting/
child_abuse.html

Domestic Violence
http://www.judicial.state.ia.us/families/domviol/dvlaws.asp

Involuntary Commitment

http://www.psychlaws.org/LegalResources/ATCriteria.htm#iowa

Licensure

http://www.counseling.org/Content/NavigationMenu/JOINRENEW/STATE
LICENSURECERTIFICATIONDETAILEDCHART/Iowa.htm

Kansas Laws

Child Abuse and Mandatory Reporting

See summaries of state laws on page 258

Domestic Violence

http://www.womenslaw.org/KS/KS_statutes.htm

Involuntary Commitment

http://www.psychlaws.org/LegalResources/ATCriteria.htm#kansas

Licensure

http://www.ksbsrb.org/pro-counselors.html

Kentucky Laws

Child Abuse and Mandatory Reporting

See summaries of state laws on page 258

Domestic Violence

http://www.womenslaw.org/KY/KY_statutes.htm

Involuntary Commitment

http://www.psychlaws.org/LegalResources/ATCriteria.htm#kentucky

Licensure

http://www.counseling.org/Content/NavigationMenu/JOINRENEW/STATE
LICENSURECERTIFICATIONDETAILEDCHART/Kentucky.htm

Louisiana Laws

Child Abuse and Mandatory Reporting

See summaries of state laws on page 258

Domestic Violence

http://www.womenslaw.org/LA/LA_statutes.htm

Involuntary Commitment

http://www.psychlaws.org/LegalResources/ATCriteria.htm#louisiana

Licensure

http://www.counseling.org/Content/NavigationMenu/JOINRENEW/STATE
    LICENSURECERTIFICATIONDETAILEDCHART/Louisiana.htm

Maine Laws

Child Abuse and Mandatory Reporting

See summaries of state laws on page 258

Domestic Violence

http://janus.state.me.us/legis/statutes/19-A/title19-Ach101sec0.html

HIV Privacy and Counseling

http://www.glad.org/rights/maine_hiv.shtml#Testing%20Issues

Involuntary Commitment

http://www.psychlaws.org/LegalResources/ATCriteria.htm#maine

Licensure

http://www.state.me.us/pfr/olr/categories/cat13.htm

Maryland Laws

Child Abuse and Mandatory Reporting

See summaries of state laws on page 258

Domestic Violence

http://www.womenslaw.org/MD/MD_statutes.htm

Involuntary Commitment

http://www.psychlaws.org/LegalResources/ATCriteria.htm#maryland

Licensure

http://www.counseling.org/Content/NavigationMenu/JOINRENEW/STATE
    LICENSURECERTIFICATIONDETAILEDCHART/Maryland.htm

Massachusetts Laws

Child Abuse and Mandatory Reporting
See summaries of state laws on page 258

General Privacy Rights
http://www.bakernet.com/ecommerce/massachusetts-p.htm

HIV Privacy Rights
http://www.glad.org/rights/massachusetts_hiv.shtml#hivprivacy

Involuntary Commitment
http://www.psychlaws.org/LegalResources/ATCriteria.htm#massachusetts

Licensure
http://www.mass.gov/dpl/home.htm

Privileged Communication
http://www.mass.gov/legis/laws/mgl/233-20b.htm

Special Education
http://www.doe.mass.edu/lawsregs/

Michigan Laws

Child Abuse and Mandatory Reporting
See summaries of state laws on page 258

Domestic Violence
http://www.cityofmarysvillemi.com/police/Laws%20in%20Michigan.htm

Involuntary Commitment
http://www.psychlaws.org/LegalResources/ATCriteria.htm#michigan

Licensure
http://www.counseling.org/Content/NavigationMenu/JOINRENEW/STATE
    LICENSURECERTIFICATIONDETAILEDCHART/Michigan.htm

Minnesota Laws

Child Abuse and Mandatory Reporting
See summaries of state laws on page 258

Domestic Violence
http://www.revisor.leg.state.mn.us/stats/518B/01.html

Involuntary Commitment
http://www.psychlaws.org/LegalResources/ATCriteria.htm#minnesota

Licensure
http://www.bbht.state.mn.us/

Mississippi Laws

Child Abuse and Mandatory Reporting
See summaries of state laws on page 258

Domestic Violence
http://www.womenslaw.org/MS/MS_statutes.htm

Involuntary Commitment
http://www.psychlaws.org/LegalResources/ATCriteria.htm#mississippi

Licensure
http://www.lpc.state.ms.us/

Missouri Laws

Child Abuse and Mandatory Reporting
See summaries of state laws on page 258

Domestic Violence
http://www.moga.state.mo.us/STATUTES/C455.HTM

Involuntary Commitment
http://www.psychlaws.org/LegalResources/ATCriteria.htm#missouri

Licensure
http://www.moga.state.mo.us/STATUTES/C337.HTM

Montana Laws

Child and Elder Protection
http://data.opi.state.mt.us/bills/mca/52/1/52-1-103.htm

Domestic Violence
http://data.opi.state.mt.us/bills/mca_toc/40_15.htm

Involuntary Commitment
http://www.psychlaws.org/LegalResources/ATCriteria.htm#montana

Mental Health
http://arm.sos.state.mt.us/37/37-14579.htm

Protection for Persons With Disabilities
http://data.opi.state.mt.us/bills/mca_toc/49_4_2.htm

Nebraska Laws

Domestic Violence
http://www.womenslaw.org/NE/NE_statutes.htm

Involuntary Commitment
http://www.psychlaws.org/LegalResources/ATCriteria.htm#nebraska

Nevada Laws

Child Abuse
http://www.leg.state.nv.us/NRS/NRS-200.html#NRS200Sec495

Child Confidentiality
http://www.leg.state.nv.us/NRS/NRS-062H.html

Involuntary Commitment
http://www.psychlaws.org/LegalResources/ATCriteria.htm#nevada

Licensure
http://www.leg.state.nv.us/NRS/NRS-641A.html

Protection of Elderly and Those With Disabilities
http://www.leg.state.nv.us/NRS/NRS-200.html#NRS200Sec495

Protection of Patients
http://www.leg.state.nv.us/NRS/NRS-200.html#NRS200Sec495

New Hampshire Laws

Child Abuse and Mandatory Reporting
See summaries of state laws on page 258

HIV Privacy
http://www.glad.org/rights/newhampshire_hiv.shtml#testing

Involuntary Commitment
http://www.psychlaws.org/LegalResources/ATCriteria.htm#newhampshire

Licensure
http://www.state.nh.us/mhpb/index.html

New Jersey Laws

Child Abuse and Mandatory Reporting
See summaries of state laws on page 258

Involuntary Commitment
http://www.psychlaws.org/LegalResources/ATCriteria.htm#newjersey

Licensure
http://www.state.nj.us/lps/ca/medical/procounsel.htm

Special Education
http://www.state.nj.us/njded/specialed/reg/

New Mexico Laws

Child Abuse and Mandatory Reporting
See summaries of state laws on page 258

Domestic Violence
http://www.womenslaw.org/NM/NM_statutes.htm

mmitment

chlaws.org/LegalResources/ATCriteria.htm#newmexico

aws

and Mandatory Reporting

ries of state laws on page 258

Involu... ry Commitment

http://www.psychlaws.org/LegalResources/ATCriteria.htm#newyork

Licensure

http://www.op.nysed.gov/mhpques-ans.htm

North Carolina Laws

Child Abuse and Mandatory Reporting

See summaries of state laws on page 258

Domestic Violence

http://www.ncleg.net/enactedlegislation/statutes/html/bysection/chapter_50b/gs_
50b-1.html

Involuntary Commitment

http://www.psychlaws.org/LegalResources/ATCriteria.htm#northcarolina

Licensure

http://www.ncblpc.org/

North Dakota Laws

Child Abuse and Mandatory Reporting

See summaries of state laws on page 258

Domestic Violence

http://www.state.nd.us/lr/cencode/t14c071.pdf

Involuntary Commitment

http://www.state.nd.us/lr/cencode/t25c031.pdf

Ohio Laws

Child Abuse and Mandatory Reporting
See summaries of state laws on page 258

Involuntary Commitment
http://www.psychlaws.org/LegalResources/ATCriteria.htm#ohio

Licensure
http://cswmft.ohio.gov/

Oklahoma Laws

Child Abuse and Mandatory Reporting
See summaries of state laws on page 258

Domestic Abuse
http://www.oscn.net/applications/oscn/deliverdocument.asp?citeID=70255

Involuntary Commitment
http://www.psychlaws.org/LegalResources/ATCriteria.htm#oklahoma

Licensure
http://www.health.state.ok.us/program/lpc/

Oregon Laws

Child Abuse
See summaries of state laws on page 258

Domestic Violence
http://www.womenslaw.org/OR/OR_statutes.htm

Involuntary Commitment
http://www.psychlaws.org/LegalResources/ATCriteria.htm#oregon

Licensure
http://www.oblpct.state.or.us/

Mandatory Reporting
http://www.oregon.gov/DHS/abuse/mandatory_report.shtml

Pennsylvania Laws

Child Abuse and Mandatory Reporting
See summaries of state laws on page 258

Domestic Violence
http://members.aol.com/StatutesP8/23.Cp.61.html

Involuntary Commitment
http://www.psychlaws.org/LegalResources/ATCriteria.htm#pennsylvania

Licensure
http://www.pacode.com/secure/data/049/chapter49/chap49toc.html

Rhode Island Laws

Child Abuse and Mandatory Reporting
See summaries of state laws on page 258

HIV Privacy Protection
http://www.glad.org/rights/rhodeisland_hiv.shtml#confidentiality

Involuntary Commitment
http://www.psychlaws.org/LegalResources/ATCriteria.htm#rhodeisland

Licensure
http://www.rules.state.ri.us/rules/released/pdf/DOH/DOH_277_.pdf

Mandatory Reporting
http://www.rilin.state.ri.us/statutes/title40/40%2D11/40%2D11%2D3.htm

South Carolina Laws

Child Abuse
http://www.scstatehouse.net/code/t20c007.htm

Domestic Violence
http://www.scstatehouse.net/code/t20c004.htm

Involuntary Commitment
http://www.psychlaws.org/LegalResources/ATCriteria.htm#southdakota

Licensure
http://www.llr.state.sc.us/POL/Counselors/

South Dakota Laws

Child Abuse and Mandatory Reporting
http://legis.state.sd.us/statutes/DisplayStatute.aspx?Type=Statute&Statute=26-8A

Domestic Violence
http://legis.state.sd.us/statutes/DisplayStatute.aspx?Type=Statute&Statute=25-10

Involuntary Commitment
http://www.psychlaws.org/LegalResources/ATCriteria.htm#southdakota

Licensure
http://www.state.sd.us/dhs/boards/counselor/

Tennessee Laws

Adult Protective Services
http://www.state.tn.us/humanserv/adpro.htm

Child Abuse and Mandatory Reporting
http://www.tennessee.gov/sos/rules/0250/0250-04/0250-04-11.pdf

Domestic Violence
http://www.womenslaw.org/TN/TN_statutes.htm

Involuntary Commitment
http://www.psychlaws.org/LegalResources/ATCriteria.htm#tennessee

Licensure
http://state.tn.us/sos/rules/0450/0450.htm

Texas Laws

Child Abuse
http://www.capitol.state.tx.us/cgi-bin/statutes/pdfframe.cmd?filepath=/statutes/
    docs/FA/content/pdf/fa.005.00.000261.00.pdf&title=FAMILY%20CODE
    %20-%20CHAPTER%20261

Domestic Violence
http://www.capitol.state.tx.us/cgi-bin/statutes/pdfframe.cmd?filepath=/statutes/
    docs/FA/content/pdf/fa.004.00.000071.00.pdf&title=FAMILY%20CODE
    %20-%20CHAPTER%2071

Involuntary Commitment
http://www.psychlaws.org/LegalResources/ATCriteria.htm#texas

Licensure
http://www.dshs.state.tx.us/counselor/default.shtm

Minor Abortion Rights
http://www.capitol.state.tx.us/cgi-bin/statutes/pdfframe.cmd?filepath=/statutes/
    docs/FA/content/pdf/fa.002.00.000033.00.pdf&title=FAMILY%20CODE
    %20-%20CHAPTER%2033

Special Education
http://www.tea.state.tx.us/special.ed/rules/tec.html

Utah Laws

Child Abuse and Mandatory Reporting
See summaries of state laws on page 258

Domestic Violence
http://www.womenslaw.org/UT/UT_statutes.htm

Involuntary Commitment
http://www.psychlaws.org/LegalResources/ATCriteria.htm#utah

Licensure
http://www.dopl.utah.gov/licensing/professional_counselor.html

Vermont Laws

Child Abuse and Mandatory Reporting
See summaries of state laws on page 258

HIV Privacy Protection
http://www.glad.org/rights/vermont_hiv.shtml#privacy

Involuntary Commitment
http://www.psychlaws.org/LegalResources/ATCriteria.htm#vermont

Mandatory Reporting
http://www.leg.state.vt.us/statutes/fullsection.cfm?Title=33&Chapter=049&
   Section=04913

Virginia Laws

Child Abuse and Mandatory Reporting
See summaries of state laws on page 258

Domestic Violence
http://www.womenslaw.org/VA/VA_statutes.htm

Involuntary Commitment
http://www.psychlaws.org/LegalResources/ATCriteria.htm#virginia

Licensure
http://www.dhp.state.va.us/counseling/

Washington

Child Abuse and Mandatory Reporting
See summaries of state laws on page 258

Confidentiality
http://www.leg.wa.gov/RCW/index.cfm?fuseaction=section&section=18.225.105

Domestic Violence
http://www.courts.wa.gov/dv/

Involuntary Commitment

http://www.psychlaws.org/LegalResources/ATCriteria.htm#washington

Licensure

https://fortress.wa.gov/doh/hpqa1/hps7/Registered_Counselor/default.htm

Mental Health

http://www1.dshs.wa.gov/mentalhealth/mentalaw.shtml

West Virginia Laws

Child Abuse

http://www.legis.state.wv.us/WVCODE/49/masterfrm2Frm.htm

Domestic Violence

http://www.legis.state.wv.us/WVCODE/48/masterfrm2Frm.htm

Involuntary Commitment

http://www.psychlaws.org/LegalResources/ATCriteria.htm#westvirginia

Licensure

http://www.wvbec.org/

Wisconsin Laws

Child Abuse

http://www.legis.state.wi.us/statutes/Stat0813.pdf

Child Privacy

http://www.legis.state.wi.us/statutes/Stat0048.pdf

Confidentiality

http://www.dhfs.state.wi.us/clientrights/ConfidTrmtRecs.htm

Domestic Abuse

http://www.legis.state.wi.us/statutes/Stat0813.pdf

Involuntary Commitment

http://www.psychlaws.org/LegalResources/ATCriteria.htm#wisconsin

Licensure

http://drl.wi.gov/prof/coun/def.htm

Wyoming Laws

Child Abuse

http://legisweb.state.wy.us/statutes/titles/title14/c03a02.htm

Involuntary Commitment

http://www.psychlaws.org/LegalResources/ATCriteria.htm#wyoming

Licensure

http://plboards.state.wy.us/mentalhealth/index.asp

References

Adeleke, T. (1997). Africa and Pan-Africanism: Betrayal of a historical cause. *The Western Journal of Black Studies, 21,* 106–116.

Adeleke, T. (1998). Black Americans, Africa and history: A reassessment of the Pan-African and identity paradigms. *The Western Journal of Black Studies, 22,* 182–183.

Adler, N., Ozer, E., & Tschann, J. (2003). Abortion among adolescents. *American Psychologist, 58,* 211–217.

Alderfer, C. (2004). A family therapist's reaction to the influences of the family of origin on career development: A review and analysis. *Counseling Psychologist, 32,* 569–571.

Ali, A., & Toner, B. (2001). Self-esteem as a predictor of attitudes toward wife abuse among Muslim women and men in Canada. *The Journal of Social Psychology, 14,* 23–30.

Almond, B. (1993). Rights. In P. Singer (Ed.), *A Companion to Ethics* (pp. 259–269). Malden, MA: Blackwell.

American Academy of Pediatrics (AAP). (1996). The adolescent's right to confidential care when considering abortion. *Pediatrics, 97,* 746–751.

American Association of Marriage and Family Therapy (AAMFT). (1998). *AAMFT code of ethics.* Alexandria, VA: Author.

American Association of Marriage and Family Therapy (AAMFT). (2001). *AAMFT code of ethics.* Alexandria, VA: Author.

American Civil Liberties Union (ACLU). (2001). *Laws restricting teenagers' access to abortion.* Retrieved June 5, 2005, from www.aclu.org/reproductiverights/youth/16388 res20010401.html

American Civil Liberties Union (ACLU). (2003a). *Why sodomy laws matter.* Retrieved December 23, 2005, from http://www.aclu.org/lgbt/crimjustice/11896res20030626.html

American Civil Liberties Union (ACLU). (2003b). *Thinking of getting married in Massachusetts?* Retrieved December 8, 2004, from http://aclu.org/getequal/rela/ massachusetts.html

American Counseling Association (ACA). (2005). *ACA code of ethics.* Alexandria, VA: Author.

American Mental Health Counselors Association (AMHCA). (2000). *Code of ethics of the American Mental Health Counselors Association.* Alexandria, VA: Author.

American Mental Health Counselors Association (AMHCA). (2003). *Code of ethics* (2000, rev.). Pacific Grove, CA: Brooks/Cole.

American Psychiatric Association. (2000). *Diagnostic and statistical manual of mental disorders IV TR.* Arlington, VA: Author.

American Psychological Association (APA). (1997). *Resolution on appropriate therapeutic responses to sexual orientation.* Retrieved December 15, 2004, from http://www.apa.org/pi/lgbc/policy/pshome.html

American Psychological Association (APA). (2003a). *Ethical principles of psychologists and code of conduct.* Washington, DC: Author.

American Psychological Association (APA). (2003b). Guidelines on multicultural education, training, research, practice, and organizational change for psychologists. *American Psychologist, 58*(5), 377–402.

American Psychological Association (APA). (2004). *Answers to your questions about sexual orientation and homosexuality.* Retrieved December 15, 2004, from http://www.apa.org/pubinfo/answers.html

American School Counselor Association (ASCA). (2004). *Ethical standards for school counselors.* Alexandria, VA: Author.

American Society of Clinical Oncology (ASCO). (1998). *Cancer care during the last phase of life.* Retrieved December 23, 2005, from http://www.asco.org/ac/1,1003,_12-002174-00_18-0010346-00_19-0010351-00_20-001,00.asp

Americans United for Life. (2003). *State parental involvement laws for minors seeking abortion.* Chicago, IL: Americans United for Life.

Andero, A., & Steward, A. (2002). Issue of corporal punishment: Re-examined. *Journal of Instructional Psychology, 29*(2), 90–97.

Arizmendi, T., Beutler, I., Shantell, S., Crago, M., & Hagerman, R. (1985). Client-therapist value similarity and psychotherapy outcome: A microscopic analysis. *Psychotherapy: Theory, Research and Practice, 22,* 16–21.

Arthur, N., & Achenbach, K. (2002). Developing multicultural counseling competencies through experiential learning. *Counselor Education and Supervision, 42,* 2–14.

Association for Specialists in Group Work (ASGW). (1998). ASGW best practices guidelines. *Journal for Specialists in Group Work, 23,* 237–244.

Atkinson, D., & Lowe, S. (1995). Asian-American acculturation, gender, and willingness to seek counseling. *Journal of Multicultural Counseling and Development, 23,* 130–139.

Austad, C., & Berman, W. (1991). Managed health care and the evolution of psychotherapy. In C. Austad & W. Berman (Eds.), *Psychotherapy in managed care: The optimal use of time and resources* (pp. 3–18). Washington, DC: American Psychological Association.

Baez, A., & Hernandez, D. (2001). Complementary spiritual beliefs in the Latino community: The interface with psychotherapy. *American Journal of Orthopsychiatry, 71,* 408–415.

Baier, A. (1985). What do women want in a moral theory? *Nous, 19,* 53–65.

Baier, A. (1986). Trust and antitrust. *Ethics, 96,* 231–260.

Baier, A. (1994). *Moral prejudices: Essays on ethics.* Cambridge, MA: Harvard University Press.

Bakon, S. (2004). Wherefore *mitzvot,* the divine commandments? *Jewish Bible Quarterly, 32*(2), 108–114.

Banja, J. (1990). Rehabilitation and empowerment. *Archives of Physical Medicine and Rehabilitation, 71,* 614–615.

Bargh, J., & Alvarez, J. (2001). The road to hell: Good intentions in the face of nonconscious tendencies to misuse power. In A. Lee-Chai (Ed.), *The use and abuse of power: Multiple perspectives on the causes of corruption* (pp. 41–56). Philadelphia, PA: Psychological Press.

Barnett, J., & Scheetz, K. (2003). Technological advances and telehealth: Ethics, law, and the practice of psychotherapy. *Psychotherapy: Theory, Research, Practice, Training, 40,* 86–93.

Barstow, A. (1994). *Witchcraze: A new history of the European witch hunts.* London: Pandora.

Battin, M. (1994). *The least worst death: Essays in the bioethics on end-of-life.* New York: Oxford University Press.

Baumrind, D., Larzelere, R., & Cowan, P. (2002). Ordinary physical punishment: Is it harmful? Comment on Gershoff (2002). *Psychological Bulletin, 128*(4), 580–589.

Beauchamp, T., & Childress, J. (1989). *Principles of biomedical ethics* (3rd ed.). New York: Oxford University Press.

Beauchamp, T., & Childress, J. (2001). *Principles of biomedical ethics* (5th ed.). New York: Oxford University Press.

Becker, E. (1999). *Chronology on the history of slavery and racism.* Retrieved February 23, 2006, from http://innercity.org/holt/slavechron.html

Bellini, J. (2002). Correlates of multicultural counseling competencies of vocational rehabilitation counselors. *Rehabilitation Counseling Bulletin, 45,* 66–75.

Belt, D. (2002). The world of Islam. *National Geographic, 201,* 76–86.

Bergeron, R., & Gray, B. (2003). Ethical dilemmas of reporting suspected elder abuse. *Social Work, 48,* 96–105.

Berlin, I. (1983). Prevention of emotional problems among Native-American children: Overview of development. *Annual Progress in Child Psychiatry and Child Development,* 320–333.

Bernard, I., & Goodyear, R. (1998). *Fundamentals of clinical supervision* (2nd ed.). Needham Heights, MA: Allyn & Bacon.

Bersoff, D. (1996). The virtue of principle ethics. *The Counseling Psychologist, 24,* 86–91.

Betan, E. (1997). Toward a hermeneutic model of ethical decision making in clinical practice. *Ethics & Behavior, 7,* 347–365.

Beutler, L. (1979). Values, beliefs, religion and the persuasive influence in psychotherapy. *Psychotherapy: Theory, Research and Practice, 16,* 79–101.

Bevan, E., & Higgins, D. (2002). Is domestic violence learned? The contribution of five forms of child maltreatment to men's violence and adjustment. *Journal of Family Violence, 17,* 223–245.

Bever, P. (2002). Witchcraft, female aggression, and power in the modern community. *Journal of Social History, 35,* 955–990.

Blackard v. Memphis Area Med. Ctr. for Women, Inc., 262 F.3d 568 (6th Cir. 2001).

Blackburn, S. (1996). *Oxford dictionary of philosophy.* Oxford, UK: Oxford University Press.

Blasi, A. (1980). Bridging moral cognition and moral action. *Psychological Bulletin, 88,* 1–45.

Blum, R., & Resnick, M. (1982). Adolescent sexual decision-making: Contraception, pregnancy, abortion, motherhood. *Pediatric Annals, 11,* 797–805.

Blummer, R. (2000). Whose constitutional rights at risk of being trampled. *Milwaukee Journal Sentinel,* p. 19a. December 19, 2000.

Bopp, J., Bopp, M., Brown, L., & Lane, P. (1985). *The sacred tree* (2nd ed.). Lethbridge, AB: Four Winds Development Press.

Bopp, J., Lane, P., Brown, L., & Bopp, M. (1989). *The sacred tree* (3rd ed.). Wilmot, WI: Lotus Light.

Bordin, E. (1979). The generalizability of the psychoanalytic concept of the working alliance. *Psychotherapy: Theory, Research, and Practice, 16*, 252–260.

Bordin, E. (1983). A working alliance based model of supervision. *The Counseling Psychologist, 11*, 35–42.

Boss, J. (2004). *Ethics for life: A text with readings* (3rd ed.). Boston: McGraw-Hill.

Bowers, M., & Pipes, R. (2000). Influence of consultation on ethical decision-making: An analogue study. *Ethics & Behavior, 10*, 65–80.

Bowker, J. (Ed.). (1997). *The Oxford dictionary of world religions.* Oxford, UK: Oxford University Press.

Brabeck, M., & Ting, K. (2000). Feminist ethics: Lenses for examining ethical psychological practice. In M. Brabeck (Ed.), *Practicing feminist ethics in psychology* (pp. 17–35). Washington, DC: American Psychological Association.

Brackley, D., & Schubeck. T. (2002). Moral theology in Latin America. *Theological Studies, 63*, 123–160.

Brennan, S. (1999). Recent work in feminist ethics. *Ethics, 109*, 858–893.

Brenner, E. (2003). Consumer-focused psychological assessment. *Professional Psychology: Research and Practice, 34*, 240–247.

Brief of the Washington State Psychological Association et al. as Amici Curiae Supporting Respondents, Washington v. Glucksberg and Vacco v. Quill, filed with the Supreme Court of the United States (Oct., 1996). Retrieved June 24, 2004, from http://www .law.washington.edu/courses/tucker/A534/Documents/Support%20of%20 Respondents%201996%20WL%20708960.pdf

Brown, P., & O'Leary, K. (2000). Therapeutic alliance: Predicting continuance and success in group treatment for spouse abuse. *Journal of Consulting and Clinical Psychology, 68*, 340–345.

Bryan, K., & Lyons, H. (2003). Experiential activities and multicultural counseling competence training. *Journal of Counseling and Development, 81*, 400–409.

Buckle, S. (1993). Natural law. In P. Singer (Ed.), *A companion to ethics* (pp. 161–174). Malden, MA: Blackwell.

Bureau of Justice Statistics. (n.d.). *Capital punishment statistics.* Retrieved June 4, 2005, from http://www.ojp.usdoj.gov/bjs/cp.html

Burian, B. (2000). Social dual-role relationships during internships: A decision-making model. *Professional Psychology: Research and Practice, 31*, 332–378.

Calderbank, R. (2000). Abuse and disabled people: Vulnerability or social indifference? *Disability and Society, 15*, 521–534.

Campbell, A. (2003). The virtues (and vices) of the four principles. *Journal of Medical Ethics, 29*, 292–296.

Campbell, C., & Fox, G. (2003). Acknowledging the inevitable: Understanding multiple relationships in rural practice. *Professional Psychology: Research and Practice, 34*, 430–434.

Cappell, C., & Heiner, B. (1990). The intergenerational transmission of family aggression. *Journal of Family Violence, 5*, 135–152.

Carter, D., & Rashidi, A. (2003). Theoretical model of psychotherapy: Eastern Asian-Islamic women with mental illness. *Health Care for Women International, 24*(5), 399–413.

Cashwell, C., Myers, J., & Shurts, W. (2004). Using the developmental counseling and therapy model to work with a client in spiritual bypass: Some preliminary considerations. *Journal of Counseling and Development, 82*, 403–409.

Castelnuovo, G., Gaggioli, A., Mantovani, F., & Riva, G. (2003). From psychotherapy to e-therapy: The integration of traditional techniques and new communication tools in clinical settings. *Cyberpsychology and Behavior, 6,* 375–382.

Catholic Medical Association (CMA). (2000). *Homosexuality and hope.* Retrieved August 1, 2004, from http://www.narth.com/docs/hope.html

Centers for Disease Control, National Center for Injury and Prevention Control. (n.d.). *Suicide: Fact sheet.* Retrieved December 26, 2005, from http://www.cdc.gov/ncipc/factsheets/suifacts.htm

Chadrow, N. (1978). *The reproduction of mothering.* Berkeley: University of California Press.

Chang, T., & Yeh, C. (2003). Using online groups to provide support to Asian American men: Racial, cultural, gender, and treatment issues. *Professional Psychology: Research and Practice, 34,* 634–643.

Chao, R. (1994). Beyond parental control and authoritarian parenting style: Understanding Chinese parenting through the cultural notion of training. *Child Development, 65,* 1111–1119.

Chappelle, W. (2000). A series of progressive legal and ethical decision-making steps for using Christian spiritual interventions in psychotherapy. *Journal of Psychology and Theology, 28,* 43–54.

Cheng Lai, A., Zhang, Z., & Wang, W. (2000). Maternal child-rearing practices in Hong Kong and Beijing Chinese families: A comparative study. *International Journal of Psychology, 35,* 60–66.

Chessick, R. (1986). Heidegger for psychotherapists. *American Journal of Psychotherapy, 40,* 83–95.

Chessick, R. (1990). Hermeneutics for psychotherapists. *American Journal of Psychotherapy, 44,* 256–274.

Chi-Ying Chung, R., & Bemak, F. (2002). The relationship of culture and empathy in cross-cultural counseling. *Journal of Counseling and Development, 80,* 154–160.

Chintz, J., & Brown, R. (2001). Religious homogamy, marital conflict, and stability in same-faith and interfaith Jewish marriages. *Journal for the Scientific Study of Religion, 40,* 723–734.

Clarfield, A., Gordon, M., Markwell, H., & Alibhai, S. (2003). Ethical issues in end-of-life geriatric care: The approach of three monotheistic religions—Judaism, Catholicism, and Islam. *Journal of the American Geriatric Society, 51,* 1149–1154.

Clark, C., & Krupa, T. (2002). Reflections on empowerment in community mental health: Giving shape to an elusive idea. *Psychiatric Rehabilitation Journal, 25,* 341–349.

Clement, G. (1996). *Care, autonomy, and justice: Feminism and the ethic of care.* Boulder, CO: Westview Press.

Cohen, A. (1975). *Everyman's Talmud.* New York: Schocken Books.

Colby, A., Gibbs, J., Kohlberg, L., Speicher-Dubin, B., & Candee, D. (1979). *Standard form scoring manual: Part three form A.* Harvard, MA: Center for the Moral Education.

Coleman, H. (1998). General and multicultural counseling competency: Apples and oranges? *Journal of Multicultural Counseling and Development, 26,* 147–156.

Coleman, H., Wampold, B., & Casali, S. (1995). Ethnic minorities' ratings of ethnically similar and European American counselors: A meta-analysis. *Journal of Counseling Psychology, 42,* 55–64.

Commission on Rehabilitation Counselor Certification (CRCC). (1997). *Code of professional ethics for rehabilitation counselors.* Rolling Meadows, IL: Author.

Committee on Professional Practice and Standards. (2003). Legal issues in the professional practices of psychology. *Professional Psychology Research and Practice, 34,* 595–600.

Commonwealth v. Colon-Cruz. 393 Mass 150 (Supreme Judicial Court, 1984).

Connor, P., & Becker, B. (2003). Personal value systems and decision-making styles of public managers. *Public Personnel Management, 32,* 155–181.

Conoley, C., & Conoley, J. (1992). Effects of consulter problem presentation and consultant training on consultant problem definition. *Journal of Counseling and Development, 71,* 60–63.

Constantine, M. (2002). Predictors of satisfaction with counseling: Racial and ethnic minority clients' attitudes towards counseling and ratings of their counselors' general and multicultural competence. *Journal of Counseling Psychology, 49,* 255–263.

Cook, D., & Wiley, C. (2000). Psychotherapy with members of African American churches and spiritual traditions. In P. Richards & A. Bergin (Eds.), *Handbook of psychotherapy and religious diversity* (pp. 369–396). Washington, DC: American Psychological Association.

Cooper, C., & Gottlieb, M. (2000). Ethical issues with managed care: Challenges facing counseling psychology. *Counseling Psychologist, 28,* 179–236.

Cooper, T. (1998). *A time before deception: Truth in communication, culture, and ethics.* Santa Fe, NM: Clear Light.

Corey, G., Corey, M., & Callahan, P. (2003). *Issues and ethics in the helping professions.* Pacific Grove, CA: Brooks/Cole.

Cottone, R. (2001). A social constructivism model of ethical decision-making in counseling. *Journal of Counseling and Development, 79,* 39–46.

Cottone, R., & Claus, R. (2000). Ethical decision-making models: A review of the literature. *Journal of Counseling and Development, 78,* 275–283.

Council for Accreditation of Counseling and Related Educational Programs (CACREP). (2001). *CACREP accreditation manual.* Alexandria, VA: Author.

Creel, A. (1977). *Dharma in Hindu ethics.* Columbia, MO: South Asia Books.

Creel, H. (1970). *What is Taoism? and other studies in Chinese cultural history.* Chicago, IL: University of Chicago Press.

Cummings, A. (2000). Teaching feminist counselor responses to novice female counselors. [Electronic version]. *Counselor Education and Supervision, 40.*

Daly, M. (1990). *Gyn/ecology: The metaethics of radical feminism.* Boston: Beacon Press. (Original work published 1978)

Dana, R. (2002). Introduction. *Journal of Personality Assessment, 79,* 195–200.

Dana, R., Aguilar-Kitibutr, A., Diaz-Vivar, N., & Vetter, H. (2002). A teaching method for multicultural assessment: Psychological report contents and cultural competence. *Journal of Personality Assessment, 79,* 207–215.

Dancy, J. (1993). *Moral reasons.* Oxford, UK: Blackwell.

Daniel, J., Roysircar, G., Abeles, N., & Boyd, C. (2004). Individual and cultural diversity competency: Focus on the therapist. *Journal of Clinical Psychology, 47,* 155–164.

Danzinger, P., & Welfel, E. (2001). The impact of managed care on mental health counselors: A survey of perceptions, practices, and compliance with ethical standards. *Journal of Mental Health Counseling, 23,* 137–161.

De Beauvoir, S. (1953). *The second sex.* New York: Knopf.

De Keijser, J., Van der lendeen R., & Jackson, J. (2002). From moral theory to penal attitudes and back: A theoretically integrated modeling approach. *Behavioral Sciences and the Law, 20,* 317–335.

Deater-Deckard, K., Lansford, J., & Dodge, K. (2003). The development of attitudes about physical punishment: An 8-year longitudinal study. *Journal of Family Psychology, 17*(3), 351–360.

Death Penalty Information Center. (2004). *State by state information.* Retrieved December 23, 2005, from http://www.deathpenaltyinfo.org/state/

Dhand, A. (2002). The dharma of ethics, the ethics of dharma: Quizzing the ideals of Hinduism. *Journal of Religious Ethics, 30,* 347–372.

Dilthey, W. (1978). *The critique of historical reason* (M. Emarth, trans.). Chicago, IL: University of Chicago Press.

Dorff, E. (2000). Ethics of Judaism. In J. Neusner & A. Avery-Peck (Eds.), *The Blackwell companion to Judaism* (pp. 373–388). Malden, MA: Blackwell.

Dornbusch, S., Ritter, P., Leiderman, P., Roberts, D., & Fraleigh, M. (1987). The relation of parenting style to adolescent school performance. *Child Development, 58,* 1244–1258.

Dubiel, H. (Fall, 2003). The remembrance of the Holocaust as a catalyst for a transnational ethic? *New German Critique, 90,* 59–70.

Duck, R., & Hunsberger, B. (2000). Religious orientation and prejudice: The role of religious proscription, right-wing authoritarianism and social desirability. *The International Journal for the Psychology of Religion, 9,* 157–179.

Dull, V., & Skokan, L. (1995). A cognitive model of religion's influence on health. *Journal of Social Issues, 51,* 49–64.

Duncan, L. (2003). Understanding leaders of repressive social movements. *Analysis of social issues and public policy, 3,* 181–184.

Elderly Persons and Persons with Disabilities Abuse Protection Act (EPPDAPA). (2003). ORS 124.005–124.040.

Elleven, R., & Allen, J. (2004). Applying technology to online counseling: Suggestions for the beginning e-therapist. *Journal of Instructional Psychology, 31,* 223–228.

Eriksen, K., Marston, G., & Korte, T. (2002). Working with God: Managing conservative Christian beliefs that may interfere with counseling. *Counseling and Values, 47,* 48–68.

Espin, O., & Gawelek, M. (1992). Women's diversity: Ethnicity, race, class, and gender in theories of feminist psychology. In M. Ballou & L. Brown (Eds.), *Personality and psychopathology: Feminist reappraisals* (pp. 88–107). New York: Guilford Press.

Esposito, J. (1999). *The Islamic threat: Myth or reality?* (3rd ed.). New York: Oxford University Press.

Evans, G., & Farberow, N. (1988). *The encyclopedia of suicide.* New York: Facts on File.

Evans, M., Boothroyd, R., Armstrong, M., Greenbaum, P., Brown, E., & Kuppinger, A. (2003). An experimental study of the effectiveness of intensive and in-home crisis services for children and their families: Program outcomes. *Journal of Emotional and Behavioral Disorders, 11,* 92–102.

Fair, D. (1959). Psychology and the Christian: An editorial. *Journal of the American Scientific Affiliation, 11,* 98–99.

Falcov, C. (1988). Learning to think culturally. In H. Liddle, D. Breunlin, & R. Schwartz (Eds.), *Handbook of family therapy training and supervision* (pp. 335–357). New York: Guilford Press.

Fawcett, S., White, G., Balcazar, F., Suarez-Balcazar, Y., Mathews, E., Paine-Andrews, P., et al. (1994). A contextual-behavioral model of empowerment: Case studies involving people with physical disabilities. *American Journal of Community Psychology, 22,* 471–496.

Fisher, C., & Fried, A. (2003). Internet-mediated psychological services and the American Psychological Association ethics code. *Psychotherapy, Theory, Research, Practice, 40,* 103–111.

Fishman, S. (2004). *Double or nothing: Jewish families and mixed marriage.* Waltham, MA: Brandeis University Press.

Flynn, C. (1993). *Regional differences in attitudes toward corporal punishment.* Paper presented at the annual meeting of the American Sociological Association, Miami Beach, FL.

Follesdal, D. (2001). Hermeneutics. *International Journal of Psychoanalysis, 82,* 375–379.

Fontes, L. (2002). Child discipline and physical abuse in immigrant Latino families: Reducing violence and misunderstandings. *Journal of Counseling and Development, 80,* 31–41.

Foot, P. (2000). *Natural goodness.* New York: Oxford University Press.

Ford, J., & Beveridge, A. (2004). "Bad" neighbors, fast food, "sleaky" businesses, and drug dealers: Relations between the location of licit and illicit businesses in the urban environment. *Journal of Drug Issues, 34,* 51–81.

Foster, G. (1960). *Culture and conquest.* Chicago, IL: Quadrangle Books.

Fowers, B., & Richardson, F. (1996). Why is multiculturalism good? *American Psychologist, 51,* 609–621.

Fowers, B., & Tjeltveit, A. (2003). Virtue obscured and retrieved: Character, community, and practices in behavioral science. *American Behavioral Scientist, 47,* 387–394.

Frame, M., & Stevens-Smith, P. (1995). Out of harm's way: Enhancing monitoring and dismissal processes in counselor education programs. *Counselor Education and Supervision, 32,* 118–129.

Freeman, S. (2000). *Ethics: An introduction to philosophy and practice.* Belmont, CA: Wadsworth.

Freeman, S. (2003). Introduction: John Rawls—An overview. In S. Freeman (Ed.), *The Cambridge companion to Rawls* (pp. 1–61). Cambridge, UK: Cambridge University Press.

Freuchen, D. (Ed.). (1957). *Book of the Eskimos.* Cleveland, OH: World.

Friedan, B. (1963). *The feminine mystique.* New York: Dell.

Friedan, B. (1981). *The second stage.* New York: Summit Books.

Fuertes, J. (2001). Future research directions in the study of counselor multicultural competency. *Journal of Multicultural Counseling and Development, 29,* 3–13.

Fuertes, J., & Brobst, K. (2002). Client's ratings of counselor multicultural competency. *Cultural Diversity and Ethnic Minority Psychology, 8,* 214–223.

Gadamer, H. (1975). *Truth and method* (trans. G. Barden & J. Cumming). New York: Crossroad.

Gale Group. (2002, May). Key moments of Islamic civilization. *New Internationalist Magazine* (345), 10–26.

Gandhi, M. (1927). *An autobiography: The story of my experiences with truth.* Ahmedabad, India: Navajivan.

Ganote, S. (1990). A look at counseling in long term–care settings. *Generations, 14,* 31–34.

Garcia, J., Cartwright, B., Winston, S., & Borzuchowska, B. (2003). A transcultural integrative model for ethical decision making in counseling. *Journal of Counseling and Development, 81,* 268–277.

Gardner, W., Scherer, D., & Tester, M. (1989). Asserting scientific authority: Cognitive development and adolescent legal rights. *American Psychologist, 44,* 895–902.

Gati, I., Krausz, M., & Osipow, S. (1996). A taxonomy of difficulties in career decision-making. *Journal of Counseling Psychology, 43,* 510–526.

Gbadegesin, S. (2001). Yoruba philosophy: Individuality, community, and the moral order. In E. Eze (Ed.), *African philosophy: An anthology* (pp. 130–141). Oxford, UK: Blackwell.

George, L., Larson, D., Koenig, H., & McCullough, M. (2000). Spirituality and health: What we know, what we need to know. *Journal of Social and Clinical Psychology, 19,* 102–116.

Gershoff, E. (2002). Corporal punishment by parents and associated child behaviors and experiences: A meta analytic and theoretical review. *Psychological Bulletin, 128,* 539–579.

Giles-Sims, J., Straus, M., & Sugarman, D. (1995). Child, maternal, and family characteristics associated with spanking. *Family Relations, 44,* 170–176.

Gilligan, C. (1982). *In a different voice: Psychological theory and women's development.* Cambridge, MA: Harvard University Press.

Gilligan, C. (2004). Recovering psyche. Reflections on life-history and history. *Annal of Psychoanalysis, 32,* 131–147.

Gilligan, C., & Attanucci, J. (1988). Two moral orientations: Gender differences and similarities. *Merrill-Palmer Quarterly, 34,* 223–237.

Gillman, R. (1991). Termination in psychotherapy with children and adolescents. In A. Schmukler (Ed.), *Saying goodbye: A casebook of termination in child and adolescent analysis and therapy* (pp. 339–354). Hillsdale, NJ: Analytic Press.

Glover, J. (1990). (Ed.). *Utilitarianism and its critics.* NY: Macmillan.

Goesling, J., Potts, S., & Handelsman, M. (2000). Perceptions of confidential violations among psychologists. *Ethics and Behavior, 10,* 363–375.

Goldstein, J., & Kornfield, J. (1987). *Seeking the heart of wisdom.* Boston: Shambhala.

Gomez, M. (1994). Muslims in early America. *The Journal of Southern History, 60*(4), 671–710.

Gone, J. (2004). Mental health services for Native Americans in the 21st century United States. *Professional Psychology: Research and Practice, 35,* 10–18.

Good, G., Dell, D., & Mintz, L. (1989). Male role and gender role conflict: Relations to help seeking in men. *Journal of Counseling Psychology, 36,* 295–300.

Gracia, J. (2000). *Hispanic/Latino identity: A philosophical perspective.* Malden, MA: Blackwell.

Granello, D. (2000). Encouraging the cognitive development of supervisees: Using Bloom's taxonomy in supervision. *Counselor Education and Supervision, 40,* 31–46.

Griffin-Carlson, M., & Schwanenflugel, P. (1998). Adolescent abortion and parental notification: Evidence for the importance of family functioning on the perceived quality of parental involvement in U.S. families. *Journal of Child Psychology and Psychiatry, 39*, 543–553.

Grimshaw, J. (1993). The idea of a female ethic. In P. Singer (Ed.), *A companion to ethics* (pp. 491–499). Malden, MA: Blackwell.

Gruber, E., & Anderson, M. (1990). Legislating parental involvement in adolescent abortion: Reexamining the arguments of Worthington and his colleagues. *American Psychologist, 45*, 1174–1176.

Gutierrez, G. (1973). *A theology of liberation.* Maryknoll, NY: Orbis Books.

Guyer, P. (1992). Introduction: The starry heavens and the moral law. In P. Guyer (Ed.), *The Cambridge companion to Kant* (pp. 1–25). New York: Cambridge University Press.

Haddad, Y. (1991). *The Muslims in America.* New York: Oxford University Press.

Haddad, Y. (1999). The globalization of Islam: The return of Muslims to the West. In J. Esposito (Ed.), *The Oxford history of Islam* (pp. 549–600). Oxford, UK: Oxford University Press.

Hadjistavropoulos, T., Malloy, D., Sharpe, D., & Fuchs-Lacelle, S. (2003). The ethical ideologies of psychologists and physicians: A preliminary comparison. *Ethics and Behavior, 13*, 97–104.

Hadjistavropoulos, T., Malloy, D., Sharpe, D., Green, S., & Fuchs-Lacelle, S. (2002). The relative importance of the ethical principles adopted by the American Psychological Association. *Canadian Psychology, 43*, 254–259.

Hall, A., & Fradkin, H. (1992). Affirming gay men's mental health: Counseling with a new attitude. *Journal of Mental Health Counseling, 14*, 362–374.

Halwani, R. (2003). Care ethics and virtue ethics. *Hypatia, 18*, 161–192.

Hansen, C. (1992). *A Daoist theory of Chinese thought: A philosophical interpretation.* New York: Oxford University Press.

Hardeman, D. (2002). Therapeutic antidotes: Helping gay and bisexual men recover from conversion therapies. *Journal of Gay and Lesbian Psychotherapy, 5*, 119–132.

Hare, R. (1963). *Freedom and reason.* Oxford, UK: Clarendon Press.

Hare, R. (1991). The philosophical basis of psychiatric ethics. In S. Block & P. Chodoff (Eds.), *Psychiatric ethics* (2nd ed.) (pp. 15–42). Oxford, UK: Oxford University Press.

Harris, C. (1997). *Applying moral theories* (3rd ed.). Belmont, CA: Wadsworth.

Harris, C. (2002). *Applying moral theories* (4th ed.). Belmont, CA: Wadsworth.

Harris, M., & Mertlich, D. (2003). Piloting home-based behavioral family systems therapy for adolescents with poorly controlled diabetes. *Children's Health Care, 32*, 65–79.

Harrison, A., Wilson, M., Pine, C., Chan, S., & Buriel, R. (1990). Family ecologies of ethnic minority children. *Child Development, 61*, 347–362.

Hassouneh-Phillips, D. (2001). Polygamy and wife abuse: A qualitative study of Muslim women in America. *HealthCare for Women International, 22*, 735–748.

Hathaway, W. (2002). Integration as interpretation: A hermeneutical-realist view. *Journal of Psychology and Christianity, 21*, 205–218.

Hathaway, W., Scott, S., & Garvey, S. (2004). Assessing religious/spiritual functioning: A neglected domain in clinical practice? *Professional Psychology: Research and Practice, 35*, 97–104.

Heaton, T., & Pratt, E. (1990). The effects of religious homogamy on marital satisfaction. *Journal of Family Issues, 11*, 191–207.

Heaven, P., & Oxman, L. (1999). Human values, conservatism and stereotypes of homosexuals. *Personality and Individual Differences, 27*, 109–118.

Held, V. (1987). Feminism and moral theory. In E. Kittay & D. Meyers (Eds.), *Women and moral theory* (pp. 111–128). Totowa, NJ: Rowman & Littlefield.

Helminiak, D. (2004). The ethics of sex: A call to the gay community. *Pastoral Psychology, 52*, 259–267.

Hendey, N., & Pascall, G. (1998). Independent living: Gender, violence, and the threat of violence. *Disability and Society, 13*, 415–427.

Henry, C. (1996). Taking an ethical position on standards. *British Journal of Guidance and Counselling, 24*, 35–45.

Hensley, L., Smith, S., & Thompson, R. (2003). Assessing competencies of counselors-in-training: Complexities in evaluating personal and professional development. *Counselor Education and Supervision, 42*, 219–331.

Herlihy, B., Gray, N., & McCollum, V. (2002), Legal and ethical issues in school counselor supervision. *Professional School Counseling, 6*, 55–61.

Hilton, N., Harris, G., & Rice, M. (2001). Predicting violence by serious wife assaulters. *Journal of Interpersonal Violence, 16*, 408–423.

Hite, R., & Fraser, C. (1988). Meta-analyses of attitudes toward advertising by professionals. *Journal of Marketing 52*, 95–105.

Ho, D. (1986). Chinese patterns of socialization: A critical review. In M. Bond (Ed.), *The psychology of the Chinese people* (pp. 1–25). New York: Oxford University Press.

Ho, F., & Johnson, R. (1990). Intra-ethnic and inter-ethnic marriage and divorce in Hawaii. *Social Biology, 37*, 44–51.

Hoagland, S. (1989). *Lesbian ethics*. Palo Alto, CA: Institute of Lesbian Studies.

Hong, G. (1993). Contextual factors in psychotherapy with Asian Americans. In J. Chin, J. Liem, M. Ham, & G. Hong (Eds.), *Transference and empathy in Asian American psychotherapy: Cultural values and treatment needs* (pp. 3–13). Westport, CT: Praeger.

Hong, G., & Friedman, M.(1998). The Asian American family. In M. Friedman (Ed.), *Family nursing: Theory and practice* (4th ed.) (pp. 547–566). Stamford, CT: Appleton & Lange.

Hong, G., & Ham, M. (2001). *Psychotherapy and counseling for Asian American clients: A practical guide*. Thousand Oaks, CA: Sage.

Hospice. (n.d.) *More About Hospice Services*. Retrieved May 27, 2005, from http://www.hospiceweb.com/info.htm

Hourani, G. (1971). *Islamic rationalism: The ethics of Abd al-Jabbar*. Oxford, UK: Clarendon Press.

Houser, R., & Ham, M. (2004). *Gaining power and control through diversity and group affiliation*. Westport, CT: Praeger.

Houser, R., Hampton, N., & Carriker, C. (2000). Implementing the empowerment concept in rehabilitation: Contributions of social role theory. *Journal of Applied Rehabilitation Counseling, 31*(2), 18–23.

Hunsberger, B. (1995). Religion and prejudice: The role of religious fundamentalism, quest, and right-wing authoritarianism. *Journal of Social Issues, 51*, 113–129.

Hunsberger, B., Owusu, V., & Duck, R. (1999). Religion and prejudice in Ghana and Canada: Religious fundamentalism, right-wing authoritarianism, and attitudes toward homosexuals and women. *International Journal for the Psychology of Religion, 9*, 181–194.

Hunsley, J. (1999). Comparing therapist and client perspectives on reasons for psychotherapy termination. *Psychotherapy: Theory, Research, Practice, Training, 36*, 380–388.

Hunsley, J., Aubry, T., Verstervelt, C., & Vito, D. (1999). Comparing therapist and client perspectives on reasons for psychotherapy termination. *Psychotherapy, 36*, 380–388.

Ibrahim, F. (1996). A multicultural perspective on principle and virtue ethics. *The Counseling Psychologist, 24*, 78–85.

Individuals with Disabilities Education Act. (1999). 20 U.S.C. §§ 1400 et seq. Implementing Regulation: 34 CFR Part 300.

Ingersoll, R. (2000). Teaching a psychopharmacology course to counselors: Justification, structure, and methods. *Counselor Education and Supervision, 40*, 58–69.

Isaacs, M., & Stone, C. (2001). Confidentiality with minors: Mental health counselors' attitudes toward breaching or preserving confidentiality. *Journal of Mental Health Counseling, 23*, 342–357.

Jackson, L., & Hunsberger, B. (1999). An intergroup perspective on religion and prejudice. *Journal for the Scientific Study of Religion, 38*, 509–524.

Jaffee, S. (2002). Pathways to adversity in young adulthood among early childbearers. *Journal of Family Psychology, 16*, 38–49.

Jaggar, A. (1991). Feminist ethics: Projects, problems, prospects. In C. Card (Ed.), *Feminist ethics* (pp. 78–106). Lawrence, KS: University Press of Kansas.

Jaggar, A. (1992). Feminist ethics. In L. Becker & C. Becker (Eds.), *Encyclopedia of Ethics* (pp. 363–364). New York: Garland Press.

Jankowski, P., & Martin, M. (2003). Reporting cases of child maltreatment: Decision-making processes of family therapists in Illinois. *Contemporary Family Therapy, 25*, 311–332.

Jones, W., & Markos, P. (1997). Client rating of counselor effectiveness: A call for caution. *Journal of Applied Rehabilitation Counseling, 28*, 23–28.

Jordan, A., & Meara, N. (1990). Ethics and the professional practice of psychologists: The role of virtues and principles. *Professional Psychology: Research and Practice, 21*, 107–114.

Jospe, A. (1995). The meaning of Jewish existence. In E. Dorff & L. Newman (Eds.), *Contemporary Jewish ethics and morality: A reader* (pp. 251–258). New York: Oxford University Press.

Kant, I. (1953). *The moral law; or groundwork of the metaphysic of morals* (Rev. ed.) (H. Paton, Trans.). London: Hutchinson. (Original work published 1785)

Kaplan, M. (1994). *The meaning of God in modern Jewish religion*. Detroit, MI: Wayne State University Press. (Original work published 1962)

Kasser, F., Koestner, R., & Lekes, N. (2002). Early family experiences and adult values: A 26 year, prospective longitudinal study. *Personality and Social Psychology Bulletin, 28*, 826–835.

Keith-Spiegel, P., & Koocher, G. (1985). *Ethics in psychology: Professional standards and cases*. New York: Erlbaum.

Kellner, M. (1993). Jewish ethics. In P. Singer (Ed.), *A companion to ethics* (pp. 82–90). Malden, MA: Blackwell.

Kellner, M.(1995).The structure of Jewish ethics. In E. Dorff & L. Newman (Eds.), *Contemporary Jewish ethics and morality: A reader* (pp. 12–24). New York: Oxford University Press.

Kelly, M. (1984). *Islam: The religious and political life of a world community.* Westport, CT: Praeger.

Kennedy, R. (2002, December). Interracial intimacy. [Electronic version]. *The Atlantic Monthly, 290*(5). Retrieved November 8, 2004, from http://www.theatlantic.com/doc/prem/200212/kennedy

Keown, D. (1995*). Buddhism and bioethics.* New York: St. Martin's.

Kermani, E., & Drob, S. (1987). Tarasoff decision: A decade later dilemma still faces psychotherapists. *American Journal of Psychotherapy, 41,* 271–285.

Kierstead, F., & Wagner, P. (1993). *The ethical, legal and multicultural foundations of teaching.* Dubuque, IA: Brown & Benchmark.

Kigongo, J. (2005). The relevance of African ethics to contemporary African society: Cultural heritage and contemporary change. Chapter 2 in *Ethics, Human Rights, and Development in Africa.* Series II(8). Retrieved January 27, 2005, from http://www.crvp.org/book/Series02/II-8/contents.htm

Kilpatrick, W. (1986). Moral character, story telling and virtue. In R. Knowles & G. McLean (Eds.), *Psychological foundations of moral education and character development* (pp. 183–199). New York: University Press of America.

Kim, B., Hill, C., Gelso, C., Goates, M., Asay, P., & Harbin, J. (2003). Counselor self-disclosure: East Asian American client adherence to Asian cultural values and counseling process. *Journal of Counseling Psychology, 50,* 324–332.

Kim, B., & Lyons, H. (2003). Experiential activities and multicultural counseling competence training. *Journal of Counseling and Development, 81,* 400–409.

King, M. (1968, February). *The drum major instinct.* Sermon delivered at Ebenezer Baptist Church, Atlanta, Georgia. Available from http://www.stanford.edu/group/King/publications/sermons/680204.000_Drum_Major_Instinct.html

Kinnier, R., Kernes, J., & Dautheribes, T. (2000). A short list of universal moral values. *Counseling and Values, 45,* 4–22.

Kirk-Greene, A. (2001). Mutumin Kirki: The concept of the good man in Hausa. In E. Eze (Ed.), *African philosophy: An anthology* (pp. 121–129). Oxford, UK: Blackwell.

Kitagawa, J., Tucci, G., & Reynolds, F. (1993). The Buddha and Buddhism. In *The new encyclopedia Britannica* (Vol. 15, pp. 270–276). Chicago, IL: Encyclopedia Britannica.

Kitchener, K. (1984). Intuition, critical evaluation, and ethical principles: The foundation for ethical decisions in counseling psychology. *The Counseling Psychologist, 12,* 43–55.

Klages, M. (2003). *Postmodernism.* Retrieved July 27, 2004, from www.colorado.edu/English/ENGL2012Klages/pomo.html

Kleespies, P., Hughes, D., & Gallacher, F. (2000). Suicide in the medically and terminally ill: Psychological and ethical considerations. *Journal of Clinical Psychology, 56,* 1153–1171.

Kluckhohn, C. (1949). *Mirror for man.* New York: McGraw-Hill.

Kluckhohn, C., & Leighton, D. (1974). *The Navaho.* Cambridge, MA: Harvard University Press.

Knapp, S. (1999). Utilitarianism and the ethics of professional psychologists. *Ethics and Behavior, 9,* 383–393.

Knapp, S., & Sturm, C. (2002). Ethics education after licensing: Ideas for increased diversity in content and process. *Ethics and Behavior, 12,* 157–166.

Kocarek, C., Talbot, D., Batka, J., & Anderson, M. (2001). Reliability and validity of three measures of multicultural competency. *Journal of Counseling and Development, 79,* 486–498.

Kohlberg, L. (1981). *Philosophy of moral development.* San Francisco: Harper & Row.

Kohlberg, L. (1984). *Essays in moral development: Vol. 2, The psychology of moral development.* New York: Harper & Row.

Kohn, L. (1993). *The Taoist experience: An anthology.* Albany: State University of New York Press.

Kohn, L. (2001). *Daoism and Chinese culture.* Cambridge, MA: Three Pines Press.

Koss-Chioino, J. (1995). Traditional and folk approaches among ethnic minorities. In J. Aponte, R. Rivers, & J. Wohl (Eds.), *Psychological interventions and cultural diversity* (pp. 145–163). Boston: Allyn & Bacon.

Kramer, S. (1990). *Positive endings in psychotherapy: Bringing meaningful closure to therapeutic relationships.* San Francisco, CA: Jossey-Bass.

Kropp, P., Hart, S., Webster, C., & Eaves, D. (1999). *Manual for the spousal assault risk assessment guide.* Toronto, ON: Multi-Health Systems.

Kubler-Ross, E. (1969). *On death and dying.* New York: Touchstone.

Kuntze, M., Stoermer, R., Mueller-Spahn, F., & Bullinger, A. (2002). Ethical codes and values in a virtual world. *Cyber Psychology and Behavior, 5,* 203–206.

Kuther, T. (2003). Medical decision-making and minors: Issues of consent and assent. *Adolescence, 38,* 343–357.

Kuykendall, R., & Day, A. (1967). *Hawaii: A history, from Polynesian kingdom to American state.* Englewood Cliffs, NJ: Prentice-Hall.

Ladany, N., Lehman-Waterman, D., Molinaro, M., & Wolgast, B. (1999). Psychotherapy supervisor ethical practices: Adherence to guidelines, the supervisory working alliance, and supervisee satisfaction. *The Counseling Psychologist, 27,* 443–475.

Ladany, N., Marotta, S., & Muse-Burke, J. (2001). Counselor experience related to complexity of case conceptualization and supervision preference. *Counselor Education and Supervision, 40,* 203–219.

Ladany, N., Walker, J., & Melincoff, D. (2001). Supervisory style: Its relation to the supervisory working alliance and supervisor self-disclosure. *Counselor Education and Supervision, 40,* 263–275.

Lakin, M. (1988). *Ethical issues in psychotherapy.* New York: Oxford University Press.

Lamb, D., & Catanzaro, S. (1998). Sexual and nonsexual boundary violations involving psychologists, clients, supervisees, and students: Implications for professional practice. *Professional Psychology: Research and Practice, 29,* 498–503.

Lamb, D., Catanzaro, S., & Moorman, A. (2003). Psychologists reflect on their sexual relationships with clients, supervisees, and students: Occurrence, impact, rationales, and collegial intervention. *Professional Psychology: Research and Practice, 34,* 102–107.

Lange, A., & Rietdijk, D. (2003). Interapy: A controlled randomized trial of the standardization treatment of posttraumautic stress through the internet. *Journal of Consulting and Clinical Psychology, 71,* 901–909.

Lanza, M. (2001). Setting fees: The conscious and unconscious meaning of money. *Perspectives in Psychiatric Care, 37,* 69–72.

Lawrence, G., & Robinson Kurpius, S. (2000). Legal and ethical issues involved when counseling minors in non school settings. *Journal of Counseling and Development, 78,* 130–137.

Lee, E. (1997). *Working with Asian Americans: A guide for clinicians.* New York: Guilford Press.

Leung, K., Lau, S., & Lam, W. (1998). Parenting styles and academic achievement: A cross cultural study. *Merrill Palmer Quarterly, 44*(2), 157–172.

Levin, B. (2002). From slavery to hate crime laws: The emergence of race and status-based protection in American criminal law. *Journal of Social Issues, 58,* 227–245.

Liebman, C., & Fishman, S. (2000). Jewish communal policy toward outmarried families. *Journal of Jewish Communal Service, 77,* 17–27.

Liebowitz, A., Eisen, M., & Chow, W. (1984). *An economic model of teenage pregnancy decision making* (Research Report No. 5. 009). Austin, TX: University of Texas Population Research Center.

Liezel, G., & Meyer, J. (2002). Career indecision amongst prospective university students. *South African Journal of Psychology, 32,* 41–48.

Lindsay, G. (1996). Psychology as an ethical discipline and profession. *European Psychologist, 1,* 79–88.

Linzer, N. (1992). The role of values in determining agency policy. *The Journal of Contemporary Human Services, 73*(9), 553–558.

Littrell, J., & Littrell, M. (1982). American Indian and Caucasian students' preferences for counselors: Effects of counselor dress and sex. *Journal of Counseling Psychology, 29,* 48–57.

Lombardi, F., & Lombardi, G. (1982). *Circle without end.* Happy Camp, CA: Naturegraph.

Lunt, I. (1999). The professionalization of psychology in Europe. *European Psychologist, 4,* 240–247.

MacIntyre, A. (1984). *After virtue* (2nd ed.). Notre Dame, IN: University of Notre Dame Press.

MacIntyre, A. (1999). *Dependent rational animals: Why human beings need virtues.* Peru, IL: Open Court.

Magnuson, S., Norem, K., & Wilcoxon, A. (2000). Clinical supervision of prelicensed counselors: Recommendations for consideration and practice. *Journal of Mental Health Counseling, 22,* 176–190.

Maheu, M. (2003). The online clinical practice management model. *Psychotherapy: Theory, Research, Practice, Training, 40,* 20–32.

Malloy, D., Hadjistavropoulos, T., Douaud, P., & Smythe, W. (2002). The codes of ethics of the Canadian Psychological Association and the Canadian Medical Association: Ethical orientation and functional grammar analysis. *Canadian Psychology, 43,* 244–253.

Margolin, G., Gordis, E., Medina, A., & Oliver, P. (2003). The co-occurrence of husband-to-wife aggression, family-of-origin aggression, and child abuse potential in a community sample. *Journal of Interpersonal Violence, 18,* 413– 440.

Marmor, A. (2001). The nature of law. In E. Zalta (Ed.), *The Stanford encyclopedia of philosophy.* Retrieved March 3, 2005, from http://plato.standford.edu/archives/sum2001/entries/lawphil-nature/

Marshall, J. (2001). *The Lakota way: Stories and lessons for living.* New York: Viking Compass.

Marshall, J. (2002). *The Lakota way: Stories and lessons for living, Native American wisdom on ethics and character.* New York: Penguin Compass.

Martin, J., & Thompson, J. (2003). Psychotherapy as the interpretation of being: Hermeneutic perspectives on psychotherapy. *Journal of Constructivist Psychology, 16,* 1–16.

Martin, N. (2001). Feminist bioethics and psychiatry. *Journal of Medicine and Philosophy, 26,* 431–441.

Maton, K., & Wells, E. (1995). Religion as a community resource for well-being: Prevention, healing, and empowerment pathways. *Journal of Social Issues, 51,* 177–193.

Mattison, M. (2000). Ethical decision-making: The person in the process. *Social Work, 45,* 201–213.

May, W. (1984). The virtues in a professional setting. *Soundings, 67,* 245–266.

Mbiti, J. (1969). *African religions and philosophy.* London: Heinemann.

McKie, A. (2004). "The demolition of a man": Lessons from the Holocaust literature for the teaching of nursing ethics. *Nursing Ethics, 11,* 138–149.

McLeod, J. (1992). What do we know about how best to assess counselor competence? *Counseling Psychology Quarterly, 5,* 359–373.

Meara, N., Schmidt, L., & Day, J. (1996). Principles and virtues: A foundation for ethical decisions, policies, and character. *The Counseling Psychologist, 24,* 4–77.

Meilander, G. (1984). *The theory and practice of virtue.* Notre Dame, IN: University of Notre Dame Press.

Melton, G. (1990). Knowing what we do know: APA and adolescent abortion. *American Psychologist, 45,* 1171–1173.

Merriam, S., Courtenay, B., & Baumgartner, L. (2003). On becoming a witch: Learning in a marginalized community of practice. *Adult Education Quarterly, 53,* 170–188.

Merskey, H. (1996). Ethical issues in the search for repressed memories. *American Journal of Psychotherapy, 50,* 323–336.

Meyer, J. (2002). Career indecision amongst prospective university students. *South African Journal of Psychology, 32,* 41–48.

Milan, S., Ickovics, J., Kershaw, T., Lewis, J., Meade, C., & Ethier, K. (2004). Prevalence, course, and predictors of emotional distress in pregnant and parenting adolescents. *Journal of Consulting and Clinical Psychology, 72,* 328–340.

Mill, J. (1970). The subjection of women. In A. Rossi (Ed.), *Essays on sex equality* (pp. 125–156). Chicago, IL: University of Illinois Press.

Miller, D. (1981). Sources of Hindu ethical studies: A critical review. *Journal of Religious Ethics, 9,* 186–198.

Miller, D. (1991). The necessity of principles in virtue ethics. *Professional Psychology: Research and Practice, 22,* 107.

Miller, J. (2003). *Daoism: A short introduction.* Oxford, UK: Oneworld.

Miller, L., & Lovinger, R. (2000). Psychotherapy with conservative and reform Jews. In P. Richards & A. Bergin (Eds.), *Handbook of psychotherapy and religious diversity* (pp. 259–286). Washington, DC: American Psychological Association.

Mio, J., Trimble, J., Arredondo, P., Cheatham, H., & Sue, D. (Eds.). (2000). *Key words in multicultural interventions.* Westport, CT: Greenwood.

Mississippi Code (1972). Sec. 43-21-105. Definitions. Retrieved December 22, 2005, from http://www.mscode.com/free/statutes/43/021/0105.htm

Mitchell, D. (2002). *Buddhism: Introducing the Buddhist experience.* New York: Oxford University Press.

Moldoveanu, M., & Stevenson, H. (1998). Ethical universals in practice: An analysis of five principles. *Journal of Socio-Economics, 27,* 721–753.

Moore, A. (2002). African-American early childhood teachers' decisions to refer African-American students. *Qualitative Studies in Education, 15,* 631–652.

Moore, M. (1996). Good without God. In R. George (Ed.), *Natural law, liberalism, and morality* (pp. 221–270). New York: Oxford University Press.

Morel, E. (1920). *The black man's burden: The white man in Africa from the fifteenth century to World War I.* Manchester, UK: National Labour Press.

Morinis, A. (2002). Musar and the path of the Mensch. *Tikkun, 17*(2), 65–68.

Mullett, S. (1988). Shifting perspectives: A new approach to ethics. In L. Code, S. Mullett, & C. Overall (Eds.), *Feminist perspectives: Philosophical essays on method and morals* (pp. 109–126). Toronto, ON: University of Toronto Press.

Muratori, M. (2001). Examining supervisor impairment from the counselor trainee's perspective. *Counselor Education and Supervision, 41,* 1–42.

Murphy, M. (2001). *Natural law and practical rationality.* Cambridge, UK: Cambridge University Press.

Najim, M. (1999). The natural law in the church's moral teaching: Physicalism or personalism. *Seminarian Writings, sem020.* Retrieved July 31, 2004, from http://www.cfpeople.org/SeminarianWritings/sem020.html

Nell, O. (1975). *Acting on principle: An essay on Kantian ethics.* New York: Columbia University Press.

Neukrug, E., & Lovell, C. (1996). Employing ethical codes and ethical decision-making models: A developmental process. *Counseling and Values, 40,* 98–104.

Neukrug, E., Milliken, T., & Walden, S. (2001). Ethical complaints made against credentialed counselors: An updated survey of state licensing boards. *Counselor Education and Supervision, 41,* 57–71.

New York Office of Children & Family Services. (2002). *Summary guide for mandated reporters in New York State.* Publication #1159. Albany, NY: Author.

Nicki, A. (2002). Feminist philosophy of disability, care ethics and mental illness. *Nursing Philosophy, 3,* 270–272.

Nicolosi, J., Byrd, D., & Potts, R. (2000). Retrospective self-reports of changes in sexual orientation: A consumer survey of conversion therapy clients. *Psychological Reports, 86,* 1071–1088.

Nightingale Alliance. (2004). *U.S. historical perspective and current trends.* Retrieved February 23, 2006, from http://www.nightingalealliance.org/cgi-bin/home.pl?article=204

Nigro, T. (2003). Dual relationship activities: Principal component analysis of counselors' attitudes. *Ethics and Behavior, 13,* 191–201.

Noddings, N. (1992). In defense of caring. *The Journal of Clinical Ethics, 3,* 14–17.

Noddings, N. (2003). *Caring, a feminine approach to ethics and moral education* (2nd ed.). Berkeley: University of California Press.

Nussbaum, M., & Glover, J. (1995). *Women, culture, and development: A study of human capabilities.* Oxford, UK: Clarendon Press.

Nyman, S., & Daugherty, T. (2001). Congruence of counselor self-disclosure and perceived effectiveness. *Journal of Psychology, 135,* 269–278.

O'Brien-Hallstein, L. (1999). A postmodern caring: Feminist standpoint theories, revisioned caring and communication ethics. *Western Journal of Communication, 63,* 32–57.

O'Flaherty, W. (1978). The clash between relative and absolute duty: The dharma of demons. In W. O'Flahery & J. Derret (Eds.), *The concept of duty in South Asia* (pp. 96–106). Columbia, MO: South Asia Books.

O'Neill, O. (2003). Constructivism in Rawls and Kant. In S. Freeman (Ed.), *The Cambridge companion to Rawls* (pp. 347–367). Cambridge, UK: Cambridge University Press.

Oakley, J. (1996). Varieties of virtue ethics. *Ratio, 9,* 128–152.

Occupational Information Network (ONET). (2004). *Summary Report for: 49-2098.00—Security and Fire Alarm Systems Installers.* Retrieved December 26, 2005, from http://online.onetcenter.org/link/summary/49-2098.00

Odell, M., & Stewart, S. (1993). Ethical issues associated with client values: Conversion and therapist value agendas in family therapy. *Family Relations: Interdisciplinary Journal of Family Relations Studies, 42,* 128–133.

Office for Civil Rights. (2003). *Summary of the HIPAA privacy rule.* Washington, DC: U.S. Department of Health and Human Services.

Okamoto, S. (2003). The function of professional boundaries in the therapeutic relationship between male practitioners and female youth clients. *Child and Adolescent Social Work Journal, 20,* 303–313.

Okin, S. (1997, October/November). Is multiculturalism bad for women? [Electronic version]. *Boston Review.* Retrieved July 28, 2004, from http://www.bostonreview .net/BR22.5/okin.html

Oldstone-Moore, J. (2002). *Confucianism.* New York: Oxford University Press.

Omonzejele, P. (2005). *African ethics and voluntary euthanasia.* (n.d.). Retrieved December 26, 2005, from http://216.239.51.104/search?q=cache:F9WgOjC3aGIJ: www.ruhr-uni-bochum.de/zme/healthliteracy/africanethics.pdf+african+ethics+ and+voluntary+euthanasia&hl=en

Oregon Death With Dignity Act. (1995). ORS 127.800–127.995.

Osborne, G. (1991). *The hermeneutic spiral: A comprehensive introduction to biblical interpretation.* Downers Grove, IL: InterVarsity.

Ozer, E., & Bandura, A. (1990). Mechanisms governing empowerment effects: A self-efficacy analysis. *Journal of Personality and Social Psychology, 58,* 472–486.

Page, S., & Tyrer, J. (1995). Gender and prediction of Gilligan's justice and care orientations. *Journal of College Student Psychotherapy, 10,* 43–56.

Pandey, S., Zhan, M., & Collier-Tenison, S. (2004). Families' experience with welfare reform on reservations in Arizona. *Social Work Research, 28,* 93–103.

Pardue, P. (1971). *Buddhism: A historical introduction to Buddhist values and the social and political forms they have assumed in Asia.* London: Collier-Macmillan.

Paton, H. (1953). *The moral law* (Rev. ed.). London: Hutchinson.

Paton, H. (1958). *The categorical imperative.* London: Hutchinson.

Pearson, Q. (1998). Terminating before counseling has ended: Counseling implications and strategies for counselor relocation. *Journal of Mental Health Counseling, 20,* 55–64.

Pedersen, P. (1995). Culture-centered ethical guidelines for counselors. In J. Ponterotto, J. Casas, L. Suzuki, & C. Alexander (Eds), *Handbook of multicultural counseling* (pp. 34–49). Thousand Oaks, CA: Sage.

Perkins, D., Hudson, B., Gray, D., & Stewart, M. (1998). Decisions and justifications by community mental health providers about hypothetical ethical dilemmas. *Psychiatric Services, 49,* 1317–1322.

Peterson, C., & Seligman, M. (2004). *Character strengths and virtues: A handbook and classification.* Washington, DC: American Psychological Association and Oxford University Press.

Peterson, N., & Gonzales, R. (2000). *The role of work in people's lives.* Belmont, CA: Wadsworth/Thompson.

Pincoffs, E. (1971). Quandary ethics. *Mind, 80,* 552–571.

Pope, K., Tabachnick, B., & Keith-Spiegel, P. (2003). Ethics of practice: The beliefs and behaviors of psychologists as therapists. In D. Bersoff (Ed.), *Ethical conflicts in psychology* (3rd ed.) (pp. 81–98). Washington, DC: American Psychological Association.

Pope, K., & Vetter, V. (1992). Ethical dilemmas encountered by members of the American Psychological Association: A national survey. *American Psychologist, 47*(3), 397–411.

Portes, A., & Rumbaut, R. (1990). *Immigrant America: A portrait.* Berkeley: University of California Press.

Punzo, V., & Meara, M. (1993). The virtues of a psychology of personal morality. *Theoretical and Philosophical Psychology, 13,* 25–39.

Quinton, A. (1973). *Utilitarian ethics.* London: Macmillan.

Rabinowitz, A. (2000). Psychotherapy with orthodox Jews. In P. Richards & A. Bergin (Eds.), *Handbook of psychotherapy and religious diversity* (pp. 237–258). Washington, DC: American Psychological Association.

Rachels, J. (1998). *The elements of moral philosophy.* New York: McGraw-Hill.

Radov, C., Masnick, B., & Hauser, B. (1977). Issues in feminist therapy: The work of a women's study group. *Social Work, 22,* 507–509.

Raguram, R., Venkateswaran, A., Ramakrishna, J., & Weiss, M. (2002). Traditional community resources for mental health: A report from a temple healing from India [Electronic version]. *British Medical Journal, 325,* 38–40. Retrieved August 25, 2004, from http://bmj.bmjjournals.com

Ragusea, A., & VandeCreek, L. (2003). Suggestions for the ethical practice of online psychotherapy. *Psychotherapy: Theory, Research, Practice Training, 40,* 94–102.

Rāhula, W., & Reynolds, E. (1993). The Buddha and Buddhism. In *The new encyclopedia Britannica* (Vol. 15, pp. 264–269). Chicago, IL: Encyclopedia Britannica.

Rao, N., McHale, J., & Pearson, E. (2003). Links between socialization goals and child rearing practices in Chinese and Indian mothers. *Infant and Child Development, 12,* 475–492.

Rassau, A., & Arco, L. (2003). Effects of chat-based on-line cognitive behavior therapy on study related behavior and anxiety. *Behavioural and Cognitive Psychotherapy, 31,* 377–381.

Rawls, J. (2001). *Justice as fairness: A restatement* (E. Kelly, Ed.). Cambridge, MA: Belknap Press. (Original work published 1971)

Reese, L. (2001). Morality and identity in Mexican immigrant parents' visions of the future. *Journal of Ethnic and Migration Studies, 27,* 455–472.

Rennison, C., & Welchans, S. (2002). Intimate partner violence. Washington, DC: U.S. Department of Justice.

Rest, J. (1983). Morality. In P. Mussen (Ed.), *Handbook of child psychology* (4th ed.) (pp. 560–629). New York: Wiley.

Rest, J. (1984). Research on moral development: Implications for training counseling psychologists. *Counseling Psychologist, 12,* 19–29.

Rest, J. (1986). *Moral development.* New York: Praeger.

Rest, J. (1994). Background: Theory and research. In J. Rest & D. Narvaez (Eds.), *Moral development in the professions: Psychology and applied ethics* (pp. 1–26). Hillsdale, NJ: Erlbaum.

Robinet, I. (1997). *Taoism: Growth of a religion.* Palo Alto, CA: Stanford University Press.

Rochlen, A., Land, L., & Wong, Y. (2004). Male restrictive emotionality and evaluations of online versus face-to-face counseling. *Psychology of Men and Masculinity, 5,* 190–200.

Rochlen, A., Zack, J., & Speyer, C. (2004). Online therapy: Review of relevant definitions, debates, and current empirical support. *Journal of Clinical Psychology, 60,* 269–283.

Rogers, J., Guelette, C., Abbey-Hines, J., Carney, J., & Werth, J. (2001). Rational suicide: An empirical investigation of counselor attitudes. *Journal of Counseling and Development, 79,* 365–372.

Rogers, M. (1992). Multicultural training in school psychology: A national survey. *School Psychology Review, 21,* 603–617.

Rosen, E., & Weltman, S. (1996). Jewish families: An overview. In M. McGoldrick, G. Giordano, & J. Pearce (Eds.), *Ethnicity and family therapy* (2nd ed.) (pp. 611–630). New York: Guilford Press.

Rosenbaum, A., & Leisring, P. (2003). Beyond power and control: Towards an understanding of partner abusive men. *Journal of Comparative Family Studies, 34,* 7–22.

Rosner, F. (2002). The Jewish view of healing. *Cancer Investigation, 20,* 598–603.

Ross, M.(1989). Feminism and the problem of moral character. *Journal of Feminist Studies in Religion, 5,* 57.

Ross, N. (1980). *Buddhism: A way of life and thought.* New York: Knopf.

Roth, S. (1995). Toward a definition of humility. In E. Dorff & L. Newman (Eds.), *Contemporary Jewish ethics and morality: A reader* (pp. 259–270). New York: Oxford University Press.

Rousseau, J. (1979). *Emile or on education* (A. Bloom, Trans.). New York: Basic Books. (Original work published 1763)

Ruggiero, V. (2004). *Thinking critically about ethical issues* (6th ed.). Boston: McGraw-Hill.

Saddhatissa, H. (1970). *Buddhist ethics: Essence of Buddhism.* New York: George Braziller.

Sampson, R. (2002). Transcending tradition: New directions in community research, Chicago style. *Criminology, 40,* 213–241.

Samuelson, N. (2001). Rethinking ethics in the light of Jewish thought and the life sciences. *Journal of Religious Ethics, 29,* 209–233.

Sanders, C. (1995). *Empowerment ethics for a liberated people: A path to African American social transformation.* Minneapolis, MN: Fortress Press.

Satcher, D. (1999). *Mental health: A report of the surgeon general.* Rockville, MD: Office of the Surgeon General.

Scaltsas, P. (1992). Do feminist ethics counter feminist aims? In E. Cole & S. Coultrapa-McQuin (Eds.), *Explorations in feminist ethics: Theory and practice* (pp. 15–26). Bloomington: Indiana University Press.

Schaeffer, K., Nottebaum, L., Smith, P., Dech, K., & Krawczyk, J. (1999). Religiously motivated sexual orientation change: A follow-up study. *Journal of Psychology and Theology, 27,* 329–337.

Schank, J., & Skovholt, T. (1997). Dual-relationships dilemmas of rural and small-community psychologists, *Professional Psychology: Research and Practice. 28,* 44–49.

Scheffler, S. (2003). Rawls and Utilitarianism. In S. Freeman (Ed.), *The Cambridge companion to Rawls* (pp. 426–459). Cambridge, UK: Cambridge University Press.

Scheffler, R., Garrett, H., Zarin, D., & Pincus, H. (2000). Managed care and fee discounts in psychiatry: New evidence. *Journal of Behavioral Health Services and Research, 27,* 1094–3412.

Schenck, E., Lyman, R., & Bodin, D. (2000). Ethical beliefs, attitudes, and professional practices of psychologists regarding parental use of corporal punishment: A survey. *Children's Services: Social Policy and Practices, 3,* 23–38.

Scher, G. (1987). Other voices, other rooms? Women's psychology and moral theory. In E. Kittay and D. Meyers (Eds.), *Women and moral theory* (pp. 178–189). Totowa, NJ: Rowman & Littlefield.

Schneewind, J. (1992). Autonomy, obligation, and virtue: An overview of Kant's moral philosophy. In P. Guyer (Ed.), *The Cambridge companion to Kant* (pp. 309–341). New York: Cambridge University Press.

Scott, C. (2000). Ethical issues in addiction counseling. *Rehabilitation Counseling Bulletin, 43,* 209–219.

Sears, S., Evans, G., & Perry, N. (1998). Innovations in training: The University of Florida rural psychology program. *Professional Psychology: Research and Practice, 29,* 504–507.

Semans, M., & Fish, L. (2000). Dissecting life with a Jewish scalpel: A qualitative analysis of Jewish-centered family life. *Family Process, 39,* 121–139.

Shanahan, T., & Wang, R. (1996). *Reason and insight: Western and Eastern perspectives on the pursuit of moral wisdom.* Belmont, CA: Wadsworth.

Shanahan, T., & Wang, R. (2003). *Reason and insight: Western and Eastern perspectives on the pursuit of moral wisdom* (2nd ed.). Belmont, CA: Wadsworth.

Shapiro, E., & Ginsberg, R. (2003). To accept or not to accept: Referrals and the maintenance of boundaries. *Professional Psychology: Research and Practice, 34,* 258–263.

Sharma, A. (1999). The purusarthas. *Journal of Religious Ethics, 27,* 223–257.

Sharma, A. (2000). Psychotherapy with Hindus. In P. Richards & A. Bergin (Eds.), *Handbook of psychotherapy and religious diversity* (pp. 341–365). Washington, DC: American Psychological Association.

Sharma, I. C. (1965). *Ethical philosophies of India.* New York: Harper & Row.

Shepard, M. (1992). Predicting batterer recidivism five years after community intervention. *Journal of Family Violence, 7,* 167–178.

Sherwin, B. (2000). Jewish ethics for the twenty-first century: Living in the image of God. Syracuse, NY: Syracuse University Press.

Shidlo, A., & Schroeder, M. (2002). Changing sexual orientation: A consumer's report. *Professional Psychology: Research and Practice, 33,* 249–259.

Shon, S. & Ja, D. (1982). Asian families. In M. McGoldrick, J. Pierce, & J. Giordano (Eds.), *Ethnicity and family therapy* (pp. 208–228). New York: Guilford Press.

Shorris, E. (1992). *Latinos: A biography of the people.* New York: Norton.

Shweder, R. (1991). *Thinking through cultures: Expeditions in cultural psychology.* Cambridge, MA: Harvard University Press.

Silk, J., Sessa, F., Morris, A., Steinberg, L., & Avenevoli, S. (2004). Neighborhood cohesion as a buffer against hostile maternal parenting. *Journal of Family Psychology, 18,* 135–146.

Simons, R., Johnson, C., & Conger, R. (1994). Harsh corporal punishment versus quality of parental involvement as an explanation of adolescence maladjustment. *Journal of Marriage and the Family, 56,* 591–607.

Simpson, P. (1997). Contemporary virtue ethics and Aristotle. In D. Statman (Ed.), *Virtue Ethics* (pp. 249–259). Edinburgh, Scotland: Edinburgh University Press.

Singer, P. (1993). Ethics. In *The new encyclopedia Britannica* (Vol. 18, pp. 492–521). Chicago, IL: Encyclopedia Britannica.

Sioui, G. (1995). *For an Amerindian autohistory: An essay on the foundations of a social ethic* (S. Fischman, trans.). Montreal, QC: McGill–Queen's University Press.

Skarderud, F. (2003). Shame in cyberspace. Relationships without faces: The e-media and eating disorders. *European Eating Disorders Review, 11,* 155–169.

Smith, H. (1991). *The world's religions: Our great wisdom traditions.* New York: HarperCollins.

Smith, H., & Novak, P. (2003). *Buddhism.* New York: HarperCollins.

Solomon, R. (1993). *Ethics: A short introduction.* Dubuque, IA: Brown & Benchmark.

Somer, E. (1999). Therapist-client sex: Retrospective reports. *Professional Psychology: Research and Practice, 30,* 504–509.

Spohn, S. (1992). The return of virtue ethics. *Theological Studies, 53,* 60–75.

Stevens, E. (1994). Marianismo: The other face of machismo in Latin America. In G. Yeager (Ed.), *Confronting change, challenging tradition: Women in Latin American history* (pp. 3–17). Wilmington, DE: SR Books.

Stewart, D., & Sprinthall, N. (1994). Moral development in public administration. In T. Cooper (Ed.), *Handbook of Administrative Ethics* (pp. 2325–2349). New York: Marcel Dekker.

Stone, R. (1990). *Adolescents and abortion: Choice in crisis.* Washington, DC: Center for Population Options.

Straus, M. (1991). Discipline and deviance: Physical punishment of children and violence and other crime in adulthood. *Social Problems, 38,* 133–152.

Straus, M., & Donnelly, D. (1993). Corporal punishment of adolescents by American parents. *Youth and Society, 24,* 419–442.

Straus, M., & Yodanis, C. (1996). Corporal punishment in adolescence and physical assaults on spouses in later life: What accounts for the link? *Journal of Marriage and the Family, 58*, 825–841.

Strom, K. (2001). *Hate crimes reported in NIBRS, 1997–99.* Washington, DC: Bureau of Justice Statistics.

Stuart, E., & Campbell, J. (1989). Assessment of patterns of dangerousness with battered women. *Issues in Mental Health Nursing, 10*, 245–260.

Sue, D., Arredondo, P., & McDavis, R. (1992). Multicultural counseling competencies and standards: A call to the profession. *Journal of Counseling and Development, 70*, 477–486.

Super, D. (1990). A life-span approach to career development. In Duane Brown and Associates (Ed.), *Career choice and development* (2nd ed.) (pp. 197–261). San Francisco, CA: Jossey-Bass.

Sussman, L., & Alexander, C. (1999). How religiosity and ethnicity affect marital satisfaction for Jewish-Christian couples. *Journal of Mental Health Counseling, 21*, 173–185.

Syse, H. (2001). *Natural law, religion, and rights.* Notre Dame, IN: St. Augustine's Press.

Szymanski, D. (2003). The feminist supervision scale: A rational/theoretical approach. *Psychology of Women Quarterly, 27*, 221–232.

Tajfel, H., & Turner, J. (1986). The social identity theory of intergroup behavior. In S. Worchel & W. Austin (Eds.), *Psychology of intergroup relations* (pp. 7–24). Chicago, IL: Nelson-Hall.

Tarasoff v. Board of Regents of the University of California. 17 Cal 3rd 425 (Cal Supreme Court, 1976).

Taylor, C. (1997). *North American Indians.* Bristol, UK: Sienna.

Throckmorton, W. (2002). Initial empirical and clinical findings concerning the change process for ex-gays. *Professional Psychology: Research and Practice, 33*, 242–248.

Tjeltveit, A. (2000). There is more to ethics than codes of professional ethics: Social ethics, theoretical ethics, and managed care. *Counseling Psychologist, 28*, 242–252.

Tombari, M., & Bergan, J. (1978). Consultant cues and teacher verbalizations, judgments, and expectancies concerning children's adjustment problems. *Journal of School Psychology, 16*, 212–219.

Tong, R. (1998). The ethics of care: A feminist virtue ethics of care for healthcare practitioners. *Journal of Medicine and Philosophy, 23*, 131–152.

Tong, R. (2003). Feminist ethics. In E. Zalta (Ed.), *The Stanford encyclopedia of philosophy.* Retrieved May 4, 2005, from http://plato.stanford.edu/archives/win2003/entries/feminism-ethics/

Trusty, J., & Niles, S. (2004). Realized potential or lost talent: High school variables and bachelor's degree completion. *Career Development Quarterly, 53*, 2–16.

Tucci, G., Kitagawa, J., & Reynolds, F. (1993). The Buddha and Buddhism. In *The new encyclopedia Britannica* (Vol. 15, pp. 263–264). Chicago, IL: Encyclopedia Britannica.

Tucci, G., Nakamura, H., & Reynolds, F. (1993). The Buddha and Buddhism. In *The new encyclopedia Britannica* (Vol. 15, pp. 269–270). Chicago, IL: Encyclopedia Britannica.

Tweed, R., & Lehman, D. (2002). Learning considered within a cultural context: Confucian and Socratic approaches. *American Psychologist, 57*(2), 89–99.

U.S. Census Bureau. (2000). *U.S. Census Bureau state and county quickfacts: Data derived from population estimates, 2000 census of population and housing.* Washington, DC: Author.

U.S. Census Bureau. (2001). *U.S. Census 2000, Summary files 1 and 2.* Retrieved December 26, 2005, from http://www.census.gov/Press-Release/www/2001/sumfile1.html and http://www.census.gov/Press-Release/www/2001/sumfile2.html

U.S. Census Bureau. (2002). *American factfinder.* Washington, DC: Author.

U.S. Census Bureau. (2004). *U.S. interim projections by age, sex, race, and Hispanic origin.* Retrieved December 26, 2005, from http://www.census.gov/ipc/www/usinterimproj

U.S. Congress. (1789). *U.S. Constitution, Bill of Rights.* Washington, DC: Author.

U.S. Department of Education. (2000). *Getting ready for college early.* Retrieved December 26, 2005, from http://www.ed.gov/pubs/GettingReadyCollegeEarly/index.html

U.S. Department of Health & Human Services. (2003). *Summary of the HIPAA privacy rule* (Last Revised 05/03). Retrieved December 27, 2005, from http://www.hhs.gov/ocr/privacysummary.pdf

U.S. Department of State. (n.d.). *Fact sheet: Islam in the United States.* Retrieved December 27, 2005, from http://www.islamfortoday.com/historyusa4.htm

Vacek, E. (1996). Divine-command, natural-law, and mutual-love ethics. *Theological Studies, 57,* 633–653.

Van Buitenen, J. (Trans. and Ed.). (1985). *The Bhagavadgita in the Mahabharata.* Chicago, IL: University of Chicago Press.

Vashon, D., & Agresti, A. (1992). A training proposal to help mental health professionals clarify and manage implicit values in the counseling process. *Professional Psychology: Research and Practice, 23,* 509–514.

Vasquez, M. (1996). Will virtue ethics improve ethical conduct in multicultural settings and interactions? *The Counseling Psychologist, 24,* 98–104.

Veatch, R. (1998). The place of care in ethical theory. *Journal of Medicine and Philosophy, 23,* 210–224.

Wachtel, P. (2002). Termination of therapy: An effort at integration. *Journal of Psychotherapy Integration, 12,* 373–383.

Walden, S., Herlihy, B., & Ashton, L. (2003). The evolution of ethics: Personal perspectives of ACA ethics committee chairs. *Journal of Counseling and Development, 81,* 106–111.

Waller, A. (1995). Health care issues in health care reform. *Whittier Law Review, 16,* 15–49.

Wang, R., Wang, H., & Hsu, M. (2003). Factors associated with adolescent pregnancy: A sample of Taiwanese female adolescents. *Pubic Health Nursing, 20,* 33–41.

Waters, A. (Ed.). (2004). *American Indian thought: Philosophical essays.* Malden, MA: Blackwell.

Watkins, C. (1994). The supervision of psychotherapy supervisor trainees. *American Journal of Psychotherapy, 48,* 417–431.

Watkins, S. (1989). Confidentiality: An ethical and legal conundrum for family therapists. *The American Journal of Family Therapy, 17,* 291–302.

Wei-Cheng, J. (2004). Cultural dimensions of career decision-making difficulties. *Career Development Quarterly, 53*, 67–78.

Welfel, E. (2002). *Ethics in counseling and psychotherapy: Standards, research and emerging issues.* Pacific Grove, CA: Brooks/Cole.

Wendell, S. (1996). *The rejected body: Feminist philosophical reflections on disability.* New York: Routledge.

Werth, J. (1999). Mental health professionals and assisted death: Perceived ethical obligations and proposed guidelines for practice. *Ethics and Behavior, 9*, 159–183.

Werth, J., & Cobia, D. (1996). Empirically based criteria for rational suicide: A survey of psychotherapists. *Suicide and Life Threatening Behavior, 25*, 231–240.

Werth, J., & Holdwick, D. (2000). A primer on rational suicide and other forms of hastened death. *The Counseling Psychologist, 28*, 511–539.

Westefeld, J., Range, L., Rogers, J., Maples, M., Bromley, J., & Alcorn, J. (2000). Suicide: An overview. *The Counseling Psychologist, 28*, 445–510.

Wester, S., Vogel, D., & Archer, J. (2004). Males, supervisors, and counseling supervision. *Journal of Counseling and Development, 82*, 91–99.

Wheeler, S., & King, D. (2000). Do counseling supervisors want or need to have their supervision supervised? An exploratory study. *British Journal of Guidance and Counseling, 28*, 279–291.

White, V., & Queener, J. (2003). Supervisor and supervisee attachments and social provisions related to the supervisory working alliance. *Counselor Education and Supervision, 42*, 203–219.

Whitman, J. (1995). Providing training about sexual orientation in counselor education. *Counselor Education and Supervision, 35*, 168–176.

Wiener, J. (1985). Teachers' comprehension of psychological reports. *Psychology in the Schools, 22*, 60–64.

Wig, N. (1999). Mental health and spiritual values. A view from the East. *International Review of Psychiatry, 11*, 92–97.

Winston, K. (2003). On the ethics of exporting ethics: The right to silence in Japan and the U.S. *Criminal Justice Ethics, 22*, 3–20.

Wolfson, E. (1999). The fee in social work: Ethical dilemmas for practitioners. *Social Work, 44*, 269–274.

Wollstonecraft, M. (1999). *A vindication of the rights of women; with strictures on political and moral subjects.* Retrieved July 27, 2004, from http://www.bartleby.com/144/index.html (Original work published 1792)

Worrell, J., & Remer, P. (1992). *Feminist perspectives in therapy: An empowerment model for women.* New York: Wiley.

Worthington, E., Larson, D., Brubaker, M., Colecchi, C., Berry, J., & Morrow, D. (1989). The benefits of legislation requiring parental involvement prior to adolescent abortion. *American Psychologist, 44*, 1542–1545.

Worthington, R. (2004). Sexual identity, sexual orientation, religious identity, and change: Is it possible to depolarize the debate? *The Counseling Psychologist, 32*, 741–749.

Yao, X. (2000). *An introduction to Confucianism.* Cambridge, UK: Cambridge University Press.

Younggren, J., & Gottlieb, M. (2004). Managing risk when contemplating multiple relationships. *Professional Psychology: Research and Practice, 35*, 255–260.

Yum, J. (1988). The impact of Confucianism on interpersonal relationships and communication patterns in East Asia. *Communication Monographs, 55,* 374–388.

Yurkovich, E., Clairmont, J., & Grandbois, D. (2002). Mental health care providers' perception of giving culturally responsive care to American Indians. *Perspectives in Psychiatric Care, 38,* 147–156.

Zabin, L., Hirsch, M., & Emerson, M. (1989). When urban adolescents choose abortion: Effects on education, psychological status and subsequent pregnancy. *Family Planning Perspectives, 21,* 248–255.

Zea, M., Mason, M., & Murguia, A. (2000). Psychotherapy with members of Latino/Latina religions and spiritual traditions. In P. Richards & A. Bergin (Eds.), *Handbook of psychotherapy and religious diversity* (pp. 397–419). Washington, DC: American Psychological Association.

Zeddies, T. (2002). More than just words: A hermeneutic view of language in psychoanalysis. *Psychoanalytic Psychology, 19,* 3–23.

Zingaro, J. (1983). A family systems approach for the career counselor. *Personnel and Guidance Journal, 62,* 24–27.

Index

introduced, 55
Tao, 61–62
yin and yang, 62
Tarasoff, Tatiana, 234
Tarasoff v. Regents, 122, 234
Taylor, C., 47
Teleological ethics, 13
Tennessee laws, 273
Termination case study, 219–226
Tester, M., 197
Texas laws, 274
Texts, interpreting, 101–102
Theft, 28–29
Therapeutic alliance, 232
Theresa (counselor), 211
Thomas (supervisor), 212–213
Thompson, J., 101, 102
Thompson, R, 243, 244
Throckmorton, W., 149
Time, 92
Ting, K., 112–113
Tjeltveit, A., 3, 12, 17
Tombari, M., 252
Toner, B., 232
Tong, R., 41, 43
Tony (supervisor), 148
Torah, 31, 79, 80
Training, counselor:
 counselor competence and, 107
 culturally differing ethics and, 7
 decision-making models and, 5
 in ethical codes, 3
 hermeneutic approach to, 6
 multicultural, 157
Trimble, J., 163
Trust:
 in African ethics, 96
 dual relationships and, 174
 ethic, 45
 fidelity and, 14
Trusty, J., 166
Truth, 13, 51–52
Truthfulness, 82, 87, 96
Tschann, J., 197, 198
Tucci, G., 71, 72, 73, 75

Turner, J., 224
Tweed, R., 59
Twenty-Sixth Amendment, 207
Tyrer, J., 9

Ummah, 233
Understanding, 103
Undesirable acts, 87
Universal connectedness, 48
Universal principle, 35–36
Universality tests, 35–36
Upanishads, 65
U.S. Census Bureau, 47, 91, 111, 112
U.S. Congress, 159
U.S. Constitution, 159, 207
U.S. Court of Appeals, 198
U.S. Department of Education, 167
U.S. Department of Health and Human
 Services, 108
U.S. Supreme Court, 197, 198
Utah laws, 274
Utilitarian ethics:
 history of, 25
 individual rights and, 120
 introduced, 9
 major concepts, 26–29
 natural law *vs.,* 22
 as preference satisfaction, 27
 problem solving with, 28–29
 spiritual life *vs.,* 67
 two basic types, 27–28
Utilitarian theory, 159–160

Values:
 code of ethics, 172
 counselors, 110–113
 family, 112
 human *vs.* biological, 23
 multicultural competence and,
  109, 157
 supervisor, 113–114
 universal human, 121, 123
Van Buitenen, J., 203
Van der lendeen, R., 29
VandeCreek, L., 132, 133

About the Authors

Rick Houser, PhD, is professor in and chair of the Department of Counseling and School Psychology at the University of Massachusetts Boston. He received his doctorate in rehabilitation counseling from the University of Pittsburgh with a minor in research methods. He has taught ethics to graduate-level counseling students for over ten years. Dr. Houser has authored and coauthored several books addressing issues such as research and counseling and the role of group affiliation and power. Additionally, much of his scholarship focus includes the intersection of social identity, social comparison, and social dominance theories. Dr. Houser is a member of the American Counseling Association. He holds licensure in mental health counseling and national certification as a Certified Rehabilitation Counselor, CRC.

Felicia L. Wilczenski, EdD, received a doctorate in education from the University of Massachusetts Amherst. She is an associate professor and director of the School Counseling Program in the Department of Counseling and School Psychology in the Graduate College of Education at the University of Massachusetts Boston. She is a member of the American School Counselor Association, the National Association of School Psychologists, and the American Psychological Association. Dr. Wilczenski is interested in service-learning applications in school-based mental health programs. Her work focuses on creating sustainable systemic approaches to character education and social-emotional education that integrate service learning. She is author of numerous articles addressing social and emotional interventions in K–12 settings. Dr. Wilczenski also teaches ethics courses in school counseling and school psychology and is interested in ethics education and professional development.

MaryAnna Ham, EdD, is a professor emeritus at the University of Massachusetts Boston. She received her doctorate from the University of Rochester. She developed the ethics curriculum at the University of Massachusetts Boston and she has taught ethics to graduate-level counseling students for over ten years. Dr. Ham was the former director and founder of the Family Therapy Program at the University of Massachusetts Boston. She has focused much of her scholarship on diversity issues and counseling. Dr. Ham has coauthored several books addressing counseling with Asian populations and the role of group affiliation and power. Dr. Ham is a licensed psychologist and licensed family therapist.

Feb14108